D0948728

Samuel Beckett, W. B. Yeats, and Jack Yeats

Two Travellers, 1942, oil on canvas, 36 × 48. Tate Gallery, London.

Samuel Beckett, W. B. Yeats, and Jack Yeats

Images and Words

Gordon S. Armstrong

PR 6003 .E282 Z5634 1990
Armstrong, Gordon S., 1935-
Samuel Beckett, W.B. Yeats,
and Jack Yeats

Lewisburg
Bucknell University Press
London and Toronto: Associated University Presses

WITHDRAWN
BALDWIN-WALLACE COLLEGE

© 1990 by Associated University Presses, Inc.

All rights reserved. Authorization to photocopy items for internal or personal use, or the internal or personal use of specific clients, is granted by the copyright owner, provided that a base fee of $10.00, plus eight cents per page, per copy is paid directly to the Copyright Clearance Center, 27 Congress Street, Salem, Massachusetts 01970. [0-8387-5141-5/90 $10.00 + 8¢ pp, pc.]

Associated University Presses
440 Forsgate Drive
Cranbury, NJ 08512

Associated University Presses
25 Sicilian Avenue
London WC1A 2QH, England

Associated University Presses
P.O. Box 488, Port Credit
Mississauga, Ontario
Canada L5G 4M2

The paper used in this publication meets the requirements of the American National Standard for Permanence of Paper for Printed Library Materials Z39.48-1984.

Library of Congress Cataloging-in-Publication Data

Armstrong, Gordon S., 1935–
  Samuel Beckett, W.B. Yeats, and Jack Yeats.

  Bibliography: p.
  Includes index.
  1. Beckett, Samuel, 1906– —Knowledge
—literature. 2. Beckett, Samuel, 1906– —
Knowledge—Art. 3. Yeats. W. B. (William Butler),
1865–1939—Influence—Beckett. 4. Yeats, Jack
Butler, 1871–1957—Influence—Beckett. 5. Art and
literature—Ireland—History—20th century.
6. English literature—Irish authors—History and
criticism. 7. Ireland—Intellectual life—20th century.
8. Ireland in literature. I. Title.
PR6003.E282Z5634   1990   828'.91209   87-48015
ISBN 0-8387-5141-5 (alk. paper)

PRINTED IN THE UNITED STATES OF AMERICA

For Jan
and for Bill, who exemplify
in every way
Continuosity, Impetuosity and Exuberance

Contents

Illustrations

Preface

DESPITE all that has been written about Samuel Beckett as a man who is clearly one of the twentieth century's best guides to the underside of the mind, the influences on his creative inspiration remain essentially undefined. Another book may seem a foolhardy enterpise, but a discussion with Alan Schneider and a visit to Paris to talk to Mr. Beckett convinced me otherwise.

Beckett's erudition is extraordinary, as befits an honors graduate of Trinity College, Dublin; a lecteur d'Anglais at L'École Normale Supérieure, Paris; a friend and confidante of James Joyce, Eugène Jolas, Hans Arp, Thomas MacGreevy, Georges Pelorson, and Jack Yeats; and an enthusiastic sponsor of many avant-garde painters, including Fauvists Bram and Geer Van Velde. There can be no question that Beckett's work is situated in the mainstream of current literary intellectual thought, but something is missing in the exegesis of his work. Attributions for his creative impulse extend from Mallarmé to Descartes, from Joyce to Geulincx, from Malebranche and the Occasionalist doctrine, from Leibnitz to Wittgenstein, from the theater of the absurd to logical positivism and the post–World War II existentialists. All these people and philosophies are presented as compelling evidence of Beckett's sources in spite of his repeated statement that his work is, indeed, a matter of fundamental sounds.

My purpose in undertaking this study was to examine Beckett's statement. I began with the hypothesis Beckett posed at the end of *Watt,* his enigmatically brilliant novel of the war years that concludes: "No symbols where none intended." Did this unassuming intellectual, who writes with infallible grace and intuitive sense on the nature of silence, language, rhythm, and form, really mean what he said?

I wanted to know if James Joyce bequeathed a literary legacy to Samuel Beckett's later work. I needed to know where the "Irish-ness" of Beckett's characters originated, and how to account for his personal antipathy toward Ireland, and his literary sympathy for it. William Butler Yeats seemed an obvious legator of "Irish-ness," but analysis of his Cuchulain plays produced significant evidence both for and against him. W. B.'s younger brother Jack kept intruding in Mr. Beckett's conversation. At first Jack Yeats seemed to be only a close personal friend of

Beckett, but a careful review of his work revealed an artist of great scope. Samuel Beckett did not exaggerate Jack Yeats's importance to him; what Yeats's unconventional stage plays explicitly lack, his later paintings state clearly. He was a realist artist of the first order, whose technique was so pure that it did not even exclude the accident of personality; whose concept of art was so clear that it did not even allow his consciousness to intrude in his finished work. Most importantly, he was an artist whose subject was unquestionably the people and the country of Ireland.

Samuel Beckett, too, has always written of the *petit peuple* of Ireland. His principal sources and his guiding philosophical lights were the Yeats brothers. Jack B. Yeats was practically a father figure—distant, revered, and much loved—for Beckett, the fledgling writer and Irish ex-patriot. The younger man paid the elder the highest praise—imitation. To know the art of Jack Yeats is to understand the work of Samuel Beckett.

W. B. Yeats is not as prominent a figure in this equation because he was absorbed in all the wrong things in Ireland's heroic, mythical past. His literary reputation, based on an elaborate symbol system behind which he hid from the world, was not conducive to high art. Symbols were used defensively as a means of warding off or transcending reality. W. B. Yeats sought archetypal connotations for his symbols that could, consciously or subconsciously, affect the words on the page. Unlike the studied prose of W. B., his brother, Jack's work (particularly in the last two decades of his life) soared free from conscious restraints to a point where prose and paint lingered at the edges of reality before departing into myth or fantasy.

There can be no question that Beckett was influenced by W. B. Yeats, both directly in subject matter, and indirectly through common literary interests. Beckett, however, disagreed with symbol systems (enemies to theatrical presence, as Robbe-Grillet suggests; mere infusion of the "voluntary imagination," as Beckett described it in his excursis of Proust) and insisted on a dramaturgy that was spare, evocative, and gesture oriented. Beckett also disagreed with W. B. Yeats's synthetic theater in which the latter used dramatic devices to demonstrate or explore philosophical postures. In Beckett's works, language functioned in limited, essentially literal ways, within conventions that derived not from the writings of W. B. Yeats, but that reflected certain techniques in the paintings and writings of Jack Yeats.

Beckett admitted, in conversation, that he turned to theater in the 1940s as a way to put limits on his imagination. In the theater he could introduce elements—lighting, gestures, scenic devices—into the darkness. The theater was, in this regard, an additive process. Beckett's novels, to the contrary, forced him into a subtractive posture as he had to ignore or discard elements of the real world to create the necessary perspective. The whole notion of "presence" in the theater, by which a spectator identifies with a dramatic situation onstage, or experiences a cathartic response to a particular moment, also intrigued Beckett, who saw in it the parallel of consciousness experiencing the presence of unconscious forces at certain moments. The theater, in this regard, became a synonym for life, for the schismatic self, for Beckett's art of the theater.

Samuel Beckett followed Jack Yeats's early lead to the spirit of man— fundamental sounds of a fundamental people who expressed fundamental relationships to self-consciousness, to each other, and to the land that sustained them. In later years Beckett surpassed his early inspiration in moments of limpid vision. In the beginning, however, Jack Yeats was everywhere in Beckett's prose fiction and early plays. The works are high praise indeed, if readers and commentators alike have the eyes to see the universal nature of Beckett's Ireland.

With the premiere of *Not I* in 1971, Beckett's treatment of subject reflected in particular the influences of Jack Yeats. In Yeats's paintings the background interacts with the principal elements and figures of the canvas and gives the viewer the sensation of observing from within the energies that led the artist to paint the scene in the first place. As Beckett saw it, Jack Yeats's work reflected not a single image but stages of an image. Portions of his canvasses were left completely bare, while other sections were filled with impasto.

Beckett applied the same techniques to his dramaticules, where he deliberately "vaguened" or neutralized an image, so that the spectator is free to choose among several possibilities. At the other extreme, Beckett presented language and images that were replete with literary and philosophical implications that one might expect from an honors graduate of Trinity College, Dublin. Scholars have filled volumes of detailed tomes, explicating the spare, multileveled images of Beckett—images that parallel Jack Yeats's layering effects in his own Irish pictorial works.

I cannot conclude the introduction without acknowledging the friendship and encouragement of Alan Schneider, who provided a Berkeley graduate student with tickets to the world premiere of *Not I* at the Forum Theater in Lincoln Center, and who—for a decade after that momentous production—shared my enthusiasm for Beckett with occasional lunches in the city, within walking distance of Juilliard.

Acknowledgments

MY first thanks are due to Samuel Beckett, who graciously put up with my impertinence on several occasions, and whose gentle Irish accent pervades every page of this book. I am also deeply indebted to Alan Schneider, who encouraged me to go to Paris to see Mr. Beckett, and who originally suggested the W. B. connection with Beckett's works.

I am grateful to Robin Skelton for his invaluable advice on Jack Yeats and John Millington Synge, and to Barton Friedman for his commentary on W. B. Yeats and suggestions for further review of my manuscript. I am also most grateful for suggestions from readers known—William Melnitz, Marvin Rosenberg and William I. Oliver—and unknown for the many kind suggestions and opinions offered my manuscript at earlier stages. Their collective advice was invaluable in the final draft of this text.

Ms. Sarah Shott of Waddington Galleries, London, and Theo Waddington have been indispensable sources of information on Jack B. Yeats's paintings. Their unfailing kindness in helping me to locate current owners of Jack Yeats's works is a principal reason the reproductions appear in this book. In this regard, Ms. Anne Yeats and Senator Michael Yeats have been most cooperative in granting me permission to use reproductions of their uncle's works. Acknowledgments are also due to the following institutions and people for reproduction permissions: The Tate Gallery, *Two Travellers;* The National Gallery of Ireland, *The Liffey Swim;* Anne Yeats, *The First Time Around;* The University of Victoria, Canada, *Circus Poster, The Tin Man, This Grand Conversation was Under the Rose* (broadsheet); Sligo Museum, *The Island Funeral;* Municipal Gallery of Modern Art, Dublin, *The Rogue;* anonymous lender, *This Grand Conversation was Under the Rose;* Mr. A. J. F. O'Reilly, *Glory.*

I am indebted to the following publishers, authors or their estates for permission to cite from their texts: Jack B. Yeats, *Sligo,* Wishart and Company; T. G. Rosenthal, Jack B. Yeats, 1871–1957, *Knowledge Publications;* Jack Yeats, *Modern Aspects of Irish Art,* Ms. Anne Yeats; Roger McHugh, ed., *Jack B. Yeats: A Centenary Gathering,* The Dolman Press; James Knowlson, *Krapp's Last Tape: Theater Workbook 1,* Brutus Books; Jacques Derrida, *Of Grammatology,* The Johns Hopkins University Press; Barton Friedman, *Adventures in the Depths of the Mind,* Princeton University Press; John Rees Moore, *Masks of Love and Death: Yeats as Dramatist,* Cornell University Press; Richard Ellmann, *James Joyce,* and *The Identity of Yeats,* Oxford University Press; Richard Ellmann, *Yeats: The Man and the Mask,* W. W. Norton; Katharine Worth, *The Irish Drama of Europe from Yeats to Beckett,* The Athlone Press, Ltd.; W. B. Yeats, *Essays and Introductions,* Macmillan Publishing Company; Robin Skelton, *Collected Plays of Jack B. Yeats,* Bobbs Merrill Company; Jack B. Yeats, *The Charmed Life,* Routledge and Kegan Paul, Ltd.; Hilary Pyle, *Jack B Yeats; A Bibliography,* Routledge and Kegan Paul; John Murphy, *Ireland in the Twentieth Century,* Irish Book Center; Samuel Beckett, *Imagination Dead Imagine,* Calder and Boyars, Limited; Samuel Beckett, *The Unnamable, Proust, Play, Not I, Murphy, How it Is, Waiting for Godot, Company,* Grove Press; Walter Asmus, "Practical Aspects of Theatre, Radio and Television," *Journal of Beckett Studies,* No. 2, Spring 1977. All paintings are courtesy of A. P. Watt Limited for Anne Yeats and Michael Yeats.

Finally, I am most indebted to my wife, Jan Armstrong, who read every page and whose editorial suggestions immeasurably improved my text. Her patience, loving care and diligence made it all possible.

Samuel Beckett, W. B. Yeats, and Jack Yeats

PART I
Samuel Beckett

1

The Modernist Temper

A voice comes to one in the dark. Imagine. . . . To one on his
back in the dark a voice tells of a past. With occasional allusion
to a present and more rarely to a future as for example, You
will end as you now are.

—Samuel Beckett, *Company*

THE voice that Beckett has translated to the stage has been disturbing
and delighting spectators and critics for fifty years. But half a century's
traffic in words has brought his audience no closer to an understanding
of the voice at the beginning of the impossible compromise that lies at
the center of Beckett's art. The voice is freedom; the voice is presence in
the absence of the consciousness that imprisons the imagination. Beckett's summons to his audience to participate in the re-creation of his (the
artist's) original impulse—which transcends the moment—is also a summons to compromise the impossible conscious moment, for which *Company* stands as a recent paradigm of Beckett's art of failure. The first
influence on Beckett is Beckett.

Beckett's inspiration has remained remarkably consistent for five decades. He devoted the 1930s and 1940s to major prose works, reviews,
anthologies of short stories, and poetry. But when he wrote the trilogy of
novels—*Molloy, Malone Dies,* and *The Unnamable*—a dramatic tension
surfaced. Michael Robinson described the new dimension in Beckett's
work as a new sense of depth, in which the author drew his characters as
if caught in a vortex that seemed to spiral downward "from all externals
to an examination of the internal silence that fills each individual
being."[1]

The vortex became *En Attendant Godot* (written between *Malone Dies*
and *The Unnamable*), which premiered at the Théâtre de Babylon in Paris
on 5 January 1953, four years after its composition. Colin Duckworth
quoted Beckett as stating that he wrote *Godot* "as a relaxation to get away
from the awful prose I was writing at that time."[2] But there is every
evidence to believe that Beckett's work on the trilogy had detonated an
explosion of dramatic energy that demanded expression. Beckett has

19

said that he wrote *Godot* "to put some limits on the darkness." Even the Manichaean doctrine, and its conflicting dualism between the realm of God—represented by light and by spiritual enlightenment—and the realm of Satan—symbolized by darkness and by material things—that plays so important a role in *Krapp's Last Tape* had already become a formidable element in Beckett's work.

In its manuscript form *En Attendant Godot* bears the dates "9 Octobre, 1948" on the first page and "29 Janvier, 1949" on the last page.[3] Beckett made his choice of a director for *Godot* when he saw Roger Blin's production of Strindberg's *Ghost Sonata,* but several years elapsed before the haunting images of Beckett's tramps reached the stage. *Godot* and its conflicting sense of presence and of absence, of void and of great fathomable depths, was not immediately acclaimed by everyone. When his audiences recognized Beckett's achievement, theaters all over the world clamored for his work. Two decades of literary obscurity ended when playwrights and critics alike applauded his first produced play. Alain Robbe-Grillet summarized the remarkable originality of *En Attendant Godot:*

> We suddenly realize, as we look at them [Didi and Gogo] the main function of theatre, which is to show what the fact of *being there* consists in. For this is what we have never seen on the stage before, or not with the same clarity, not with so few concessions and so much force. A character in a play usually does no more than *play a part,* as all those about us do who are trying to shirk their own existence. But in Beckett's play it is as if the two tramps were on the stage without a part to play. . . . They are free.[4]

Beckett's exposition of the inner landscapes of experience reflected one aspect of a particularly modern dilemma. Arnold Hauser noted the same phenomena in his survey of art history: "Everything stable and coherent is dissolved into metamorphoses and assumes the character of the unfinished and fragmentary."[5] Decades before the concept of deconstructive analysis, Beckett's creatures became a measure of process in the midst of a gigantic impersonal universe, a Kafkaesque state in which

> we are in the situation of travellers in a train that has met with an accident in the tunnel and this at a place where the light of the beginning can no longer be seen, and the light of the end is so very small a glimmer that the gaze must continually search for it and is always losing it again, and furthermore, both the beginning and the end are not even certainties. Round about us, however, in the confusion of our senses, or in the supersensitiveness of our senses, we have nothing but monstrosities and a kaleidoscopic play of things that is either delightful or exhausting according to the mood and injury of

each individual. What shall I do? or: why should I do it? are not questions to be asked in such places.[6]

Kafka's victims of a nightmarish accident in the heart of a train tunnel paralleled the situation in which Beckett's creatures find themselves in *Godot;* they are obligated to wait in another kind of hell for unending process to end. While process continues, the tramps endure their moments by examining the silences of their own beings in the ineluctable presence of self-awareness.

Beckett incorporated silence in his plays as an integral part of their dramatic structure. The final moments of *Krapp's Last Tape* are filled with silence; the blank tape whirls on the turntable and a silent Krapp stares dumbfounded into darkness. Pierre Chabert, who acted the part of Krapp in Beckett's 1975 production of the play in Paris, commented on Beckett's extraordinary control of all elements of the production, including the play's silences that almost became "a voiceless body listening." Chabert described the playwright's sensitivity:

> Beckett's stage poetics is dominated . . . by establishing a physical relationship between the character and speech, the character and his body, between the body, space, and objects. This relationship is controlled and kept at a distance by the importance that is ascribed to music and rhythm, even in the movements of the body and in gesture.[7]

The cadence of silence and sound in *Godot* is even more pronounced. In one particularly poignant moment, Vladimir and Estragon speak of their dead voices, which render them incapable of keeping silent:

Didi. They make a noise like wings.
Gogo. Like leaves.
Didi. Like sand.
Gogo. Like leaves.
  Silence.
Didi. They all speak together.
Gogo. Each one to itself.
  Silence.
Didi. Rather they whisper.
Gogo. They rustle.
Didi. They murmur.
Gogo. They rustle.
  Silence.
Didi. What do they say?
Gogo. They talk about their lives.
Didi. To have lived is not enough for them.
Gogo. They have to talk about it.
Didi. To be dead is not enough for them.

Gogo. It is not sufficient.
  Silence.
Didi. They make a noise like feathers.
Gogo. Like leaves.
Didi. Like ashes.
Gogo. Like leaves.
  Long silence.
Didi. Say something!
Gogo. I'm trying.
  Long silence.
Didi. (in anguish). Say anything at all!
Gogo. What do we do now?
Didi. Ah!
  Silence.[8]

According to Reid, "The elaborate fugues of point and counter-point, strophe and anti-strophe, silence and sound," of this passage lead to an inescapable comparison with music notations.[9]

The structure of this portion of *Godot* forms a rhythmic pattern of sound and silence: 4 lines/silence/2 lines/silence/4 lines/silence/6 lines/ silence/4 lines/silence/2 lines/silence/4 lines (4:2:4:6:4:2:4). Within that structure the second line is repeated in each four-line sequence except the last, where the first line ending—"all!"—rhymes imperfectly with Estragon's final "Ah!" In the six-line sequence the third and fifth lines rhyme while the second and fourth lines are the present and past tenses of a single thought—"they talk" and "they have talked." Similarities do not end there; the noise of leaves that occurs in the first four-line sequence is repeated in the third four-line sequence, as is the qualifications: "they make a noise." And finally, the entire fugue, to use Alec Reid's appropriate designation, is tied together by sibilance—the noise of wings, leaves, sand, whispers, rustles, feathers, leaves (again!), "ashes. . . . Say something! . . . Ah!" Beckett's absolute control of language rhythms that allowed him to place silences within a text as a painter might alternate light with shadow, also allowed him to produce work that is rightfully described as music, and more carefully described as language imagery that fills the canvas of his theater.

The notion of silence and sound, language and meaning, in Beckett's work does not begin and end with his plays. He spent a long apprenticeship dueling with words. In *Murphy* the young hero "works up" the rocking chair to appease his body in order to set his mind free. The pleasure he gains thereby is such that "pleasure [is] not the word."[10] *Murphy* contains undifferentiated silence, a "mote in the dark of absolute freedom" (112). *Watt,* on the other hand, is a question mark. The creature of the novel is in need of semantic succor; one "who [has] not seen a symbol, nor executed an interpretation, since the age of fourteen, or fifteen," but who, at every opportunity, exhausts the possibilities of language.[11] Beckett creates a mathematical cipher hero whose every movement is governed by all possible permutations and combinations, but can be defined by none. Watt is the ultimate creature of the imagination, meaningless except in the measure of the transition that creates the illusion of dimension. John Pilling argued that *Watt* "suffers from being too clear, too allegorical"; far from there being "no symbols where none intended," there are symbols everywhere inviting the reader, like Watt, to explain and exorcise.[12] *Watt* does not deal in symbol, but in the interstices of language. The exhausting *brio* of *The Unnamable* is presaged in Watt's meeting with the Galls, father and son:

> a thing that was nothing had happened, with the utmost formal distinctness, and that it continued to happen, in his mind, . . . inexorably to unroll its phases, beginning with the first (the knock that was not a knock) and ending with the last (the door closing that was not a door closing) . . . (76).

Beckett's deconstruction of external phenomena gradually centers on Watt himself.

In part three of *Watt,* which is really part four inverted, after Watt's train trip and his arrival at the sanitarium, he and Sam converse inversely; part three ends at the beginning, and begins at the end of Watt's story, when he is transferred to another pavilion. Watt begins by walking and talking backward, his scalp torn by thorns, his face and hands bloodied: "Wonder I, said Watt, panky-hanky me lend you could, blood away wipe" (159–60). At this moment the narrator has a strange sensation:

> suddenly I felt as though I were standing before a great mirror, in which my garden was reflected, and my fence, and I, and the very birds tossing in the wind, so that I looked at my hands, and felt my face, and glossy skull, with an anxiety as real as unfounded (159).

This is Sam in Beckett-land, passing through the looking-glass. Watt and Sam begin to pace together, deconstructing both language and movement:

> Then I placed his hands, on my shoulders, his left hand on my right shoulder, and his right hand on my left shoulder. Then I placed my hands, on his shoulders, on his left shoulder my right hand, and on his right shoulder my left hand. . . . And so we paced together between the fences, I forwards, he backwards, until we came to where the fences diverged again. And then turning, I turning, and he turning, we paced back the way we had come . . . (163).

As Watt walks he talks, inverting letters, words, sentences, periods.

At the eighth level Watt reaches the interstices of language, where all syntax is in flux; his arrival parallels his meeting with the Gall family that was not a meeting, but a nothing—the final chop-logic of naught but language and circumstance. In this House of Knott silence is meaning. There are no symbols because Watt exhausts all appearances of reality until reality vanishes, inverted, as he reverses field, or tires, or ends in inconclusion. Grave's story of Earnest Louit's defense of his dissertation, "The Mathematical Intuitions of the Visicelts," before the endlessly shifting board of examiners—Mr. O'Meldon, Mr. Mageshorn, Mr. Fitzwein, Mr. de Baker and Mr. MacStern—demonstrates Beckett's skill at permutative hyperbole. The ultimate achievement of the Visicelts is represented by an ancient, Mr. Nackybal (whose real name is Tisler), whose skill at cubing roots in his head is traced to his having memorized the cubes of one to nine. This is hardly earth-shaking material. Language is traversed, reversed, and inversed until nothing is left but the onion skin of process.

Beckett explores the bonding of creatures of the imagination with chance forms of consciousness in the world of *How It Is,* a world of a succession of victims, tormentors, and incessant inversions in the nuclear glue of cerebral functions:

> words quaqua then in me when the panting stops bits and scraps a murmur this old life same old words same old scraps millions of times each time the first how it was before Pim before that again with Pim after Pim before Bom how it is how it will be all that words for all that in me I hear them murmur them[13]

The narrator of *How It Is* is words, a dramatic conduit of consciousness-shaping images. Whatever the words say, the narrator becomes. When he is Pim, he *is* Pim; when he is tormentor of another, he *is* tormentor, as he states. There is no other way of being. Until the victim understands this process, consciousness has no name. Until the sounds are shaped into meaning, the murmurs are undistorted reflections, memory traces that language summons. In *How It Is* consciousness is torment of the freedom of the imagination, which in turn torments other images from the past. An endless procession of summonings and discardings—in which Pim, the image, is summoned and jettisoned by Bom, the tormentor, according to the needs of reality—concludes as it begins. Process is the last word.

Even the narrator's apparently prescient knowledge does not change the endless procession of Pims and Boms. In part two, Pim's approach to the narrator is identical to the narrator's own approach to Bom in part four (assuming that the novel continues). And just as Pim gives up his identity for that of Bom, the narrator gives up his "Pim-ness" to become, in turn, Bom, the tormentor:

> the one I'm waiting for oh not that I believe in him I say it as I hear it he can give me another it will be my first Bom he can call me Bom (60)

The train of intelligence that this external dance reveals does not show the slightest hope of acquiring any insight into what it means to be conscious. Language and form are knee-jerk reactions of successive victims and their tormentors:

> no other goal than the next mortal cleave to him give him a name train him up bloody him all over with Roman capitals gorge on his fables unite for life in stoic love to the last shrimp (62)

Once the persecutor encounters and traps the victim, the training regime begins with very specific lessons:

> first lesson theme song I dig my nails into his armpit right hand right pit he cries I withdraw then thumb with fist on skull his face sinks in the mud his cries cease end of first lesson (62)

After the persecutor accomplishes a circumnavigation of Pim's body, the second of eight lessons elicits Pim's voice. Words are agonizing to Pim but life-giving to Bom. The narrator devours little scenes of life from long ago that Pim recalls. The training regime continues until Pim's lessons have been completed. What was once freedom is trapped in language, a habit of being:

> one sing hails in armpit two speak blade in arse three stop thump on skull four louder pestle on kidney five softer index in anus six bravo clap athwart arse seven lousy same as three eight encore same as one (69)

At the end of the sequence civilization and literature triumph once again.

Beckett makes it abundantly clear that language cannot provide an answer to process. Silence is always broken by murmurs; beauty and the perfectability of the world are subject to decay and putrefaction, the inevitable concomitants of the world of exterior reality. Even the mind itself, freed from the confines of the body, exists only in its promise of "continuosity." Equally limiting, the body changes endlessly in its intercourse with eternity. Beckett's creatures are confronted with the anachronistic Cartesian concept of mind-body dualism. Accommodation to

Cartesian ethics is impossible; negation is absurd; affirmation is intellectually dishonest. But the imagination, in which forms of memory rise
and fall away undiminished by the passage of years, is the way to
freedom.

The 1965 publication of the French version of *Imagination Dead Imagine* marked a new departure. In it Beckett examines the modern Cartesian mind-body dualism that plagued Geulincx, Malebranche, and
Leibnitz in a manner that defies language:

> No trace anywhere of life, you say, pah, no difficulty there, imagina-
> tion not dead yet, yes, dead, good, imagination dead imagine.[14]

With the imagination "dead" he describes the *agon* with mathematical
precision: two bodies, that of a man and a woman, are contained within
"two diameters at right angles AB CD divide the white ground into two
semicircles ACB BDA" (7). The narrator continues his description, in
which he brings the art of the novel to a state of high technology:

> the head against the wall at B, the arse against the wall at A, the knees
> against the wall between B and C, the feet against the wall between C
> and A, that is to say inscribed in the semicircle ACB, merging in the
> white ground were it not for the long hair of strangely imperfect
> whiteness, the white body of a woman finally (12).

He similarly describes a man within the semicircle BDA.

Beckett describes the site of the work and the palpable white background against which its figures pulsate with the accuracy of a mathe-
matician: "White too the vault and the round wall eighteen inches high
from which it springs. Go back out, a plain rotunda, all white in the
whiteness, go back in, rap, solid throughout, a ring as in the imagination
the ring of bone" (8). He scrupulously observes the positions in which
the two bodies lie within their semicircles—on their right sides, holding
left leg with left arm, left arm with right hand a little above the elbow, in
the light and heat, the gray and cool, the black and cold—with all the
variations of light and heat, dark and cold, vibrations and resonances.
He codifies reality to death. And something is missing:

> Only murmur ah, no more, in this silence, and at the same instant for
> the eye of prey the infinitesimal shudder instantaneously sup-
> pressed. . . . no question now of ever finding again that white speck
> lost in whiteness, to see if they lie still in the stress of that storm, or of a
> worse storm, or in the black dark for good, or the great whiteness
> unchanging, and if not what are they doing (13–14).

The irony of *Imagination Dead Imagine* derives from the knowledge that consciousness is the *prey* of imagination, which defines itself in the absence of the other. An end of imagination is an end of the recurring images that form, or constitute, consciousness. As Beckett jettisons the old he installs the new, and renews the struggle for dominance that consciousness and unconsciousness represent, whether in the convulsive light of external reality or in the dark of absolute stillness within. Without bonding, life as it is now known does not exist.

The bonding in *How It Is* and *Imagination Dead Imagine* recalls that historical Pleistocene moment in the development of man when humanity crossed the "threshold of reflection": when something in man "turned back on itself and—so to speak—took an infinite leap forward."[15] That moment of reflection, when man first perceived the mind's eye, was the original moment of drama, from which all mimetic, scientific, and artistic forms derived. The binary moment when the image of the mind was united in consciousness with an image on the retina of the eye made the dominant species on earth. The first drama, in that sense, was a binary moment in the mind's eye in which, through the operation of the imagination, an image of the past united to an image of external reality in a moment of insight.

Man achieves many things in the conscious world. Artists have always pressed the boundaries of the imagination, through the development of self-awareness in the area that lies, or intervenes, between artists and their subject matter. The influences of the Yeats brothers—Jack Yeats in particular—on Beckett's early development was essential. But of the early predecessors influencing Beckett in the field of self-awareness, none was more prominent than James Joyce.

Maria Jolas, the American widow of Eugène Jolas, the 1930s editor of *Transition* magazine, the Paris-based literary review that published Beckett and Joyce, recalled the friendship between them:

> When I read Sam today . . . his writing . . . seems to bridge the gap for me between now and Joyce. I hear the same soft Dublin voice, I sense the vast cultural past, the same ferocious but as often very gentle irony, the same humanity and rare wit that makes me laugh out loud as I read. Like Joyce he is also a Christ-haunted man, not yet of the new barbarism. . . .
> But there is a fundamental difference. Joyce could still say yes, whereas Sam's answer is definitely no.[16]

An American critic, Ruby Cohn, also noted the influence of Joyce in Beckett's art, and quoted Beckett: "Joyce had a moral effect on me—he made me realize artistic integrity."[17] But similarities of accent and of moral responsibility cannot conclude the issue of artistic indebtedness. Samuel Beckett's art is not subsumed in the writings of James Joyce.

Beckett, of course, has been unfailingly generous in acknowledging literary influences, where they exist. But he has also been very particular in noting dissimilarities between other artists and himself. In November 1980 he remarked, "Joyce dealt with maxima; I deal with minima."[18] In an early review of Beckett's work, Ihab Hassan commented on the dissimilarities between Beckett's and Joyce's work, which multiplied as time went on:

> [Beckett] begins by parodying the inventories of *Ulysses* and the puns of *Finnegan's Wake* and ends by devising a system of combinations and permutations more pure than any Joyce could have invented.[19]

Finally, Richard Coe cited an essential difference between the work of the two artists from quite another perspective:

> Like Joyce, [Beckett] is intrigued by words, but whereas for the author of *Finnegan's Wake,* language was an intimate part of the mystery of creation, for Beckett words are the chief ingredient of the art of failure; they form that impenetrable barrier of language which forever keeps us from knowing who we are, what we are.[20]

An excruciating awareness of self—the space that intervenes between object and representer—prevented Beckett from embracing language in the same way Joyce did. Beckett knew, almost from the first publication of his literary career, what the parameters of his own art would be: "For the artist who does not deal in surface . . . the only possible spiritual development is in a sense of depth."[21]

Samuel Beckett wrote *Proust,* his first extended piece of literary criticism, in 1931. "Shrinking from the nullity of extracircumferential phenomena," he plunged "into the core of the eddy," in an excavatory search that was diametrically different from Joyce's efforts in verbal calisthenics. The subject matter both authors chose was the Irish people. But their works of art are signally different. In a 1967 letter to Sighle Kennedy, Beckett expressly and emphatically stated his own direction: "I simply do not feel the presence in my writing as a whole of the Joyce and Proust situation."[22]

Richard Ellmann cited an important similarity between the work of James Joyce and Samuel Beckett that he believed derived from the friendship the older writer shared with the struggling young poet—they shared the same sentiments about their subject. Ireland was "an old sow that [ate] her farrow."[23] Surely his feelings gave Beckett good reason to find in his art a rationale for external chaos in his art. However, his remark does not justify his vision of language as a medium of communication ill-suited to its purpose. The origin of that idea can be traded at least as far back as the 1931 publication of the "Poetry in Vertical" manifesto in *Transition* magazine. Among the manifesto's signatories were Thomas MacGreevy (who introduced Beckett to Joyce), Jack Yeats, and Samuel Beckett.[24] According to the Verticalists,

> The final disintegration of the "I" in the creative act is made possible by the use of a language which is a mantic instrument, and which does not hesitate to adopt a revolutionary attitude toward word and syntax, going even so far as to invent a hermetic language, if necessary.[25]

Realist art of the nineteenth and twentieth centuries strives to reduce the artist's subjectivity to zero in exactly the same way the Verticalists sought to limit all the artist's ego functions.

The Verticalists' manifesto also implies the limitations of language in the definition of things. Indeterminacy of meaning has occupied deconstructive critics for years, as Geoffrey Hartman succinctly pointed out:

> We assume that, by the miracle of art, the "presence of the word" is equivalent to the presence of meaning. But the opposite can also be urged, that the word carries with it a certain absence or indeterminacy of meaning.[26]

The principle of indeterminacy has long been known to science as the Heisenberg principle of uncertainty. The discoverer of quantum mechanics, Heisenberg declared that to measure an object (an atom, for example) is to change it. In a review of *En Attendant Godot*, Gabor Mihalyi noted Beckett's success in applying the Verticalists' theory to his art:

> Beckett takes stylization to the utmost limit; all matter is dissolved in form. . . . Even speech is deprived of its function as a medium of communication, being reduced to a formal element, like structure or atmosphere.[27]

The translation of images into a mantic language that dissolved self-consciousness occupied Beckett for the next four decades.

Joyce and Beckett both saw memory as the key to their art, in which they arranged images from the past in new configurations. But Joyce moved his images horizontally, across the boundaries of language and syntax, whereas Beckett moved his images vertically, into the recesses of the unconscious. The similarities that commentators have found in the works of Joyce and Beckett are primarily a matter of common subject matter and of final objectives. Their means of achieving their artistic goals were quite distinct.

So were their respective approaches to the world. Ultimately reflected in their art, their individual attitudes were also evident in their "conversations" with each other. Both men were addicted to periods of quiet. Critics have noted with amusement the resistible silence meeting the plausible pause:

> They engaged in conversations which consisted often of silences directed toward each other, both suffused with sadness, Beckett mostly for the world, Joyce mostly for himself. Joyce sat in his habitual posture, legs crossed, toe of the upper leg under the instep of the lower; Beckett, also tall and slender, fell into the same gesture. Joyce suddenly asked some such question as "How could the idealist Hume write a history?" Beckett replied, "A history of representations."[28]

Joyce wanted to expand the self into consciousness in more complex ways than had ever before been achieved; Beckett, in contrast, wanted to shrink the role of the self. Beckett's goal was to find the limits of self-awareness as an expression of consciousness. Joyce's sadness for himself reflected the world's failure (in his eyes) to recognize his genius. Beckett's sadness reflected the impossibility of communication, of the world, of the self, of self-consciousness, in even the simplest exercise. There can be no question of Joyce's influence on Beckett. But there were many more.

James Joyce and Samuel Beckett were not the only Irishmen who explored the underside of the mind in the twentieth century. One of the foremost Irish poets of the period, William Butler Yeats, also developed his dramatic vocabulary in the mind's eye of the imagination. Yeats was the dominant literary figure during Beckett's early years as a literateur. James Joyce practically established his reputation by insulting the older poet in person. Beckett, ever the gentleman, once remarked that he admired the late work of W. B. Yeats, and recalled with pleasure Yeats's favorable review of one line of *Whoroscope*.

The relationship between Beckett and W. B. Yeats was not always one of mutual admiration, however. Certainly the exchanges between the two men never reached the acerbity of the Joyce-Yeats contretemps. Nevertheless, Beckett felt that Yeats was too pompous and postured in his early days, and too inclined to slobber fatuously over all the wrong aspects of Irish society.[29]

Beckett was offended by many of the personal mannerisms of the elder Yeats brother. But for Beckett there were other, more important, literary lessons to be learned from W. B. Yeats. Those lessons influenced the entire course of Beckett's career, slightly acknowledged though they were. John Montague noted the particular interest Beckett displayed for Yeats's works in 1961, twenty-two years after the poet's death:

The Metal Man, c. 1912, pen and ink and watercolor on card, 11¾ × 13¼. Sen. Michael Yeats.

Glory, 1952, 40 × 60. Mr. A. J. F. O'Reilly, Castle Martin, County Kildaire, Ireland.

Circus Poster, **Courtesy Special Collections, University of Victoria.**

A BROAD SHEET

AUGUST, 1903

PICTURES BY JACK B. YEATS AND OTHERS.

An Chraoibhin or Hanrahan in The Twisting of the Rope

HANRAHAN.

There is a pearl of a woman giving light to us;
She is my love, she is my desire.
She is fair Oona, the gentle queen-woman,
And the Munstermen do not understand half her courtesy.

These Munstermen are blinded by God;
They do not recognise the swan beyond the grey duck.
But she will come with me, my fine Helen,
Where her person and her beauty shall be praised for ever.

Arrah, wisha, wisha, wisha! isn't this the fine village? isn't this
the exceeding village? The village where there be that many rogues
hanged that the people have no want of ropes with all the ropes
that they steal from the hangman!

> The sensible Connachtman makes
> A rope for himself;
> But the Munsterman steals it
> From the hangman;
> That I may see a fine rope,
> A rope of hemp yet,
> A stretching on the throats
> Of every person here!

*Translated by Lady Gregory from Douglas Hyde's "Twisting of
the Rope."*

THE GRAND CONVERSATION UNDER
THE ROSE.

As Mars and Minerva were viewing some implements,
Belona stepped forward and asked them the news;
Or were they repairing those fine warlike instruments,
That now are growing rusty for want of being used?
Saying the money is withdrawing, and the traffic is diminishing,
Mechanics they are walking without shoes or hose;
Come, stir up a war, and the world will be flourishing—
This grand conversation was under the rose.

See how they transact in the States of America,
Renowned independence there sits on the throne;
They are not misguided by the schemes of their ministry,
That would extract the marrow from the centre of the bone.
Let us enlarge that hero that set the world a-trembling,
Whose name was a terror to his imperious foes;
Although the day is lost, 'twas by dissembling—
This grand conversation was under the rose.

He was a fine statesman, and noble, fine general,
His equal was never in influence before;
His abilities are brighter than a diamond or mineral,
As thousands can verify that lie in their gore.
The active Napoleon did make the money fly about,
Until came combining policy, at last did him depose.
These numbers who contested him would now rejoice to see him out—
This grand conversation was under the rose.

The Farm and Comedian would wish the great Bonaparte
Was brought on the stage to act a new play.
They find their industry drawn by ministerial art,
But all is not sufficient their vast debts to pay.
He had not been contested with more than Alexander done,
But planting requisition, just as he did propose;
But the All-seeing Eye would not let him o'er the world run—
This grand conversation was under the rose.

Old Irish Song.

THE DEAD MAN'S POINT.

Hand coloured. Post free. 12s. 6d. a Year. Published Monthly. A Specimen Copy may be had, 13 Pence, post free.
PORTFOLIOS, to hold 24 copies, may be had, price Two Shillings each, or Two Shillings and Sixpence Post Free,
in the United Kingdom.
A few Sets of A BROADSHEET for 1902 may still be had.
PUBLISHED AND SOLD BY ELKIN MATHEWS, VIGO STREET, LONDON, W.
No. 20   **All Rights Reserved**
                       FAIRCHOUSE & SON, PRINTERS CROYDON

*This Grand Conversation was held
under the Rose,* **1903, broadsheet. Courtesy Special Collections, University
of Victoria.**

He usually read through the entire canon of a particular author, and at this time, he was absorbed in W. B. Yeats's *Collected Poems*. In the past, he had deliberately shunned Yeats's poetry and knew only his most famous poems—those which no Irishman living in Dublin could avoid—and had concentrated on the plays, for which he had great respect and admiration. There were lines in *The Countess Cathleen* that he knew by heart, and passages from *At the Hawk's Well* that never failed to move him.[30]

Beckett's own literary fortunes had remarkably improved in the intervening years. He was disposed to think well of the difficult times he had survived, when even the thought of writing a laudatory note in honor of a successful friend had depressed him.[31] The influence of Joyce was past. Beckett was finally able to judge dispassionately W. B. Yeats's long career and the formative influence he had had on the youthful Trinity graduate.

The bearing Joyce had on Beckett's relationship with W. B. Yeats can be judged from Yeats's painful account of his first meeting with the arrogant twenty-year-old Joyce who was at the time seventeen years his junior. Joyce was determined to establish his mark in Irish letters immediately, and wasted little time in demolishing the reputation of a man he believed unworthy, or at the very least, no longer worthy of it. Richard Ellmann reported Yeats's summary of their meeting:

> He [Joyce] had thrown over metrical form, he said, that he might get a form so fluent that it would respond to the motions of the spirit. I praised his work but he said, "I really don't care whether you like what I am doing or not. It won't make the least difference to me. Indeed I don't know why I am reading to you."
>
> Then, putting down his book, he began to explain all his objections to everything I had ever done. Why had I concerned myself with politics, with folklore, with the historical settings of events. . . ? I felt exasperated and puzzled and walked up and down explaining the dependence of all good art on popular tradition. . . .
>
> I looked at my young man. I thought, "I have conquered him now," but I was quite wrong. He merely said, "Generalizations aren't made by poets; they are made by men of letters. They are no use. . . . I have met you too late. You are too old."[32]

The attack was not defensible. Ellmann made short work of Joyce's petty insouciance. The poet's integration of individualized consciousness with historical and popular images, the basis of much of Yeats's work, would one day be the nadir of Joyce's own creations.[33]

Yeats was stung by the attack, remarkable more for the honesty with which he preserved it than for its inherent value. He himself knew that much of his early work had not accomplished all he had hoped it would. He himself commented on his shortcomings with equal honesty:

> I had set out on life with the thought of putting my very self into poetry, and had understood this as a representation of my own visions and an attempt to cut away the non-essential, but as I imagined the visions outside myself my imagination became full of decorative landscape and of still life.[34]

His attempt to "cut away" the nonessential elements of poetic truth, which Yeats subsequently labeled "an increase of the masculine element at the expense of the feminine component," was characteristic of his late work, and provided a link between the mature poet and Samuel Beckett that Beckett himself acknowledged many years after W. B.'s death.

The divergence between Yeats and Beckett was never more apparent than in their development of the artistic equation from its primary sources: Yeats exploded into decorative landscapes and still life; Beckett imploded into inner-scapes of light and darkness, imaginative forms that might best be described as "more than screams than song."[35] Yeats's early perception of the imagination as the site of twentieth century art was prescient enough, but his expansion of the boundaries of the supersensual faery world created problems for him, as Joyce—and Beckett after him—did not hesitate to point out.

Following their initial encounter, the relationship between Joyce and Yeats did not noticeably prosper. However, with age and a reputation no longer shining, Joyce improved his manners, if not his opinion of the older poet. W. B. Yeats died on 8 January 1939. After his funeral one wreath arrived late. It was from James Joyce, adjudged by the critic Richard Ellmann to be "a fellow symbolist who believed with equal intensity in natural things."[36] *Res ipsa loquitur.*

In conversation Beckett acknowledged the importance of W. B. Yeats's later work, in which he simplified his dramatic constructions and symbol systems. Analysis of Yeats's plays and writings reveals additional evidence of the influence he had on Beckett's development as a playwright. The influence was, of necessity, selective, as W. B.'s legendary eclecticism posed its own structural problems. His occultism and corollary "mumbo jumbo," for example, has been fashionably discounted for years.[37] The phases and gyres and tinctures of Yeats's elaborate symbol systems obscured more than they revealed. But his Cuchulain cycle plays were useful sources for Beckett's own art. The elder Yeats brother may have focused on all the wrong aspects of modern Ireland, but he did focus on Ireland and on the Irish imagination, for which both Jack Yeats and Samuel Beckett were indebted to him.

W. B. Yeats's influence on Beckett was partially attributable to his use of theater space. The stagescape of Yeats's plays was the mind's eye; the subject of his late plays was the Irish people of the twentieth century. The site he chose for his plays was the threshold of consciousness, depicted in the theater as nightfall. In his late plays he attempted to unite the spectator's mind with the actor's virtual presence. His last plays, *Purgatory* and *The Death of Cuchulain,* were a triumph of stagecraft. Yeats's ironic perspective was sharpened by years during which his countrymen neglected him. He had spent long arduous years learning his craft and exploring the legends of ancient Ireland. At Yeats's death the legends passed into history; his craft, however, passed to Beckett.

In his last years Yeats felt betrayed by his countrymen, and he freely expressed his anger at a new individualistic generation of Irishmen who ignored Ireland's ancient myths. His feeling of betrayal infused his writing with bitterness. He described himself, in "The Tower," as having finished his "dog's day. An ancient bankrupt master of this house." In "Among School Children," Yeats derided his stature (as Ireland's national poet) as that of "a comfortable kind of old scarecrow," betrayed by a new generation. In his introduction to "Fighting the Waves" in *Wheels and Butterflies* (1934), Yeats summed up his career as a dramatist:

> I wrote in blank verse, which I tried to bring as close to common speech as the subject permitted, a number of connected plays—*Deirdre, At the Hawk's Well, The Green Helmet, On Baile's Strand, The Only Jealousy of Emer.* I would have attempted the Battle of the Ford and the Death of Cuchulain, had not the mood of Ireland changed.[38]

Yeats did, in fact, write *The Death of Cuchulain* in 1938 and 1939. It was his last play, and it depicts the aging poet as Cuchulain, going forward to battle for the last time, against death itself.

Yeats's characterization of himself as a figure of legendary Ireland was not unusual. Cuchulain was a central feature of Yeats's mask as an artist. Richard Ellmann noted, for example, that Yeats was a man who almost dreamed himself into becoming the poet his imagination originally projected: "[Yeats's] timidity as a young man, encouraged him to nourish his imagination. . . . Then, with great courage and will, he tried to become the hero of whom he had dreamed and to instill into Ireland a heroic atmosphere."[39] His concentration of effort brought the sharpest of reactions from Joyce, Beckett, and others among his countrymen; but, in the beginning, Yeats had great hopes.

In an 1897 letter to William Sharp (known by the pseudonymn "Fiona MacLeod"), Yeats proclaimed a new theory of poetical "legendary drama" that utilized only symbolic and decorative settings: "A forest, for

RITTER LIBRARY
BALDWIN-WALLACE COLLEGE

instance, should be represented by a forest pattern and not by a forest painting. One should design a scene which would be an accompaniment not a reflection of the text."[40] Two years earlier, Yeats had protested vigorously against the current fashion in drama. He had no use for Ibsen and realism, which Beckett would later describe in *Proust* as "the grotesque fallacy of realistic art—'that miserable statement of line and surface,' and the penny-a-line vulgarity of a literature of notations."[41] Yeats was convinced that an age of imagination, of emotion, of moods, and of revelation was at hand: "And when the external world is no more the standard of reality, we will learn again that the great passions are angels of God . . . for art is a revelation." He felt that art, in its highest moments, was "pure life; and [that] every feeling [was] the child of all past ages."[42] Hence Yeats returned to ancient Irish legend—the old fantastical expression—for inspiration, "for in literature, unlike science, there are no discoveries, and it is always the old that returns."[43]

The greatest source of difficulty for Yeats was the actor, who kept intruding his nature into the expression of Yeats's archetypal ideas. His "über marionettes" broke in everywhere on the poet's schemata for the theater. Yeats proclaimed the sovereignty of the actor over the stage decor, but placed poetry at the apex of his dramatic triad, to upstage both character and setting. Nothing was to be allowed to interfere with the transmission of the poet's ideas from the page of the text to the mind's eye of the spectator. On one occasion Yeats went to extraordinary lengths to ensure the compliance of his actors:

> I understood these things in which actors kept still enough to give poetical writing its full effect upon the stage. I had imagined such acting, though I had not seen it, and had once asked a dramatic company to let me rehearse them in barrels that they might forget gesture and have their minds free to think of speech for a while.[44]

Yeats did not record the actors' opinions of his training sessions, nor of the successful effect of his innovations on the finished production. Beckett had other reasons for putting Hamm's aged parents in ashcans. But it is interesting to speculate on this comic echo; *Endgame*'s Nagg and Nell have absurdist antecedents, if not cursed progenitors, of their own.

W. B. Yeats's theory of the stage bore a marked resemblance to that of his friend, Edward Gordon Craig, who believed that an actor's emotional makeup was an impediment to real communication in the theater. But Yeats also had a philosophical basis for his art that he had derived from introspective analysis. For him theater was a revelation of self and anti-self, of demon, and of mask. "Man and Daimon are wed," according to Yeats, "when the man has found a mask whose lineaments permit the expression of all the man most lacks, and it may be dreads, and of that only."[45] The power of the imagination, in certain states of revery, exposed the demon and the mask. In his plays Yeats mounted those states of revery onstage, and proclaimed that his vision was the "Anima Mundi"—the soul of the world—that would liberate the jaded urban intellectual from the world of university life or of busy city thoroughfares.

Following Swedenborg, W. B. Yeats developed theories of an afterlife that compounded the complexity of his symbol systems. His predilection for strategies and for elaborately patterned symbols of external reality directly contradicted his goal of reaching through the imagination to a meditative state in which the scenery was like that of the earth: "human forms, grotesque or beautiful, senses that know pleasure and pain."[46] Yeats never tired of describing the meditative state:

> There as here we do not always know all that is in our memory, but need angelic spirits who act upon us there as here, widening and deepening consciousness at will, can draw forth all the past, make us live again all our transgressions and see our victims "as if they were present," together with the place, words, and motives; and that suddenly, as when a scene bursts upon the "sight" and yet continues "for hours together" . . . all the pleasures and pains of sensible life awaken again and again, all our passionate events rush up about us and not as seeming imagination, *for imagination is now the world* (emphasis added).[47]

His guide for tracing footprints through the sands of somnambulistic archetypes was first Swedenborg, then "Indian and Japanese poets, old women in Connaught, mediums in Soho and lay brothers."[48]

W. B. Yeats's most important influence on Samuel Beckett's development came from the elder man's belief in the power of the imagination and his faith in revelation. For him imagination was the key to unlocking the secret doors of the soul, and even those of the afterlife. In his introduction to "The Cat and the Moon," Yeats argued for a lunar symbol for the soul:

> Perhaps some early Christians . . . thought as I do, saw in the changes of the moon all the cycles: the soul realizing its separate being in the full moon, then, as the moon seems to approach the sun and dwindle away, all but realizing its absorption in God, only to whirl away once more: the mind of a man separating itself from the common matrix, through childish imaginations, through struggle—Vico's heroic age—to roundness, completeness, and then externalising, intellectualising, systematising, until at last it lies dead. . . .[49]

Taking the moon as symbol of the reflective soul, Yeats quickly developed an elaborate thesis of successive incarnations. He saw twenty-eight possibilities:

> corresponding to the phases of the moon, the light part of the moon's disc symbolizing the subjective and the dark part . . . the objective nature, the wholly dark moon (called phase 1) and the wholly light (called phase 15) symbolizing complete objectivity and complete subjectivity respectively.[50]

For Yeats the course of a man's life was a series of lives, an elaborate fugue that typically consisted of thirteen cycles of twenty-eight incarnations each. Souls that failed to find a rhythmic body after centuries of life, were condemned to be born again, and to be instructed further in the nuances of time and space. The complexity of his scheme did nothing to improve the quality of Yeats's tragedy, but it did allow him to express, in symbolic form, the impossibility and the incompleteness of daily life.

Yeats's belief in the power of revelation was his effort to engage the universal soul, the Anima Mundi, as the inspiration for his writings. Three hundred years of Cartesian logic—the "provincial centuries"—had completely neglected the imagination as the principal source of artistic creation. W. B. was anxious, in his work, to make amends, for he believed religion to be the true basis of drama—not formal religion, but the faith in an order of things that gave man a destiny more mysterious and significant than that of any single human consciousness.[51] It is a relatively simple matter to watch Yeats, through the medium of the trance state, move his mind's eye across the corpus callosum, from language to sign, from left hemisphere to right, and to observe a world he subsequently described as imagination:

> If you suspend the critical faculty, I have discovered, either as a result of training, or, if you have the gift, by passing into a slight trance, images pass rapidly before you. . . . Those who follow the old rule keep their bodies still and their minds awake and clear, dreading especially any confusion between the images of the mind and the objects of sense; they seek to become, as it were, polished mirrors.[52]

This reflective act gave the poet his unity of being. The unexcelled quality of the finely articulated images that passed before the mind's eye became the basis for Yeats's theater pieces. He created a symbol system to portray scenes from his trance state in order to communicate what Peter Ure so aptly described as "that which hides itself continually in the depths of the soul."[53] W. B.'s solution was a major problem that vexed

Yeats all his life. His subject matter was the mind's eye, which Beckett subsequently adapted to his own purposes. However, the communication of the subject matter, a question of technique and of theatrical sense, marked the differences between the two poets.

Yeats's predilection for strategies and for elaborately patterned symbols protected him from the world. Unlike Yeats, Beckett chose to embrace the freedom of pure chance and chaos, and to become, in the words of *Murphy,* "a point in the ceaseless unconditioned generation and passing away of line . . . a mote in its absolute freedom."[54]

Yeats also differed from Beckett in his development of a poetic based on the substantive material of Irish legend. The poet justified his actions by using techniques he ascribed to Shakespeare and to the Greek playwrights of the classical era. In "At Stratford-On-Avon," W. B. Yeats suggested that Shakespeare was primarily interested in creating "a personal myth, depicting the alienation suffered by the artistic personality."[55] Yeats believed that the great Elizabethan bard suffered the shortcomings of his age, which Yeats described as a Renaissance heritage of continental influences that tainted the pure English strain of language and of history. Yeats was determined not to follow the Shakespearean model, but to look to the chanted odes of ancient Greek drama—"actors with masks upon their faces, and their stature increased by artifice *[kothurnes]*."[56] However, he followed the Elizabethan precept of theater that laid great stress on delivering language "to delight the ear" to the spectator. In *The Poet and the Actress,* he restated his principles for an Irish drama, which included a reluctant nod to the Shakespearean agon:

> In every great play—in Shakespeare for instance—you will find a group of characters—Hamlet, Lear, let us say, who express the dream, and another group who express its antagonist and to the antagonist Shakespeare gives a speech close to that of daily life.[57]

Characters in Yeats's early plays embodied the opposites of dream and of daily life. The Fool and the Blind Man of *On Baile's Strand* (1904) and Cuchulain and Conchubar of *The Only Jealousy of Emer* (1919) were examples of the opposition (on one level of interpretation) of the folly and strength of youth to the wisdom and debility of old age. Yeats hoped that these symbols would have the power to transform passion into tragic revery. But instead of increasing the dramatic tension, his images from Ireland's heroic past distanced the spectator and negated the bond between the stage picture and the spectator's mind's eye.

Yeats's theory of the stage limited the actors' scope, not only in gesticulative freedom, but also in facial expression. The players wore masks and acted in settings that accompanied, but did not reflect, the dramatic text. Nothing was allowed to interfere with the communication between playwright and spectator. The myth of the heroic figure took center stage, represented by the actor, not the character. Communication was a shared experience between artist-playwright and artist-spectator; the medium was the artist-actor, who mirrored the soul of Emer or Cuchulain or Conchubar:

> All art is the disengaging of a soul from place and history, its suspension in a beautiful or terrible light to await the Judgment, though it must be, seeing that all its days were the Last Day, judged already.[58]

Yeats was very certain of what he wanted his audience to experience: to look into the mind's eye was to revive common ancestors and to take part in the creative process itself. The experience of sharing the artist's creative moment promised to be one of near-religious frenzy. But Yeats's belief in predestination and the disengagement of the soul gave his plays a neoclassical sound that neutralized their passion. The neutralization was carefully contrived by the poet, who believed that unfulfilled passion became vision: "and . . . vision, whether we wake or sleep, prolongs its power by rhythm and pattern, the wheel where the world is butterfly."[59] The conflicting intentions of Yeats's theater, in which he generated the white heat of artistic conception only to temper it by his use of remote mythological characters and his removal of emotional content from his subject, made it seem less than genuine. The poet's theory of the stage had a special meaning: artificially inflamed passion was intentionally muted and transformed into an emblem of the past—empty, stratified, and always symbolic. One might almost assume that had Yeats not been rejected by Maud Gonne, the great love of his life, he would have invented her out of whole cloth.

An aesthetic for the theater based on abstract conceptions of the mind's eye and the determination to translate these images into romantic figures of Ireland's heroic past posed understandably grave problems for Yeats. His conception for theater was clear, but his implementation of it took decades of frustration and extraordinary strength of will and spirit to resolve. When he wrote on theater in the 1890s Yeats began well:

> After all, is not the greatest play not the play that gives the sensation of an external reality but the play in which there is the greatest abundance of life itself, of the reality that is in our minds?[60]

But his belief in tragic revery as the site of true drama led him to demand static production elements and symbols that provided action and movement into the mind's eye. In 1899 he wrote mistakenly:

The theatre of art, when it comes to exist, must . . . discover grave and decorative gestures, such as delighted Rossetti and Madox Brown, and grave and decorative scenery that will be forgotten the moment an actor has said, 'It is dawn,' or 'it is raining,' or 'the wind is shaking the trees;' and dresses of so little irrelevant magnificence that the mortal actors and actresses may change without much labour into the immortal people of romance.[61]

Unlike romantic poets of the past, Yeats eventually found a way to stage what Barton Friedman called "the deeps of the mind."[62] But in his earlier demand for grave and decorative gesture and scenery he ignored the transforming power of the actor. Instead of creating theatrical moments that would transcend time through the art of performance, Yeats created symbols that stopped time and left his characters and settings covered in a mantel of psychic Irish dust.

For Yeats the dramatist the happy discovery of Japanese Noh drama in the second decade of the twentieth century was an important one. Until that time he had forced his symbolism to carry the entire weight of the action in his theater, and it had crushed his theater. Richard Ellmann described Yeats's difficulty from a slightly different perspective:

The world which Yeats builds up in the 'nineties is . . . a skilful evasion, neither here nor there. His professed object was, like Mallarmé's, to evoke an unseen reality; and symbols were the only way to do it. But in practice, Yeats used the symbols primarily to hide this world rather than to reveal another one. . . . Symbolism, instead of providing a means for balance and reconcilement, furnished an elaborate robe to cover a wretched young man. . . . Instead of manipulating his symbols, he drowned himself in them.[63]

It took Yeats years to recover "theatricality" in his plays; the last of the Cuchulain plays was his best and most "theatrically" successful.

W. B. Yeats's strategy of accommodation to the world and his method of communicating material to the stage differed significantly from those of Samuel Beckett. Nonetheless, the two poets shared a common belief in the doctrine of purgatory that was particularly Irish. Yeats asserted his belief that purgatory derived from early Christianity and Neoplatonism, could be linked to twentieth-century psychical research, and was "a countryman's belief in the nearness of his dead 'working out their penance' in wrath or at the garden end."[64] However, the pain of Yeats's purgatory was Beckettian bliss. The younger poet found his inspiration in the figure of Belacqua Shuah. In Beckett's earliest collection of short stories, *More Pricks than Kicks,* Mr. Shuah was the prototype for a whole kin-group of tramps descended from a character in Dante's *Purgatorio.* Having left his repentance until the last moment, the original Belacqua is condemned to spend a second lifetime waiting at the base of the mountain of Purgatory before beginning his arduous upward climb. "Waiting" is a typical occupation for Beckett's characters; in *En Attendant Godot* Vladimir and Estragon are luminaries for other similar creatures who, like Belacqua, spend

> a whole lifetime resting and daydreaming in the shade of a rock without having to do anything. Belacqua is often mentioned with envy by Beckett's heroes as one who has successfully abandoned everyday life to live in a world of his own imagination.[65]

Beckett's Belacqua, who finds irony and enjoyment in a situation Dante and Yeats's twin characters find painful, adds a richly comic ingredient to his author's work. Much to the detriment of his own work, W. B. Yeats injected purgatory, parapsychology, mediums, and the transmigration of the soul into his poetry and his plays. The influences on Yeats the man— (catalogued by Kathleen Raine) Swedenborg, Blake, the faery faith of Ireland, "book of the people" theosophy, Cabalism (the Order of the Golden Dawn), Plato, Plotinus, Noh plays of Japan, *The Tibetan Book of the Dead*, the Vedas—scarcely left room for Yeats the poet-playwright.[66]

The analysis of levels of consciousness to which Beckett and Yeats both subscribed had an interesting nineteenth-century advocate in Charles L. Dodgson (1832–98), pseudonymously Lewis Carroll, Oxford don, cleric, and writer, who declared that the human being was capable of at least three physical states (with varying degrees of consciousness):

> a. the ordinary state, with no consciousness of the presence of Fairies;
>
> b. the "eerie" state, in which, while conscious of actual surroundings, he is *also* conscious of the presence of Fairies;
>
> c. a form of trance, in which, while *un*conscious of actual surroundings, and apparently asleep, he (i.e. his immaterial essence) migrates to other scenes, in the actual world, or in Fairyland, and is conscious of the presence of Fairies.[67]

Carroll's work predated Yeats's major work by half a century, and Beckett's by seven decades. Fairies and forms of consciousness have been in the air for a long time. While no direct connection should be made between Lewis Carroll's *Alice's Adventures in Wonderland* and Yeats's *At the Hawk's Well* or Beckett's *En Attendant Godot*, the wet stones and the sprouted tree are evidence that someone or something passed through the looking glasses of both the latter playwrights' imaginations. Yeats adopted the trance state as a principle of life:

I know we are approaching some kind of philosophy which will deal with the social state. But I avoid politics merely because I feel that our opinions will not hold. To my way of thinking, speculative interests are our true interests for the time being. The more I ponder it, the more I am confident that the only salvation for the world is to regain its feeling for revelation. . . . We must bring ourselves to distrust general principles, and strive to get some sort of spiritual basis. Until we do there is no hope.[68]

At the beginning of his career Beckett found a similar voice. The young hero of Beckett's *Murphy* binds himself with seven scarves in his rocking chair, relaxing his body to free his mind:

Thus as his body set him free more and more in his mind, he took to spending less and less time in the light, spitting at the breakers of the world; . . . and more and more and more in the dark, in the will-lessness, a mote in its absolute freedom.[69]

The remarkable consistency with which each playwright maintained a singular vision through a long career testifies to the strength each derived from an inner sight, whether of the mind's eye of the imagination or of images induced in a trance state. Whatever its source, Yeats and Beckett never tired of describing the process. In many instances, the process was the artwork, an artistic expression of right-hemisphere thought. While they might have been colorful, mediums, old Connaught women, and Japanese poets were not necessary.

W. B. Yeats's attempt to portray his interpretation of William Blake's "sympathetic will" on the stage was limited only by the medium he chose—a symbol system personified by figures from the Celtic twilight.[70] But Blake's imagination was much richer, much deeper and more encompassing than Yeats's cerebral fantasies. Symbols could not be used as a substitute for reality. Instead of using symbols to create tragedy in the mind's eye, Yeats might have presented the mind's eye as reality onstage as Beckett did in his best dramatic pieces. Both poets inhabited the same stagescape; the differences between them were differences of technique and of theatrical sense. Yeats's long struggle to convey the images of the mind's eye to the patrons of the Abbey Theatre did not end until 1938, when an older W. B. Yeats put aside old symbols and spoke again from his heart.

Presence, Myth, and Discourse in Beckett's Dramaticules after *Not I*

Then it will not be as now, day after day, out, on, round, back, in, like leaves turning, or torn out and thrown crumpled away, but a long unbroken time without before or after.

Samuel Beckett, *No's Knife*

THERE was nothing novel in the notion that Beckett's art changed, circa 1945, from a struggle to represent the accommodations of art to life to a mature vision of an artist struggling with the very possibility of expressing artistic forms of relations in a meaningful context. After the premiere of *Not I* in 1971, the context of Beckett's dramaticules shifted away from the stage picture to the picture plane of the spectators' mind's eye. Presence and discourse, the traditional mimetic embellishments of the theater, began to serve a dual function of explicating the play and reflecting the processes of comprehending the play. Becket's theater became meta-theater of the mind's eye: "I see how I say it as I say it" became a hallmark of Beckett's postmodern works for the theater. There is no question but that he began to write within and beyond the bounds of modernism.

Beckett was not the first to discover the truism that art is not a better or worse copy of nature but an aggregate of traditions, illusions, and devices that represent the world's value systems. The history of modernism is, in fact, the history of representations of interior exploration, in an era whose dominant figure is still Ibsen, in an age that has already discounted realism and modernism in favor of postmodernism—the organicism composed of elements of interiority, realism, and classicism in their romantic, transformational guise. But Beckett was among the first to situate his distinctive theatrical mode in 1945 when he described the paintings of Bram van Velde as exemplary of the artist, whose goal is

to force the deep-seated invisibility of exterior things to the point where invisibility itself becomes a thing. . . . That is a labor of diabolic complexity, which requires a framework of suppleness and extreme lightness, a framework which insinuates more than it asserts.[1]

The line of relationships between pictorial and dramatic art in Beckett's work in the theater stem from his early studies, begun in the thirties with the van Velde brothers. The remains of the modernist context that Beckett regarded as the ruins of a vulgar penny-a-line literature of notations, were nevertheless anchored in objective reality. Beneath that reality Beckett worked tirelessly to portray the deep-seated invisibility of images and objects.

In *The Irish Drama of Europe from Yeats to Beckett*, Katharine Worth argued for the literary indebtedness of Beckett to W. B. Yeats and *fin de siècle* Symbolists.[2] Worth overstated the issue. Artists work within and beyond their traditions, and a case can be made for any era's responsive adaptation to a previous era's aesthetic values. What Worth did not see, although she came very near to uncovering it, was the influence of pictorial artists, and in particular of Jack B. Yeats, the younger brother of W. B. Yeats, on the young Samuel Beckett.

Beckett himself regarded Jack Yeats as a source of artistic inspiration. In 1945, at a critical moment in Beckett's artistic career, he visited Jack Yeats in Ireland. They took a long walk and talked about art. It was Beckett's first trip to Ireland since the late thirties. Their conversation profoundly affected Beckett's attitude toward artistic creation and the limits of intentional creative consciousness. In *Cahiers d'art* (1945), Beckett immediately raised the issue of the necessity of an "insulating framework" for art. But it would be several decades before the full impact of Jack Yeats's insights into creative processes would find their way into Beckett's dramaticules—beginning with *Not I* (1972.) The focus in Beckett's works of figure and ground relationships, and of the virtual destruction of the mind's eye's pictorial plane—the movement from a modernist drama to a postmodern art form—coincided with Beckett's return to his homeland at the conclusion of World War II, and his discussion of art with the younger Yeats brother.

The broad outlines of modernism, the twentieth century's dominant art form, can be seen in the emergence of London's Bloomsbury Group in 1909. Virginia Woolf, the most distinguished member of the Bloomsbury set, whose luminaries included Lytton Strachey, E. M. Forster, Clive and Vanessa Bell, and John Maynard Keynes, defined the direction of the new avant-garde with an image of the modernist temper: "Life," she announced in 1919, "is a luminous halo."[3] In her more serene moments, when she refrained from flicking food at startled dinner guests. Ms. Woolf declared the world to be "a semi-transparent envelope surrounding us from the beginning of consciousness to the end." Woolf's modernist definition of an irradiated objective reality, a post-Freudian device to represent the world's appearances, was one solution to the problems posed by the Cartesian outer shell—*cogito ergo sum*—that had split man's consciousness for three centuries.

Woolf challenged her compatriot craftsmen and artisans to break through the envelope of reality and to convey

> this unknown and uncircumscribed spirit, whatever aberration or complexity it may display, with as little of the alien and external as possible.[4]

However, the alien and external qualities that Woolf sought to avoid in pursuing her modernist aesthetic become the very basis of Beckett's postmodern processes. In fact, Beckett probed precisely those forms which accommodated the very mess of causal process in the hope that something less tangible would seep through, and that a more vertical perspective would emerge from the interstices of objective reality.

In this kind of communication Beckett's dramatic forms are translucent enough to make the attentive spectator question the myth-bearing potential of his images. In the collapse of the pictorial plane, a technique that Beckett borrowed from the visual arts, he elicited sensibilities beyond the old symmetries of language and of feeling:

> without . . . light or dark, from or towards or at, the old half knowledge of when and where gone . . . only a voice dreaming and droning on all around . . . the voice that was once in your mouth.[5]

In Beckett's late works he tore away the envelope of modernism, leaving only fragments of an old literary formula. His goal was still to represent the world's appearances. But his means had changed.

"Eleutheria," Beckett's earliest unpublished work for the theater, bears no resemblance to his late great dramaticules. Written within two years of Beckett's 1945 conversation with Jack Yeats and the publication of Beckett's painting critique of Bram van Velde, the typescript is a long (135 pages) unremarkable drama in three acts. The final measure of Beckett's skill as a dramatist did not appear until the 1972 premiere of *Not I* at Lincoln Center. In Beckett's case, a period of artistic gestation was apparently essential for his move from the critical to the narrative (*From an Abandoned Work,* 1957), to the dramatic posture of *Not I*.

Linda Ben Zvi has described the complex nature of Mouth in *Not I* as an expression of "the schismatic self," a concomitant refusal "to say I because of a me that cannot be covered by the personal pronoun and cannot be verbalized."[6] The schismatic self is expressed in more than grammatical terms. Beckett deliberately *vaguens* (obscures) his modernist landscapes to the point where dramatic images intersect with language. Figure and ground relationships are reversed. The Auditor hovers in the air downstage left. Mouth's red lips seem to float in space upstage (or downstage—in the dark, one is not certain), as language gushes in torrents from her painted lips. By collapsing the conventional picture plane, Beckett invites spectator participation. There is room for insinuation, for the permeability of a diaphanous presence, in the midst of Mouth's messianic, multidimensional discourse. The lips of Mouth may serve as "figure," but what is the relationship of Auditor? And are both Auditor and Mouth "figure" to the "ground" of the spectator's imagination? One cannot be certain. Beckett had deliberately vaguened the images in his work, visually and grammatically.

Martin Esslin, an early and insightful critic of Beckett, has noted the compression and power of images that he demonstrated in this work. In *Not I*, Beckett had become a master of the orchestrated image, adding to or deliberately obscuring an image with the skill of a pictorial artist. One realizes immediately the importance of Jack Yeats to Beckett as the latter "paints" his stage portraits. According to Esslin, who sensed rather than elucidated Beckett's technique,

> *Not I* is an immensely important work. It contains substance which lesser writers would have needed three or four hundred hours on the stage or a 500-page novel (at least!) to encompass, and moulds the wealth of human suffering a whole lifetime of human experience, into an image so telling, so graphic, into words so brilliantly meaningful, that a bare quarter of an hour suffices to communicate it all.[7]

In contrast to *Not I*, "Eleutheria" did not display the compression and power so clear in Beckett's later works. "Eleutheria" required a *mise en scène* of two distinct places—a principal action and a marginal action—the latter almost entirely silent except for a few short phrases. In three acts these two juxtaposed scenes can be progressively seen from different angles, the principal action always mounted on the right (stage left), and the marginal action on the left. Hence the Krap salon—a sitting-room corner—is dominant in act 1; Victor's room—a solitary bedframe—is dominant in act 2—the set presumably being designed to revolve. Act 3 has no marginal action. Beckett gave the reason in his play notes—the Krap setting, with its round elegant table, four period chairs, arm chair, candelabra, and sconce, have all fallen into the pit on the last revolve, a kind of *deus ex machina* of the naturalistic set.[8]

As Beckett's art developed, his drama moved inward from the objective to the subjective realm of the imagination. In *Not I*, the *mise en scène* no longer consisted of two external realms—a principal action and a marginal action—but of two levels of consciousness: "not I," and "she." Beckett's technical virtuosity in dealing with a dehiscent self in *Not I* stood in sharp contrast to the split-focus setting of "Eleutheria." The vertical thrust of *Not I,* the collapse of the picture plane of reference in the play, and the demand for audience collaboration to complete the imagery, orchestrated by the delineation of stages of an image through language and gesture, set off the latter work.

Beckett's problem in "Eleutheria" was one not of "fixing up" the script but of translating its images into more adequate vehicles of communication. This is probably the reason why the play has remained unproduced. In *Waiting for Godot,* Beckett's second play (and first produced), he "found the trick." Now the virtual world of the imagination carried more meaning than the real world of external reality. The playwright allowed the spectator to enter a real world within the imagination, rather than the virtual world translated into the real world. Beckett worked to make this point clear:

> *Estragon.* Charming spot. *(He turns, advances to front, halts facing auditorium.)* Inspiring prospects.
>
> (10A)

The virtual world of the mind's eye is opened directly:

> *Vladimir.* All the same . . . that tree . . . *(turning toward auditorium)* that bog. . . .
>
> (10B)

In act 2 Beckett breaks the aesthetic distance of the stage once again in an attempt to establish a virtual link to the imagination, this time more tentatively:

> *Vladimir.* . . . . Not a soul in sight! Off you go! Quick! *(He pushes Estragon towards auditorium. Estragon recoils in horror.)* You won't? *(He contemplates auditorium.)* Well I can understand that.
>
> (47B)

There is, of course, one moment of actual reality that Beckett did include in *Godot:*

> *Vladimir.* I'll be back.
> *He hastens towards the wings.*
> *Estragon.* End of the corridor, on the left.
> *Vladimir.* Keep my seat.
> *Exit Vladimir.*
>
> (23B)

Unique among plays in the modern repertoire, *Godot* contains actual exits that exist in a specific theater in Paris, and virtual exits that do not exist in any theater in the world:

> *Vladimir/Estragon.* Let's go. *They do not move.*
>
> (35B, 60B)

As the odd couple in *Godot* remark, there is no lack of void or of compartments of virtual reality in the mind's eye. There are also more reasons than ever to acknowledge finally the theater games played by a dehiscent double image:

> *Estragon.* We always find something, eh Didi, to give us the impression we exist?
>
> (44B)

These images derive from Beckett's first explorations of a split stage of "Eleutheria." Until Beckett can dramatize his split subjective presence and accommodate the audience's participation in his stage picture, lessons he learned in part from Jack Yeats, Beckett's stage is static, distorted, and convoluted. The physical collapse of half the set into the pit in act 3 can be a metaphor for the play as a whole.

Beckett's exploration of the limits of communication were not the conventional exploration of imagery from within the imagination to the limits of consciousness, but delving of a communication of the presence that extends from within the imagination to the limits of the unconscious—within to "in." In *Waiting for Godot,* intervals of speech and action serve as punctuation points, grammatical signposts that anchor the work to external reality. In time the work he began in *Godot* became a kind of game in which theater stood as a paradigm for Beckett's external reality. Paul Lowry, for example, has noted Beckett's strategy in *Fin de Partie:* "The game is language, and the play is about the struggle with this inevitably defunct tool of perception and survival."[9] Words and images tyrannize Clov, as Lowry perceptively remarks in his analysis. But these same words and images also tyrannize the spectators with their illusions of false realities. At one point Beckett practically dares the audience to leave the theater:

> *Clov.* What is there to keep me here?
> *Hamm.* The dialogue.[10]

That is the conventional limit. But there is another limit within, the subjective presence that lies beneath verbal constructs. Lowry notes that Hamm has learned an "endgame" of words, to which he is

no less subject to the tyranny of language than his own slave. . . .
Language used to be Hamm's slave; he "invented" it, used it to build
himself a refuge that would protect him from the devastated outside,
and taught it to his slaves.[11]

Clov represents movement, just as Hamm represents language—
"hamming it up with words." Once words and actions are abolished on
stage, the drama ceases to exist. The old tyrannies are at an end. In
conventional terms, the movement of the play becomes solipsistic. The
external world is reduced to a void. Language is dispensed with, finally:

> Hamm. . . . speak no more.
> *(He holds handkerchief spread out before him.)*
> Old stauncher!
> *(Pause.)*
> You . . . remain
> *(Pause. He covers his face with handkerchief, lowers arms to armrests, remains motionless.)*
> *(Brief tableau.)*
> CURTAIN
>
> (84)

For Beckett, as for his audience, the play does not end with the words
and actions dispensed. "You"—that indefinable presence of the within—
"remain." The cloven feet and the hammy mouth are gone, signaling
consciousness's freedom from the tyranny of words and actions. That
does not limit the communicative content of *Endgame*, although it might
be argued that Beckett's solution effectively ends this play's game of
words and actions in the external sphere of things. But the game begins
anew when Hamm removes the handkerchief from his eyes.

The initial search for freedom from the tyranny of consciousness was
analyzed in chapter 6 of *Murphy* (1937), Becket's first novel. In *Murphy*,
Beckett described forms of the "less conscious" as a flux of forms,
constantly rising and falling away.[12] In the presence of this significant
absence in *The Unnamable*, the third novel of his 1948 trilogy, Beckett
attempted to resolve the "Eleutheria" dilemma of portraying, at one and
the same moment, the me and the I of the self. Beckett described this
presence as a dream of reality:

> . . . perhaps its a dream, all a dream, that would surprise me, I'll wake,
> in the silence, and never sleep again, it will be I, or dream, dream
> again, dream of silence. . . .[13]

Beckett's presentation of this game of the schismatic self appears to work
better in narrative form because it articulates now the I, now the me, of

the self in a complex process of identification and interpretation. Situations unfold, characters emerge, tones build, sensibilities portray a continually evolving self. Communication takes place in the interstice of language images. As Beckett developed his concept in his dramaticules, his dramatic mode gained intensity through the collapse of perspective of the stage image, and through the audience's instantaneous identification with those processes on stage and in the mind's eye.

Eric Levy, in *Beckett and the Voice of Species*, defined the same situation in *The Unnamable* that Hamm will explore provisionally in *Endgame* a decade later:

> Each word pushes his existence a little farther, and so comes out with great effort and intensity. There is nothing to fall back on, not even his previous words, for there is no clear end to which they lead and no certainty from which they spring. The difficulty of ending grows more apparent. Words are all the narrator has, but, having them, he loses himself. . . . Each word, borrowed from the community of men, compromises the isolation of which he tries to speak and, by translating the purity of an experience uniquely his own into the coarser terms of a public language, subverts the very purpose of narration.[14]

In the narrative posture, the situation results in an impasse. When Beckett examines the importance of image and words in the theater with the example of Jack Yeats's work before him, new possibilities emerged. *Endgame* was not the end of a game but a game of endings that Beckett would clarify in later theater pieces.

Studies by Barbara Gluck and David Hayman described James Joyce's influence on the youthful Samuel Beckett, which he successfully discarded as a mature *literateur*.[15] Hayman in particular noted a similarity in subject matter that links the two Irishmen with Kafka and Proust through the creation of a sort of "intercranial discourse that characterizes [Beckett's] later prose."[16] As evidence of this, Hayman cites *Finnegan's Wake*, which (like Beckett's trilogy of novels) "is the individual psyche of a stylized individual and by extension that of the reader." In Beckett's theater, spectators demonstrate Hayman's thesis of a dichotomized self in a similar fashion. The narrative and dramatic roots of Beckett's art found nourishment in the febrile minds of Kafka and Proust. But in Beckett's theater, there is much more. When he developed his dramatic technique, the creative processes were not those of a novelist applied to the stage, but those of a pictorial artist.

Billy Whitelaw, one of Beckett's favorite actresses, described his creative processes in her notes on rehearsals to play W1 in *Play* (1964,) Mouth in *Not I* (1972,) and May in *Footfalls* (1976.) The latter two productions were directed by Beckett; the part of May was written for Ms. Whitelaw, who commented:

> In *Footfalls*, I felt like a moving, musical Edvard Munch painting—one felt like all three [athlete, musician, painter]—and in fact when Beckett was directing *Footfalls* he was not only using me to play the notes, but I almost felt he did have the paintbrush out and was painting, and, of course, what he always has in the other pocket is the rubber [erasure], because as fast as he draws a line in, he gets out that enormous India-rubber and rubs it out until it is only faintly there.[17]

S. E. Gontarski noted the same pictorial effect in Beckett's manuscript for *Happy Days,* in which the playwright made the notation "vaguen it" beside certain passages of the text.[18] Whitelaw's description of his use of "India rubber" in *Footfalls* is just a more painterly elucidation of the "vaguen it" technique Beckett adapted from pictorial artists like Munch, Jack Yeats, and van Velde brothers.

Beckett's later deliberate efforts to obscure the structural and thematic concerns of his plays and to create a kind of absence, whiteness, and transparent silence coincides in every respect with the development of his friend Jack Yeats, who began his artistic career with precise line drawings, but concluded it with paintings rich in impasto or bare to the canvas, depending on the moment's inspiration. This application of a heavy layer of emotion to segments of a scene or the stripping away of specifics that alleviates the acuteness of a scenic image—"the great inner real where phantoms quick and dead, nature and void, all that ever and that never will be, join in a single evidence for a single testimony"—becomes the basis for Beckett's late dramaticules, in which image is paramount and language serves as a conduit to a schismatic self.[19]

As early as the writing of *Waiting for Godot* in 1948, Beckett practiced the lessons he learned from Jack Yeats. In *The Making of Godot,* Colin Duckworth noted specific details that Gontarski later summarized in his study of Beckett's *Happy Days* manuscript:

> One of the important observations Colin Duckworth makes about *Godot* is that the arrangement for Vladimir and Estragon to wait for Godot was not originally verbal, but written down, and by Godot himself. . . . Beckett originally envisioned the two characters to be waiting for a real reason.[20]

This deliberate attempt to obscure images and create ambiguities in the action and the language of the play was Beckett's attempt to break through the envelope of reality, that vulgar container of modern art so meaningfully described by Woolf a generation earlier.

Modern art was not, of course, the only victim of an absolutist credo for defining the limits of consciousness. In the 1930s modern science sought to duplicate the modernist envelope by creating perfect mathematical formulations. This attempt by Bertrand Russell and others to capture in a single system all the valid principles of mathematical reasoning, whereby all possible true consequences would flow from a small set of axioms, based on a well-defined set of rules, was paralleled in the pictorial arts by artisans who sought to develop, or to express complete artistic statements on, the nature of self and of self-consciousness.

Austrian logician Kurt Godel discredited Russell's thesis on the perfectability of a mathematical formulation by demonstrating that there are undecidable propositions in any axiomatic system; the self, for example, cannot be observed entirely by the self any more than one can look at one's own visage in a mirror with eyes closed. Some quotient must remain separate and distinct from the system in order that the machine can proceed; the viewer can come close, but no closer, than Zeno's paradoxes.[21]

In the opening of *Endgame,* Clov pursues this irreducible image as he speculates on Zeno's ever-shrinking heap of millet, moving from a relative value toward the impossible, absolute value of nothing. The heap, in this case, also refers to the build-up of words and images—and in a more particular sense, of positive entropy and the games that nature plays with man—that Beckett discovered on reading Erwin Schrödinger's *What is Life? The Physical Aspects of a Living Cell* in 1946. In one passage of the book Schrödinger noted that everything that goes on in Nature "means an increase of the entropy of the part of the world where it is going on. Thus a living organism continually increases its entropy—or, as you may say, produces positive entropy—and thus tends to approach the dangerous state of maximum entropy, which is death."[22] Clov's narrative on Zeno's millet heap, the build-up of positive entropy in *Endgame,* is amplified visually by Beckett in *Happy Days.* In this latter play, Winnie's heap, where she finds herself stuck "up to her diddies," is only a more graphic depiction of Schrödinger's positive entropy. Not simply confined to Zeno's impossible heap of millet, as *The Student's Guide to the Plays of Samuel Beckett* suggests, the mound is also a heap of broken literary tradition, of faulty memories of favorite romantic poets, of words themselves, and of time as it imposes itself on the silence that so terrifies all of Beckett's characters.

Hassan recorded the devastating effect language has on Beckett's figures. They are creatures of habit, seduced by the mesmerizing images of irreconcilable opposites, that of the vision of transitory permanence and that of the reality of their lives as habit-driven automatons:

Sentences end by denying the assertions with which they began. Questions receive further questions for an answer. Misunderstandings, contradictions, repetitions, and tautologies abound. The syntax is often the syntax of nonsense, the grammar of absurdity. And silence, literal silence, invades the interchanges between human beings.[23]

In Beckett's works, language is a smoke screen to protect the self from too much realization—as if that were really possible. Winnie's "prattling" represents little more than a series of "banalities, cliches, half-remembered literary quotations and misquotations," as Gontarski noted in his manuscript study of *Happy Days:* "And the titular phrase, repeated *ad nauseum* throughout the play, is the most hollow of banalities."[24] This "impenetrable barrier" of words, as another commentator, Richard Coe put it, is both balm and bane to its victim. As bane, it protects the habit of being from the constant threat of dislodgement; as balm, it accommodates the chaos of the world in logical, compartmentalized phenomena.[25] In terms of Beckett's "Dante . . . Bruno. Vico . . . Joyce" essay, published three decades before *Happy Days,* Winnie's "language-kitten" is still chasing its classics' "tail" through a succession of "the Almighty's little jokes." James Knowlson saw Winnie's rising of the sun, which opens yet another day, as "ushering in a further period of suffering for countless millions and a further period of time from which there seems to be no escape—except in conscious or unconscious self-delusion.[26] When words fail, and habits of a lifetime decline in their efficient disposition of her daily chores, what terrors of the mind lie ahead?

In Winnie's case there are none. Gontarski's analysis of the relation of habit and self-awareness in *Happy Days* provides the key to the work's central dramatic irony, the final crushing blow to Winnie's desperate fear that, at the end of it all, no change will have occurred, and salvation will be no nearer at hand. (Of course that is the very point Beckett wishes to leave the spectator, who, with Winnie, summons the remnants of her classics and shares in her frustrations.) Gontarski summarized:

> We are all being buried by time. Habit is Winnie's defense against the agony of consciousness and the impossibility of finishing. But Winnie never fully realizes her plight. That lack of awareness . . . also deprives her of any tragic dimension. Awareness and recognition are crucial to tragedy. . . . And although the lack of knowledge makes her happiness possible and keeps her from being tragic, it also blocks her victory.[27]

Winnie's fragmented memories of the classics become even more disjointed in act 2, reflecting the continual disintegration of her personality and the build-up of positive entropy. The more time passes, the more habit deadens all possibility of change, until presumably even the memory of change once thought possible dims into a forgotten past—of

Keats's "beechen green" and Mr. Shower or Cooker, she cannot now recall, and the classics that have degenerated from the great poets to "such sentimental versifiers as Charles Wolfe."[28] So Beckett merges science and art in his depiction of uncompromising reality that, in truth, eluded earlier artistic interpreters of the twentieth century. In Beckett's works one is left not with great tragedy, but with great pathos of the *petit peuple* of the world—the subject of all of Beckett's plays and the subject of Jack Yeats's works in painting, literature, and drama.

Beckett's vaguening of images and his obliteration of specific dramatic details in order to coalesce the self into a context—even if only in its absence—has been discussed by other commentators. In "God and Samuel Beckett," Richard Coe suggested that there is a physical counterpart to the psychic context of Murphy's mind in Beckett's first novel:

> Beckett's characters allow themselves to be mutilated, becoming armless, legless, featureless . . . now bedridden, now propped up against walls, now stuck in vases like sheaves of flowers, in order to escape from the tyranny of movement and its despotic corollaries: or else they try to die, and dying, strive to detach their "selves" from the unhappy accident of incarnation only to discover that their "personality" against all odds survives.[29]

Beckett's artistic obligation and its expression in communicative terms— as language in his narrative works and as less conscious language and gestures in his dramaticules—leaves the attentive spectator with only words and images in a never-quite-ending game of word-refuges and play-images, outside of which is death. In this regard, the final goal of Beckett's art begins to approach the dictum of Jack Yeats as it was assessed by his more famous brother. W. B. Yeats noted that, as regards Jack's 1935 novel, *The Charmed life,* his younger brother pursued "all that—through its unpredictable, unarrangeable reality—least resembles knowledge." Once again the modernist "envelope of reality" was broken by an artist attempting to see beyond the reality of "the old half-knowledge of where and when" of objective, Cartesian reasoning processes.[30] In an article on the work of Jack Yeats, John Pilling noted the same sense of deliberate indirection—a "vaguening" of the texts—as in the work of W. B. Yeats. There is an inconsequentiality in the novels of Jack Yeats. Pilling commented, where the author seems to

> follow the drifts of the mind, not in any excavatory spirit, as Joyce did, but out of a much simpler, almost childlike, amazement at the material it can throw up.[31]

And, in a key phrase that is particularly apt for an understanding of

Beckett's art, Pilling suggested that Jack Yeats "follow[s] the haphazard windings of the mind in the hope of catching those moments *when the mind is bringing its reality into being*" (emphasis added). Jack Yeats began, of course, as a pictorial artist. Only in later years did he begin a career as a novelist and playwright, at a moment in his artistic development when he had begun to experiment with techniques to express what he described as the "ante-room" and the "shadow-land" of pictorial art. The contrasting impasto and bare canvas paintings of Jack Yeats's late period of painting also had their counterpart in his novels and his plays, although to a lesser degree. Beckett's first dramatic effort to express a "shadow-land" or "ante-room" of dramatic art resulted in a play in which a principal action and a marginal action existed simultaneously but not altogether successfully. One common difficulty in Jack Yeats's plays and in "Eleutheria" was the authors' problems of erasing extraneous details of presence onstage while maintaining sufficient tension. Until the notion was accomplished of imaging the dichotomized self as a formulation both of the stage and of the spectator, and the collapsed pictorial plane was reassembled (as Beckett did in *Not I*), the nettlesome difficulties remained.

Critics' support for and against W. B. Yeats as a dominant influence on Samuel Beckett's work is about equal, despite Beckett's own assertion that Yeats's focus was on all the wrong things. Ronald Rollins discussed both poets briefly in a journal article entitled "Old Men and Memories," while Thomas Kilroy compared the work of both men in *Irish Studies*.[32] In a more extended commentary, Barton Friedman pointed out that the syncopated dialogue of Yeats's *The Green Helmet* is echoed in Beckett's *Waiting for Godot*.[33] The most interesting of the texts in terms of focus was that of Katharine Worth's *The Irish Drama of Europe from Yeats to Beckett*. Worth boldly supported W. B. Yeats's worthiness as the father of modern drama. She also saw him as the precursor of Beckett's achievement in the theater:

> Yeats's evolution of a modern technique of total theater and his use of it to construct a "drama of the interior" make him one of the great masters of twentieth-century drama. . . . *Waiting for Godot* is in the same line of country as *At the Hawk's Well*.[34]

Worth described Beckett's later plays as complete Yeatsian "movements;" "ghost plays [as Beckett tells us] more and more emphatically with every play."[35] Furthermore, Worth made the intriguing point that W. B. Yeats realized the limitations of language in his theater, and sought continually to coalesce all the elements of drama in a synthesis of sounds, gestures, images, and silences that could approximate the complexity of the human mind. "Eleutheria," one would have to admit, is in "this line of country." But the complexities of the human mind that W. B. Yeats sought to portray, compared to the analysis of the schismatic self that Beckett depicted in his later dramaticules, suggest that more refined analysis of dramatic terms and a more sensitive approach to the acknowledged difficulties in both poets' theater pieces is now necessary.

In terms of historical influences, Worth was particularly helpful in cataloguing W. B. Yeats's debt to *fin de siècle* Symbolists:

> Performers were now testing Rimbaud's dream of a language "of the soul . . . containing everything, smells, sounds, colors;" Pater's dictum that all art aspires towards the condition of music; the Nietzschean concept of Dionysian unity, "whereby actor becomes transformed into dancer, dancer into musician, musician into lyric poet."[36]

These ideas found their way into Yeats's work, according to Worth, as a source of nourishment for his revolutionary drama. For W. B. Yeats, the symbol was a way of presenting the timelessness of his drama onstage, an impersonal mode of communication that led finally to his adoption of Gordon Craig's puppetlike *über marionette* acting style for his plays. The consequence, already noted, reportedly led to actors rehearsing his plays standing in barrels, so that nothing could detract from the inner spiritual expressiveness of his works. In a contrary approach, Beckett, in works like *Proust,* found timelessness through the recovery of involuntary memory and an immediacy of emotional context that was completely personal and total, without being intellectual or rational. The contrast on this point could not be more extreme: Yeats carried his audience toward the impossible expression of the "invisible hypnotist" within, relying on language and symbolic gestures to chart his way; Beckett worked out from within, using a narrator or scribe to "translate" the impossible *unself* of the artist to his spectators.

These processes of language and gesture in the theater can be described in semiotic terms, whereby the mind's eye of interpretation—even at the level of connoted, coded symbols (conventional language and gesture) of Yeats's *The Death of Cuchulain,* for example—reflects the Old Man who, in turn, reflects the creative process. Yeats's summing up of a lifetime of tumult in the theater in his last play presented the viewer with a mélange of objective truths and subjective dreams, designed to tantalize the participant into the deep of the mind and to evoke a total drama of the interior. But in fact, the viewer perceives images on the level of uncoded iconographic signs that his or her habit of perception transforms into symbols of intellectual comprehension. That is how one customarily thinks and perceives images in context. Beckett's goal as an artist, in working out from within, was to freeze the image at the level of the sign, where the form was the principal ingredient and not the primary conduit to rational thought, and where language was seen as the impossible transformation of the artist's intent. Beckett's interview with Tom Driver, printed in *Columbia University Forum* in 1961, confronted this issue. Becket said, in part:

> . . . there will be new form . . . and this form will be of such a type that it admits the chaos and does not try to say that the chaos is really something else. . . . That is why the form itself becomes a preoccupation, because it exists as a problem separate from the material it accommodates. To find a form that accommodates the mess, that is the task of the artist now.[37]

An earlier formulation of this same principle of language as a barrier to real communication appeared in *Le Monde* in 1945, where Beckett announced:

> each time that one wishes to make words do a true work of transference, each time one wishes to make them express something other than words, they align themselves in such a way as to cancel each other out.[38]

In the communicative process, Beckett began deeper than W. B. Yeats, and Beckett stayed deeper than Yeats's division of the stage into self-conscious and unconscious elements. By 1972, in *Not I,* Beckett had found the elusive form that could accommodate the mess of language. The voice had become the translator of the old woman's passions. Beckett presented the spectator with the form—images of a dehiscent self—that the spectator reassembled as everyday reality.

As a consequence, Beckett productions occur in a less-conscious landscape. Where W. B. Yeats found language and symbols useful transports to the threshold of the real, Beckett imaged man's entrapment in language as a corollary to man's entrapment in the life cycle.[39] In the former, language brings the actor to the Marmorean stillness of the life beyond; in the latter, language is simply a hindrance that must be absorbed in the form of the sign itself, wherein language and gesture is purposely eroded until "that which lurks behind it . . . begins to trickle through."[40]

Some documentation exists on the strain imposed on actors working within the boundaries of each playwright's perception of an ideal production mode. Despite the claim that W. B. Yeats required his actors to rehearse while standing in barrels, he was remarkably open to im-

provisational stimuli for his actors. Worth recorded that Yeats was imbued with amateur revolutionary fervor for his theater, and wrote:

> after all with amateurs in mind—the Abbey Theater was for a time a
> semi-amateur venture—and although he acquired professional per-
> formers of very high standing as he went along, he always retained his
> sense of the plays as particularly open to performance by untrained
> people who loved poetry.[41]

Records of Beckett's experience in the theater as playwright-director
reveal a precise craftsman. James Knowlson, looking at the production
processes of Samuel Beckett's own staging of *Krapp's Last Tape,* included
in *Theatre Workbook* the comments of Donald Davis, who played the role of
Krapp in that play's American premiere in January 1960:

> Beckett is quite specific, of course, giving precise directions. In the
> process of rehearsal at first, we thought, "Oh my goodness. That won't
> hold, it's going to be boring. We had better elaborate."—I don't mean
> grossly elaborate—but we'd put in little bits of business like this and
> that. And then when we got more familiar with it and were able to run
> it, we discovered that we were constantly stripping away all the stuff
> we had added.[42]

Beckett's precision contrasted directly with W. B. Yeats's improvisational
freedom. The architectonics of gesture in a Beckett dramaticule are as
important as the text. Pierre Chabert, who played the role of Krapp in
La Dernière bande under Beckett's own direction in 1975, commented on
the manner in which the playwright envisaged the realization of his texts
on stage:

> Beckett's stage poetics is dominated by a concern to transform speech
> into scenic object, and into sonorous and spatial material. . . . The text
> and the staging are organized according to or around repetition,
> around "as simple a pattern as possible, reproducing its effects con-
> tinually and indefinitely. . . ." Beckett as director will never introduce
> an action of the body, a movement or a gesture or a handling of objects
> without repeating it—sometimes in the elementary form of simple
> repetition (twice). Yet between these bodily actions, gestures, move-
> ments and so on, each repeated twice, a whole network of repetitions
> and echoes is built up. (For example, [in *Krapp's Last Tape*] there are
> two bananas, two glasses, two shudders, two looks backstage into the
> darkness, etc.)[43]

Beckett dealt specifically with each actor's gestures and speech, as well
as the smallest detail of the stage set. Evidence gleaned from rehearsal
notes of *That Time* and *Footfalls* in 1976, under Beckett's direction in

Berlin's Schiller-Theater Werkstatt, showed the author-director's minute attention to details in his discussions with the technical director and the chief lighting technician:

> Beckett describes precisely the rhythm of the lights in both pieces. In *Footfalls* the unit of time should be seven seconds each time, in *That Time* ten seconds. The bell at the beginning of *Footfalls* dies away in seven seconds, then the light comes up during seven seconds and one can see May walking. At the end of the three parts the light fades out each time inside seven seconds, the bell dies away in seven seconds, and the light comes on again in seven seconds. At the end of the third part, the light comes on again after the bell, lights up the empty strip for seven seconds and then fades out. In each part, the light will be somewhat darker than in the preceding one. Therefore it is darkest when the strip is lit up without May at the very end. Correspondingly, the bell gets slightly softer each time.[44]

Beckett's directions for the actor playing the part of May were equally precise. In Berlin that year Hildegard Schmahl played the part of May and at first had difficulty with the text. But Walter Asmus reported the director's reassuring and revealing response to his actor: "The walking up and down is the central image." That is the basis of the play. "The text," according to Beckett, *"the words were only built up around this picture"*[45] (my emphasis). When days later Hildegard continued to have difficulties: "Tears run over her face: 'I don't want to make it unpleasant for you. I'm not crying . . . it's just the tension inside, in my head. My God, what torture. . . .'" Beckett again reassured her, in terms that seem to come more from the visual arts than from conventional dramatic technique:

> *Beckett.* Try gradually, while you speak the words, to see the whole inwardly. It has a visionary character . . . it is an image which develops gradually. When you begin to narrate the story, you don't yet know the end. . . . It is too easily narrated. . . . I will leave you alone for a few days.[46]

The results were impressive. On the evening of the final dress rehearsal, with an invited audience in attendance, the actor was clearly as in control of her situation as Beckett would wish her to be:

> Even from the first sounds, one senses that H is on the right track. Nothing soft, nothing which is not binding, nothing accidental in her way of speaking. A great coldness and tautness without sentiment. May stands independent of her surroundings as a concentrated bundle on the strip of light. Her superfluous movement distracts, the tension communicates itself to the observer, one is drawn into the undertow of her story—the concentration is passed on and challenges

the observor to an absolute concentration. Beckett is satisfied with the result. "You have found the trick" is his comment.[47]

Beckett's mastery of his craft was visibly reflected in this production, in which he demonstrated control of all movement, all emotional responses that absolved even the accidents of personality.

The tortuous route the actor must follow to reach this epitome of internal concentration developed out of two decades of experimental dramaturgy. The most obvious example of these processes at work can be seen in *Endgame* and in *Happy Days,* where the restraints the playwright imposes on the actor are physical. But the same dynamic tension was also the principal focus of "Eleutheria," his first work for the theater, where the emphasis on restraint and inward tensions was somewhat mistakenly placed on the setting. In this early work Beckett left the audience to intuit the sense of presence intended in the peripheral set. He seems to have followed a succession of steps in defining the schismatic self, beginning with the two-part divided set of "Eleutheria," followed by the physical confinement of the actor in *Endgame*'s ashcans, *Play*'s funeral urns, *Happy Days*' earthen mound, to name several examples, and concluding with the dissection of the actor's presence in *Not I.*

In each case, the isolation was intended to focus the spectator's concentration on the fact that something "less conscious"—to cite Beckett's favorite expression in quoting Jack Yeats—was taking place. The elliptical remarks at the end of each act of *Waiting for Godot*—"Let's go. *They do not move.*"—signify no less the movement within that has already been noted. His late plays make much clearer the ambiguity that Beckett was unable or unwilling to resolve in his first masterwork for the theater.

The scrupulous honesty Beckett manifested in his plays was a direct product of common influences that he and Jack Yeats shared in the 1920s and 1930s. Beckett steadfastly refused to alter his work or to permit a liberal interpretation of his basic play format by even devotées of his works. In fact, he has gone on record as being opposed to the dramatization of his novels out of context, or otherwise changed according to popular taste. The principal reason for his objection to the adaptation of his work would seem to be that his plays cannot be reduced to symbols any more than a painting of a horse can be studied as an exercise in drawing sheep.

Beckett's images for the theater were hard and precise. He studied his art consciously for two decades before committing it to manuscript form. Among his studies was a 1936 review of Jack Yeats's novel, *The Amaranthers.* Beckett's review noted Jack Yeats's internal development of the novel form to draw pictures for the mind's eye: "There is no symbol . . . but stages of an image."[48] Almost like a motion picture caught between frames in which discrete images flow upon a plane of light, the spectator puts it all together to tell the final story. Hildegard Schmahl's desperate attempt to gradually develop an image in *Footfalls,* to "see the whole inwardly," as Beckett explained it to her, is clearly a product of Beckett's adaptation of Jack Yeats's "stages of an image" developed forty years earlier.

William Butler Yeats also experimented with his Abbey Theatre actors, sometimes permitting them great freedom, and other times physically restraining the actors during rehearsals. The problems of spontaneity and restraint in W. B. Yeats's theatrical vision was tied to his philosophy of art, one that did not define the limits of what he called the deep of the mind. In W. B. Yeats's Abbey Theatre productions, inspiration took its course. The actors improvised on the symbols provided by the poet. But at certain times W. B. Yeats's vision of the action took precedence; the actors did not experiment with movement or actions but were relatively transfixed, while the poet's language transported the spectator. The result was a confusion of purposes not at all clarified by Yeats's own description of his artistic processes:

> . . . as I write the words "I select," I am full of uncertainty, not knowing when I am the finger, when the clay. Once, twenty years ago, I seemed to awake from sleep to find my body rigid, and to hear a strange voice speaking these words through my lips as through lips of stone: "We make an image of him who sleeps, and it is not he who sleeps, and we call it Emanuel."[49]

This near-mystical union of the self and unself lay at the center of W. B. Yeats's theater. Jack Yeats explored the same psychic territory but in a much more precise manner. The stages of an image in Jack Yeats's art, as Beckett described them, were hard, concrete, definable, and bound together by the spectator's vision. In W. B. Yeats's works, the spectator is transported to some other realm of experience, one that is never clearly defined beyond its symbolic state. In W. B. Yeats's dramas, the central issue of the play, the mimetic performance in which actors are engaged as agents of the action to represent some segment of reality, never appears except as an incidental ingredient. Samuel Beckett followed the same course in "Eleutheria," with similarly disappointing results. Only when Beckett returned to his original inspiration and worked with the notion of sequential images presented in a spare setting—and *Waiting for Godot's* two acts represent two sets of images that were only later reduced to Vladimir and Estragon as principals—did the theater work for an apprentice playwright. With the production of *En Attendant Godot* at the Théâtre de Babylon in Paris on 5 January 1953, the die was cast.

Samuel Beckett's guides in the literary exploration of the nature of the unself were not confined, of course, to the brothers Yeats, nor to the inhabitants of the Celtic twilight. Aside from those in the circle surrounding James Joyce, whom Beckett knew in Paris after 1929, the earliest important influence on his work was Marcel Proust. Certainly the rosetta of Beckett's early writings was *Proust*, composed in 1931, in which he introduced three important elements: hieroglyphic time, demotic habit, and Greek memory.[50] Proust's concept of multiple selves, which derived from a reading of Anatole France's literary pieces, was partially reflected in Jack Yeats's idea of an image in stages. In this sense, Beckett's revolutionary art was at least a century old in its origins. Marcel Proust's influence on him declined after 1945 as Beckett began thinking about a career in the theater, and moved away from the passivity inherent in Proust's concept of voluntary and involuntary memory. Minor critics' claims that *Proust* contains the core of the major Beckett plays is simply not substantiated by analyses, however common these two artists' creative processes, however passionate their disclaimer of the vulgarity of realistic art. "Eleutheria" was the first exception and the case in point.

In *Proust* Beckett recovered the hieroglyphs of time through a constant process of decantation "from the vessel containing the fluid of future time, sluggish, pale and monochrome, to the vessel containing the fluid of past time, agitated and multi-colored by the phenomena of its hours."[51] Present time, however, is visible in *Proust* only as a succession of habits, organized to protect the personality from the suffering of being. The world is created every minute and every second of every day by a succession of habits, organized to protect the personality from the suffering of being. The world is created every minute and every second of every day by a succession of habits "concluded between countless subjects that constitute the individual and their countless correlative objects."[52] The only way to escape demotic (vulgar) habit and hieroglyphic time is either through the refusal to submit to new habit (Beckett explains the process)

> between this death and that birth, reality, intolerable, absorbed feverishly by his consciousness at the extreme limit of its intensity, by his total consciousness organized to avert the disaster, to create the new habit that will empty the mystery of its threat—and also of its beauty;[53]

or through the refusal to remember the succession of paradises lost to habit: when memory fails and involuntary memory floods the victim, "an explosive . . . immediate, total and delicious deflagration."[54]

The artist should avoid the voluntary memory of intelligence, for its images are as pale and monochromatic as the speculative fluids of future time, "washed out" by the pendulum swings of habit. Involuntary memory, to the contrary, retains its vitality since it has not been forgotten, but is reconstituted accidentally:

> Then the total past sensation, not its echo nor its copy, but the sensation itself, annihilating every spatial and temporal restriction, comes in a rush to engulf the subject in all the beauty of its infallible proportions.[55]

Only in this way, argued Beckett, can one experience the world free of its intellectual components—time, habit, and memory.

In the text of *Proust*, Beckett argued that reality is the mock experience of habit, and that habit is continually displaced by man's successive accommodations to the world *within*, while the real—the essence of being—is unleashed in the magic of involuntary activity of mind, of memory, of sleep, of waking madness. Consequently, an objective evaluation of the world is worthless because conscious perception is "a series of events on which we can throw no light, a series of problems that cannot be solved."[56] Proust, of course, found his truth in involuntary memory and the necessary verbiage that surrounds its moment. Beckett was forced to another conclusion: "There is no communication because there are no vehicles of communication." Language is an intellectual process, as are images of being and becoming. Furthermore, the poet of the unself continued,

> even on the rare occasion when word and gesture happen to be valid expressions of personality, they lose their significance on their passage through the cataract of personality that is opposed to them. Either we speak and act for ourselves—in which case speech and action are distorted and emptied of their meaning by an intelligence that is not ours, or else we speak and act for others—in which case we speak and act a lie.[57]

According to Beckett, the only possible artistic statement is the expression of the "spiritual assimilation of the immaterial," extracted from life within and applied to the "so-called material and concrete" without. The hero of *Murphy* celebrates waking madness, finally incinerating himself accidentally, thereby rejoining the "chaosmos" within. Taking the opposite tack in a search for meaningful experience, *Watt* is a paean to voluntary memory, whose hero comes to naught (a "what-not") in the House of Knott or conscious awareness. "Eleutheria" presented a dichotomous theatrical frame that was relatively unsuccessful. Beckett's spiritual assimilation of the immaterial into the theater remained elusive for two decades until he dissected the nature of the stage image, and communication became almost a dysfunction of the intellect.

Beckett's early dramatic themes did not negate the premise that, at least as far as influences on his work were concerned, Proust's star fell as Jack Yeats's rose in 1945. Portents of *Play*, for example, whose figures are enclosed in funeral urns and tormented or edited by the light, a unique inquisitor, can be found in *Proust* in Beckett's description of the recovery of the most trivial experiences of involuntary memory, "encrusted with elements that logically are not related to it." At appropriate moments in the life of an individual the vases of experience, "filled with a certain perfume . . . and suspended along the height of our years," are inundated and we are "flooded by a new air and a new perfume (new precisely because already experienced), and we breath the true air of Paradise, of the only Paradise that is not the dream of a madman, the Paradise that has been lost."[58] The funeral urns signify the death-in-life experience of the real, in terms of everyday reality, obliterating the inner life of the unself in the process of extracting language from it. Even the foundations of *Film*—Beckett's solitary excursion into the world of celluloid, which introduces a protagonist "sundered into Object (O), and Eye (E), the former in flight, the latter in pursuit"—can be extrapolated from a passage in *Proust* (to say nothing of *Imagination Dead Image*):

Imagination, applied—a priori—to what is absent, is exercised in vacuo and cannot tolerate the limits of the real. . . . Nor is any direct and purely experimental contact possible between subject and object, because they are automatically separated by the subject's consciousness of perception, and the object loses its purity and becomes a mere intellectual pretext or motive.[59]

In a recent journal article on *Film*, Sylvie Henning suggested that Beckett essentially agreed with Bishop Berkeley's line of thought that in our modern God-less world, "to be is to be perceived, since even when everything else has been successfully avoided, there is always perception by the self." The problem with this admirable argument, of course, is that Beckett begins with the unself and the impossibility of communicating the experience of it through the warren of habits in intellectual time, and that any attempt to escape from objective perception leads to the perception by the auditor or editor or translator—the "he, not I," or conversely, the "I, not he"—of the unself. In this event one has returned to the notion of the schismatic self that began the discussion: Beckett refutes Bishop Berkeley in *Film* as surely as he does Descartes in *Watt*, or Proust in *Not I*. Beckett exposed the habits of perception and the intellectual imperatives of the imagination that can thrust the individual into the darkness of time and habit and intelligence in their conscious orientation.

Not I presents its viewers with Beckett's most radical dramaturgy for the theater, not only regarding the development of the schismatic image, discussed elsewhere, but also regarding the virtuoso performance of what has become a triad of Beckettian consciousness—the two "vaguened" split images and the similarly "vaguened" gesture. In the case of *Not I,* the split image is that of a mouth that is also perhaps a vagina; the gesture is that of an acquiescent auditor/editor and also perhaps an interrogator.

The origins of the split focus can clearly be traced back to "Eleutheria," where the principal action and the marginal action of one stage consciousness compete for the spectator's attention. But the more interesting origin of this unlikely dynamic is *Murphy* and Beckett's famous excavatory analysis of Murphy's split brain, as outlined in chapter 6: the "hollow sphere" that contains within its boundaries a perfect microcosm of the external world, "already present as virtual, or actual, or virtual rising into actual, or actual falling into virtual." There are two components:

> The mind felt its actual part to be above the bright, its virtual beneath and fading into dark. . . . The mental experience was cut off from the physical experience. . . . It was made up of light fading into dark, of above and beneath, but not of good and bad. It contained forms with parallels in another mode and forms without, but not right forms and wrong forms. It felt no issue between its light and dark, no need for its light to devour its dark. The need was now to be in the light, now in the half light, now in the dark. That was all.[61]

In Beckett's art, the philosophical implications of Murphy as a post-Cartesian, and the influences of Malebranche and Geulincx or the Occasionalists' philosophy with its curious blending of rationalism and mysticism, did not obviate particular inherent dramatic potentials of Murphy's archetypal situation, and of the means (to quote Beckett) "in which it might be exploited" in his novels—and later, in his plays.[62] In point of fact, the latent power of the dramatic image of Murphy's brain is unleashed the moment that Beckett determines that the issue between light and dark is crucial, and the challenge between both halves of the split brain becomes the focus of the work.

When Beckett rejected his initial attempt to focus first on the body, then on the mind, in favor of an examination of the relations between the two halves of this gravamen of mind-stores, all the difficulties of "Eleutheria" began to disappear. The zones of light, half-light, and dark within which increasingly he, Murphy, felt himself to be "a mote in the

dark of absolute freedom," and that led directly to "Eleutheria"—
"freedom" in its Greek translation into English—simply did not contain
any dramatic interest, or even stage the *agon* of any dramatic context.
The issue of presence on the stage, as Robbe-Grillet so astutely noted,
was only a hint of the difficulties that Beckett posed for himself in
translating *Murphy* and his heirs into their theatrical counterparts.
Translation is too loose a term, as is transformation. Rather, the infusion
of the unself into a theatrical framework, in which immediacy and
gesture were primary constituents and language was always servant to
the image, finally brought Beckett to the point where he could examine
the processes of Murphy's mind as a stage dynamic. Beckett was helped
toward this goal by the ideas of pictorial artists—the van Veldes in the
late 1930s, and the work of Tal Coat, Masson, and Bram van Velde,
which was summarized and published by Beckett in "Three Dialogues"
in 1949.[63] Behind all was the figure of Jack Yeats, softening, obscuring,
vaguening the images.

Criticism of *Not I* in the 1970s and 1980s focused correctly on its
theatricality. Hersh Zeifman noted, for example, that for the audience,
the Auditor represents a kind of Greek choral figure, "the visual symbol
of . . . the attempt to make the Mouth admit the truth about herself—as
well as being a witness to its failure."[64] But Zeifman's analysis breaks the
dramatic image of the stage picture that Beckett intended. Mouth's
schismatic "She—not I" debate is the central focus of the play. The
Auditor may or may not be an intelligible resource, but he may not be
isolated as an external commentator to the action as Zeifman suggested.
In Zeifman's view, the Auditor could be removed from the play without
doing damage to Mouth's communicative posture. However, isolating
the Auditor in this manner leads to the static situation of "Eleutheria,"
and the dramatic problem that Beckett posed for himself in *Not I*—that
of the means of articulating both aspects of the ego (as Linda Ben Zvi[65]
characterized it in her review of the play)—is lost.

A principal measure of Beckett's art in the 1970s was his development
of a dramatic technique from its roots in Murphy's split mind, graph-
ically demonstrated in *Not I* and in *Footfalls* as well. One commentator
remarked that "the very structure of these works derives from the
interplay between the two views of the self and the battle for pronoun
dominance: I or she in *Not I*, May or voice of Mother in *Footfalls*."[66]

The contrast between Beckett's astute analysis of dramatic situation
early and late in his career—the acquiescent states of Murphy's mind
(the Oblomov experience of no contentious issues between the varying
states of consciousness and semiconsciousness) and the mature dramaticules that contain a classical *agon* of the self's opposing sides—could not
be sharper. There is no retreat to narrative, as some critics have insisted.

To the contrary, the validity of *Not I* is confirmed only in production. Analysis of *Not I* in terms of a counterpoint between text and stage image is unnecessary. Paul Lowry insisted in his review of *Not I* that "the story of 'she' contrasts with the stage image of 'I': the stage image is, as it were, magnetic . . . unignorable, attracting the text to itself and thus insisting upon a present tense dimension to the story."[67] Professor Lowry grappled with the difficulties that Beckett resolved in his art as he moved from the narrative posture of "Eleutheria" to the dramatic cohesion of *Not I,* but he impaled his critique on what he called a passive text that ignored both the immediacy and the completeness of the schismatic dramatic image.

Adequate interpretation of *Not I* is dependent on the spectator's comprehension of the triad of consciousness, comprising both halves of the schismatic self and the figure of the auditor (who serves as the translator/intervener of "I" and of "me"). In the collapse of the imagination's pictorial plane, elements of consciousness are set free. In external reality the subjective "I" of the self has no difficulty in asserting itself. But in a moment of seizure, or at such times as would stop the mind's censor from channeling unspoken thoughts into articulate speech, the objective self—the inner "me" that watches and reports but has no independent articulation of being—is suddenly freed from all restraint. The momentary recognition of that identity onstage as a nonself collides with the spectator's recognition of his or her imagination's unself.

Beckett's *Not I* is a startling mirror image of conventional reality. In production ("ground zero" for the interpretation of any dramatic work), the subjective "I" becomes the outsider, the objective "she" takes center stage, and the spectator is forced to decode the signals. Beckett showed us what Jack Yeats described as "the shadow land of the rose," a world viewed from its innermost perspective. The identity of the questioner who incessantly interrupts Mouth is the subjective "I" that the spectator habitually identifies as the self, but is in this case the schismatic self that is—uncustomarily—the outsider. And finally, the translation of the inner objective "me" that has no voice but "I" is personified in the presence of the Auditor, who permits "me" to become "she" for the spectator, thereby completing the triad of consciousness in one of its possible, knowable, imagistic forms.

In her review of *Not I,* Katherine Kelly noted that Mouth seems to represent a particular kind of hell that is shared by all of Beckett's heroines, "created by their eternally thwarted desire for love, mercy and renewal, yearned for in the form of children, spring and morning. Winnie, Maddie and Mouth are all Earth Mothers of sorts."[68] But this cry of pain at the things that give rise to beauty and fall away again is not confined to the women in Beckett's plays. Krapp, surrounded in his dotage by children and an old dog in front of the fire, is another vision that Beckett rejected. The alternative is scarcely better. Indeed, it might be suggested that one of Beckett's great cries of rage came from the pain of knowledge that lasting truths have no physical counterparts. An accumulation of positive entropy permeates every aspect of man's search for truth, beauty, and permanence. The end is always dust and ashes.

Beckett's hell is universal, and not confined—as Professor Kelly suggested—to womankind alone. The subtle identity of Mouth with "she" and the physical correspondence between her story and *Not I*'s onstage spectacle was carefully developed:

> . . . speechless infant . . . (. . .) . . . nothing of any note till coming up to sixty when- . . . what? . . . seventy? . . . good God! . . . coming up to seventy . . . wandering in a field . . . looking aimlessly for cowslips . . . to make a ball . . . a few steps then stop . . . stare into space . . . then on drifting around . . . when suddenly . . . gradually . . . all went out . . . all that early April morning light . . . and she found herself in the— . . . what? . . . who? . . . no! . . . she! . . . (*pause and movement 1*) . . . found herself in the dark . . . and if not exactly . . . insentient . . . insentient . . . for she could still hear the buzzing . . . (. . .) . . . but so dulled . . . feeling . . . feeling so dulled . . . she did not know . . . what position she was in . . . imagine![69]

Four parts of the play repeat pause and movement, a fifth repeats only pause, but no movement, by the Auditor.

The unremarkable story of *Not I* tells of the supposed life of a near mute who, on stumbling in cow dung on an early April morning, falls face first into a grassy field. She hears voices, sounds that come from her apparently, that she scarcely recognizes as her own. This steady stream of words, vowels, glottal stops, truncated phrases, and broken syntax that she tries to deny are affirmed each moment by her sense of her lips and tongue moving. *Not I* is a reversal of the Cartesian ethic, not *cogito ergo suum* but "the machine": "I feel, therefore I am."

Professor Kelly's contribution was to both relate the events Mouth describes to Beckett's visible stage image and, in addition, to situate the audience as a subjectivity within Mouth's commentary. The ray of light, shining always on the same spot, corresponds to the spotlight that illuminates Mouth onstage; the inability of Mouth to note what position she is in corresponds to the spectator's inability to situate Mouth, or the Auditor, within a frame of reference, or even to determine whether Mouth is not another orifice of the body.

Kelly's commentary defines the specific dramatic context within which the play must be interpreted, without the removal of elements for the sake of textual-dramatic counterpoint. An insistence on this unity of interpretation allows the triad's consciousness's identity to be completed by the spectator. A performance text cannot be separated from its dramatic functions. The subjective I of the schismatic self, which in the case of the old woman is that identity associated with the near mute, is subverted by her fall in the meadow. The me that lies behind the I, but that can never be fully amplified in "I," becomes the objective self "she" through the intercession of an auditor/translator. The stream of words from the old woman's mouth, and the buzzing in her head, following her fall in the cow slops, represents the uncontrollable nature of the unself, that other peripheral consciousness Beckett sought to portray in "Eleutheria," as a first instance in its dramatic form, and in Murphy's split mind in *Murphy,* in narrative form. In performance, the spectator grapples with the images and with the words in the same uncomprehending way as Mouth, thereby duplicating in the viewer's and listener's mind's eye the identical duality of the schismatic self Beckett created onstage. The spectator's recognition of that transformation makes dramatic gesture experiential, not intellectual. Any notion that Mouth's refusal to relinquish the third person because she is addicted to story-telling, or that she uses language to distance herself from the chaos of her past memories and experiences, is qualified stage tension Beckett created in opposing both halves of the self, creating internal dynamics that are more compelling than the passive acceptance or rejection of thoughts springing from a single consciousness. Beckett's world does not begin nor end in solipsisms.

An interesting commentary on Mouth's escape from her predicament, signaled by the larks flying in the sky to represent freedom from a world of sensory confinement, comes at the heart of the play, just after *(pause and movement 2)*. Mouth senses the return of feeling: ". . . starting at the top . . . then working down . . . the whole machine . . ." (p. 19 in *Not I, Odds and Ends*). The description of the half-mute lying insentient, catatonic except for the babel of words coming from her orifice as from *a machine,* is a distant echo of Beckett's first public commentary on the nature of the universe. In *Our Exagmination,* the series of essays composed in 1929 by James Joyce's friends to celebrate the forthcoming publication of his "Work in Progress," *Finnegan's Wake,* Beckett's essay included the remark that "on this earth that is Purgatory . . . the machine proceeds. And no more than this: neither prize nor penalty; simply a series of stimulants to enable the kitten to catch its tail. And the partially purgatorial agent? The partially purged."[70] The audience, watching Mouth perform, fulfills the dictum of the machine, the tail-catching kitten, in an unending sequence of events whose subject is both victim and persecutor, at the same moment, in the same act, of the same consequence. When the word stimulants end, only the larks remain: ". . .

back in the field . . . April morning . . . face in the grass . . . nothing but the larks . . . pick it up—*Curtain fully down.*" Purgatory has ended.

In addition to the similarities in Beckett's adaptation of stage methods and in Jack Yeats's late painting technique to communicate the inner division of the self and the vortex of energies that reached out from within a subject, another painter also played a crucial role in the genesis of *Not I.* Beryl Fletcher hinted at the artist's influence in his description of the dynamics of *Not I* and their effect on the spectator: the tension between the memory of an event and its immediacy in involuntary recall—which Beckett explored extensively in *Proust*—is grafted onto the spectator's consciousness by Mouth's verbal and visceral expression of her sense of being. "We are plunged," according to Fletcher, "into the situation ourselves. As audience we mirror the same anguish as Mouth and pass through the same stages that she is describing." Beckett's spectator becomes not only an observor, but also a participant in his drama's anguish and its dilemma. In similar circumstances, Jack Yeats would confront viewers of his paintings and ask each of them in turn, "Now, what does this mean to you?" In *Not I,* the figure that permits this intrusion beyond the proscenium arch, a violation of the ideal aesthetic distance in theater, is the Auditor. Described as the figural presence of a translator who serves as Mouth's intercessor for a less conscious means of expression, the "me" obscured in the "I" as "she" is proclaimed by Mouth. According to Fletcher, the source of this Auditor figure is Caravaggio's painting *The Beheading of John the Baptist,* in the Valletta Cathedral in Rome, "where a shadowy group in the background observes the beheading."[71]

Conversation with Beckett confirmed this source. But the passive nature of the background figure and the notion that the Auditor played the role of a silent witness, are quite contrary to Fletcher's statement. In his view, one is back in the same posture as Krap in "Eleutheria," confronted with an undefined presence on stage. In fact, the Auditor serves the figural function of Mouth's past, Mouth's present moment as she relates her anguish, and the promised future spectator's participation in the turmoil of Mouth's mind—until words are forsaken, images are relinguished, and *the machine* ends its purgatorial existence on earth.

Beckett's description of his viewing of Caravaggio's painting in Italy is the key to deciphering the Auditor's function. According to Beckett, "Some years ago I visited the Valetta Cathedral in Rome to view Caravaggio's *The Beheading of John the Baptist.* I stood there a long time in front of the painting. Gradually I noticed that I was not alone, that behind the screen at the side of the church [in the painting] was the face of a man watching me observe the scene of beheading."[72] The image of the hidden figure, at first appearing only in the guise of a lamp or an urn behind the barred wall, left a powerful impression on Beckett, not so much in Caravaggio's realization of the horrific beheading scene as in the fact that he, the spectator, had been observed watching, feeling, and experiencing in the most secret recesses of his soul, a mirror image of himself—"not I but he, watching me watch a visceral assault on another individual." Caravaggio's communication, and Beckett's interpretation, of the baroque experience with its emphasis on excessive sentimentality and emotion that strained beyond the boundaries of the pictorial image, provided exactly the right medium in which to situate the Auditor vis-à-vis the spectator. The Auditor's identity as an integral part of Mouth's triad of consciousness was suddenly disturbed by the realization that the spectator also mirrored the stage action, and that the Auditor incorporated the visceral feelings of the spectator into his purgatorial realm, from which there was no escape until the stage context was finally dissolved.

The concept of presence and its dissolution as an objectifiable reality in Beckett's plays—implicit in the "vaguening" notations of the playscripts and in the actors' comments on the playwright's "painterly" qualities as a stage director—has been evident for decades. James Knowlson noted the concern for immanence in Beckett's works as far back as the 1930s. Knowlson commented on the composition of *Murphy,* which involved the search for a credible reality that might be discovered when all the layers of illusion were stripped away:

> From *Murphy* onward, all Beckett's people are, in the most profound sense, exiles, excluded from some inner reality of the self which, if it exists at all, and they feel, in spite of everything, that it does, or, at the very least, that it should, would lie outside the dimensions of time and space, somewhere in that strange inner world that Murphy was already seeking to plumb in his willing acquiescense to the darkness with its "chaosmos of forms," so that he might become a "mote in the dark of absolute freedom."[73]

In Beckett's plays, the *fear* that presence will vanish and the illusions of a lifetime will dissipate into waking madness is a recurrent theme. In *Waiting for Godot,* Estragon's dreams are a constant threat for Vladimir:

> *Estragon.* I was dreaming that—
> *Vladimir.* (violently). Don't tell me!
>
> (57B)

This exchange echoes a moment in act 1, when both character motivation and playwright intention is explicitly spelled out:

Estragon wakes with a start.
Estragon. (restored to the horror of his situation). I was asleep!
   (Despairingly.) Why will you never let me sleep?
   . . .
   I dreamt that—
Vladimir. DON'T TELL ME!
Estragon. (gesture towards the universe). This one is enough for you! *(Silence.)* . . .

(11A)

An even more pervasive sense of presence that is something other than reality, or life as a nightmarish dream of reality, also has its earliest manifestation in *Godot,* where Vladimir muses on the sleeping form of his companion:

> *Vladimir.* . . . The air is full of our cries. *(He listens.)* But habit is a great deadener. *(He looks again at Estragon.)* At me too someone is looking, of me too someone is saying, He is sleeping, he knows nothing, let him sleep on. *(Pause.)* What have I said?
>
> (53A, B)

An echo of Vladimir's musings appeared in subsequent plays. In *Happy Days,* Winnie notes that her head is always full of cries: "Faint confused cries. *(Pause.)* They come. *(Pause.)* Then go. *(Pause.)* As on a wind. *(Pause.)*" (56). There is even an acknowledgment of another, an audience watching her, in the opening words of act 2:

> *Winnie.* Someone is looking at me still. *(Pause.)* Caring for me still. *(Pause.)* That is what I find so wonderful."
>
> (49)

The bell in *Happy Days* is replaced by the light's editorial function in *Play,* and the interior dialogue in *Not I,* all derived from the immanence Beckett's creatures cannot grasp, the sense of an inner presence just beyond conscious grasp.

Existential critics and proponents of absurdist theater have followed other approaches in dealing with the troubling presence of the actor, or of the character who maintains the ghost of the actor within the portrayal, or of the playwright, whose absence is denoted precisely in proportion to the presence of the actor, or of the character. Martin Esslin noted, for example, Beckett's affinity to the Absurdists is the playwright's tendency "towards a radical devaluation of language, towards a poetry that is to emerge from the concrete and objectified images of the stage itself. . . . What happens on the stage transcends, and often contradicts, the words spoken by the characters."[74] Devaluation of language is certainly one method by which to assess the Beckett canon; but devaluation of gestures—an even more radical departure from the norm than Esslin has heretofore acknowledged—is closer to the *Murphy* paradigm so markedly in evidence in Beckett's late dramaticules.

In a 1980s journal article, Bert States proposed a more analytic and ultimately a more useful approach to the problem of presence.[75] States argued that the actor in the theater could be phenomenologically understood as a kind of storyteller, who *is* the story he is telling:

> Presumably, the transitional "voice" between the true story teller and the actor would be the rhapsode who tells his story (or rather someone else's) directly to the audience, simulating the more exciting parts of it in the manner of the First Player in *Hamlet,* who gets so carried away by the plight of Hecuba. With the actor, of course, the narrative voice . . . disappears entirely, and we hear only the fictitious first-personal voice . . .—rather, we *overhear* it, since the voice is no longer speaking to us. The audience is now an implicit or unacknowledged "you,". . . . This is, of course, what bothered Rousseau so much, that the actor was the final step in the disintegration of presence and direct discourse.[76]

Apart from the question of what constitutes the "dramatic voice," States took the important step to establish terms of relations that could serve as a paradigm for analyses of theatrical presence.

The context of the dramatic event consists of the exterior world, the theater world, and the play world. Within this triad, States located a discourse dialectic—also a triad of possibilities: Speaker ("I," "Actor," "Character"), Spoken To ("You," "Audience," "Other Character/Self"), and Spoken Of ("He," "Character," "Absent Character/Event"). In States's view, the actor's presence can only speak to the audience in one of three pronominal modes, "because they are all that discourse contains."[77] In the self-expressive mode, the "I" (actor) performs on his or her own behalf, and one is aware of the artist in the actor challenging himself or herself to measure up to the role's potential. In the collaborative mode, the audience is included as a necessary ingredient of production, with a dramatic standing equal to that of the fictional stage characters. In States's final pronominal mode, the actor is completely intent on becoming his character. This is the representational mode, in which the goal is to reenact significant human experience.

States was the first to admit that his system did not offer a complete phenomenology of the actor's art, but he does not hesitate to suggest that speech discourse is "one might say, . . . our behavior—that can be broken down into the pronominal triad."[78] Furthermore, he admitted to a broader interest than his topic in his allusion to the transformational qualities of the actor's art that allow

us briefly to live another life, peculiarly inserted into our own, which produces an entelechial completion, dimly like the effect of an out-of-body experience.[79]

These quantum leaps are necessary to States's analysis if it is to be effective as a tool for dramatic theory. But the leaps propel the investigator past the problem: the notion of presence in the theater and the place of the actor in the dynamic equation.

Beckett struggled with the problem in "Eleutheria" by proposing that the central action and the marginal action complement each other. Solutions to interpretations of performance elements are no easier. The problem of the actor in the theater is a problem *precisely* because he or she is there, before the audience, *all at once,* "doing artificially what the rest of us do naturally: in one sense the primary medium of the theater, in another its end and purpose."[80] But what is the dramatic "voice," beyond States's opinion that the actor represents the final step in the disintegration of presence and direct discourse? In an analysis of *Not I,* the figural qualities of the Auditor present a strong clue that much more is happening in Beckett's plays than States's pronominal triad can accommodate. In Beckett's works, the site of the drama has switched from the actor's art to the spectator's participatory art, more so than States's collaborative mode indicated, and much more than his leap of faith that declared there is a transitional "voice" between the true storyteller and the actor.

Beckett was at pains to differentiate between the form of the communication (myth versus drama) and the means of communication (narrative versus dramatic voice.) In his plays, the essential transformation into the spectator's participatory art comes not from the voice, which is of secondary importance, but from the form that permits what States described as the entelechial completion. There is a diachronous exchange between myth and drama; a synchronic substitution of storyteller and actor allows for that exchange alone. But the transformational qualities of a scene linking the spectator to the character on stage are missing from States's system. Beckett's work up to the 1940s focused on States's intellectual dilemma; thereafter, and into the 1970s, the focus shifted to the spectator's participation.

In an important note to *The Student's Guide to the Plays of Samuel Beckett,* Beryl Fletcher stated that Beckett's works "are meditations on the human condition—and he is interested in mythologies for their own sake, without any commitment to them whatsoever."[81] This is a point on which Beckett and Jack Yeats disagreed. Jack was aghast at Beckett's indifference, feeling that commitment was incumbent on the artist. Beckett refused to be concerned. Fletcher's confirmation of myth as a source of Beckett's art, a notion that few critics have discussed in print at length, also provides answers to the narrative postures of deconstructive critics, who link the actor to the storyteller by means of the "overheard voice." The establishment of a transitional "voice" between a true storyteller and an actor severely limits the importance of the stage image in the spectator's mind's eye. Beckett's was well-known for having trafficked with painters rather than with playwrights as he endeavored to master drama's gestural mode, to which linguistic adornment is, in a literal sense, an afterthought.

Analyzed in terms of synchronic substitution, the actor is indeed the final step in the disintegration of direct discourse. But he is also an intermediary, bringing the spectator to the edge of silence and to the disintegration of presence within the image—which one interprets with linguistic and scenic adornment. Bert States's propositions on the nature of discourse are an invaluable contribution to the study of presence in the theater. But they carry one only to the outer edges of the Beckettian equation, where the perspective on the mythic qualities of his work is seen from the other side, an absent image, working its way back to a *vaguened* prospect.

In *Not I,* for example, the triad of possible speech discourses expands, from the predictable categories delimiting "speaker," "spoken to," and "spoken of"—categories of the external world: "I," "you," and "she"; the theater world of "actor," "audience," and "character"; and the playworld of "character," "other character/self," and "absent character/event"—to include three entirely new catagories of discourse based on the schismatic self. The theater world remains constant, consisting of "actor," "audience," and "character" as expected, but the external world is now composed of speaker: "not I," spoken to: "s/he," and spoken of: "I," indicating in the playworld a speaker: "subjective self," spoken to: "objective self," and spoken of: "absent event/objective self," respectively. The audience listens to a subjective self attempt to recover its objective self, but it is unable to do so. The vehicles for communication are almost gone because the objective self has no mechanism by which to communicate until the subjective self provides the energy: neither does the subjective self have any control over the speed or content of its communication since comprehension lies above emotion, and language above image, in the hierarchy of communicative gestures. The caesura between emotional context and its verbal facilitation is the real site of *Not I,* and not a moment earlier—while the material remains a part of the myth of consciousness—nor a moment later—when language begins its metaphoric and symbolic flight toward the banal.

The triad of speech discourse within the three pronominal modes of conventional objective reality could be diagramed as follows:

speaker	I	actor	character
spoken to	you	audience	other character/self
spoken of	s/he	character	absent character/event

The world of a stage as a subjective dichotomy breaks down quite differently, and its diagram might appear as follows:

speaker	not I	actor	character
spoken to	s/he	audience	other character/self
spoken of	"I"	character	absent event/objective self

In this model the myth of consciousness is exposed as exactly that: the communication of "I" as spoken of is the objective self quite different from its conventional role as another event, or as a character spoken of or alluded to in the abstract. Beckett indicated very clearly that consciousness plays the role of moderator of an unself continuum, which is the real unacknowledged force in determining presence.

In this sense *Not I* is the perfect textbook example of theatrical deconstruction of possibly the most dominant myth since the age of Sigmund Freud. The sense of presence indicated by the missing "I" of "Not I" that Mouth alludes to four times in the dramaticule, the important caesura between image and its articulation, provides the spectator with a network of relations that is, in effect, a mathematical identity of the viewer's own process—as well as an identity of the caesura that separates the spectator from the stage. The recognition of that moment, and the transformation of that recognition into an image of comprehension, as the viewer becomes an act of spectating himself or herself, is one measure of Beckett's achievement in *Not I*.

The exploration of the schismatic self in *Not I* was a further development of concepts that Beckett examined in *Play*, in which the sense of presence was indicated by the intrusion of a "unique inquisitor" that demands answers and orchestrates a repeat of the play, in double time, through the use of or at the behest of (it is never certain) the light. W1, W2, and M respond to the editorial function of the spotlight beaming from one face to another, suggesting that a catastrophic dilemma is created in the delivery of speech (the light) from a more tranquil realm. The spectator remains isolated from the action. But in *Not I*, the Auditor replaces the spotlight, and the viewer becomes central to the process as the site of the dramatic exchange—the notion of presence—is sharply defined in the schismatic self.[82] The undifferentiated self of *Play*, which seemingly demands answers and ignores responses, and is inquisitor, editor, and automaton all at the same moment (unless the light *is* the characters' responses), is separated into its components in *Not I*. The spotlight's insistent demand, representing language and intelligence, was replaced in *Not I* by the spectator's inquiry. In this schemata the Auditor represents the fading passivity of the objective self, which is scarcely a factor in Mouth's world any longer.

Jacques Derrida's *Of Grammatology* articulated the origins and relations between image and language in terms that seem particularly appropriate for an understanding of the concept of "presence" in Beckett's stage works. The formulations in *Play* and in *Not I* exemplify the leading edges of an argument that posits the myth-bearing potential of an image as an *a priori* condition of language—despite the misgivings of a romantic theorist like Rousseau, who was forced to concede that:

> to the degree that needs multiply, that affairs become complicated, that light is shed [knowledge is increased], language changes its character. It becomes more regular and less passionate. It substitutes ideas for feelings. It no longer speaks to the heart but to reason.[83]

Rousseau speaks of a "performance art" in his description of the fundamentally passionate nature of the image, as opposed to the sterile clarity of language, "that lodging of writing." The precision and exactitude of speech is contained, above all, in "literalness." And, according to Derrida, "a precise and exact language should be absolutely univocal and literal [propre]: nonmetaphorical."[84] The conclusion Derrida drew from this analysis is that language originally derives from its mother, passion: therefore, the first language had to be figurative, and the claims advanced by States and others that a phenomenological orator stands behind the protagonist of a play, "whose specialty is that he is the story he is telling," are only marginally significant. The myth, and its myth-making potential, are at center stage. To cite Rousseau once more:

> As man's first motives for speaking were of the passions, his first expressions were tropes. Figurative language was the first to be born. Proper meaning was discovered last. One calls things by their true name only when one sees them in their true form. At first only poetry was spoken; there was no hint of reasoning until much later.[85]

In the later Beckett dramaticules typified by *Not I* there are no symbols, or properly speaking, no complete symbols in the dehision of language and gesture and fragmented concepts, as they pass through the subjective self toward pure communication, leaving in their wake the "presence" indicated by "Not I's" absence. The identity of light with intelligence and the sterility of its inquiry in *Play* completely accorded with Rousseau's doctrine. At the end of the play one knows scarcely more than at its outset—only that a play of possibilities has taken place, possibilities of completely arbitrary significance as the light "edits" text:

> *M.* Mere eye. No mind. Opening and shutting on me.
>   Am I as much—
>   *Spot off M. Blackout. Three seconds. Spot on M.*
>   Am I as much as . . . being seen?[86]

W2 complains equally:

> *W2.* Are you listening to me? Is anyone listening to me? Is anyone looking at me? Is anyone bothering about me at all?
>
> (17)

And W1 takes the light's unresponsiveness as perhaps indicative of a personal affront she has made unwittingly:

> *W1.* Is it something I should do with my face, other than utter? Weep?
>
> (18)

But the appeal to the urn-creatures' vanity and the habits of a lifetime of conscious intellectual perceptions as a basis for living is the trap Beckett lays for the unwary spectator. No communication takes place in *Play;* the narrative is stillborn within the subjective self, in a perpetually frozen pseudo-triologue of three isolated voices. The play of intelligence on a trope of figurative language—or on an image *before* it is reduced to metaphor by intellectual processes—is the frame of Beckett's startling image of consciousness. The process could not be otherwise, for as Rousseau asserted: "One does not begin by reasoning, but by feeling." In Beckett's theater, it is up to the spectator to provide the passionate framework that finally integrates *Play* as a dramaticule, by retracing the paths of the work's metaphor, vaguened or adumbrated as necessary, to reveal "the great inner real" so clearly displayed in the works of Jack Yeats. With regard to the metaphor, the frontier *behind which* Beckett works, Derrida had the last word:

> Metaphor must therefore be understood as the process of the idea or meaning (of the signified, if one wishes) before being understood as the play of signifiers. . . . Before it allows itself to be caught by verbal signs, metaphor is the relation between signifier and signified within the order of ideas and things, according to what links the idea with that of which it is the idea, that is to say, of which it is already the representative sign. Then, the literal or proper meaning will be the relationship of the idea to the effect it *expresses*. And it is the *inadequation of the designation* (metaphor) which *properly* expresses the passion.[87]

In the last analysis, one returns to Bert States's entelechial completion, an "out-of-body" sensation—the true catharsis of drama—which Derrida described as the inadequacy of even metaphoric language to contain the emotional context of image-myths.

Woolf's "envelope of consciousness," which began the modernist credo to explore consciousness "with as little of the alien and external as possible," came full circle in a postmodernist, deconstructionist and "accommodationalist" aesthetic as it functioned in the art of Samuel Beckett. Even the terms of relations of artist to his subject matter presented Beckett with a labor of "diabolical complexity" if they were to function properly. In a Beckett dramaticule, interpretation carried the spectator from myth to image to language, from the denoted uncoded iconographic sign to the connoted iconographic coded symbol that is conventional language. In this process, the image was paramount in the passage from the *within* (less conscious) to the *in* (consciousness) of language forms. But the real source of Beckett's art, his attempt to come to terms with the human condition in other than arbitrary terms, lies beneath the image in the sense of "presence" communicating through discourse that has, at its roots, some mythic materials of the human species that can only be translated, edited, or otherwise received as an indirect communication. Hence the irony of Beckett's best works, masquerading as essays of the utmost seriousness, tempts the spectator and the critic into postures that are intellectually defensible but dramatically absurd and solipsistic.

Marilyn Gaddis Rose analyzed this sense of irony in "The Sterne Ways of Beckett and Jack Yeats," where she proposed convincingly that "all these Anglo-Irish writers are far too complicated as ironists and rhetoricians to be . . . open with the reader, and they certainly would avoid themselves the traps which they set for the reader."[88] The specific traps Beckett sets for the reader/spectator are double-pronged: on the one hand, Beckett abhorred a literature of notations, the "penny-a-line vulgarity" of realistic art; on the other hand, he developed the concept of metatheater, wherein the spectator was an integral part of the performance. Such a dichotomy provided the playwright with ammunition to explode the myth of Cartesian mind-body dualism as the viewer became the act involved, and the language of the actor became the discourse of the spectator.

James Knowlson noted this basic schism in Beckett's works, from which much of his ironical posture springs. Knowlson found that there was a sense

that there exists a profound rift between the inner and the outer world, together with the feeling that, if reality is to be discovered anywhere at all, it certainly does not lie in the unpalatable "mess" in which physical man finds himself embroiled.[89]

However, Knowlson's explication of the "rift" only hinted at the larger problem that he never addressed: one cannot "discover" reality any more than one can stop time or entomb sound. At best, the clever playwright can describe reality and bear witness to it. In fact, the entire notion of presence in Samuel Beckett's theater could be set within an ironic framework, in which the playwright teased the spectators' sensibilities. For in truth, the spectator is the principal subject of a Beckett work.

The most direct link in a literary sense—or rather, to be more accurate, in an imagistic sense—was Jack Yeats, the master of insubstantial context, of the probing "accidental" revelation of the *petit peuple*, who fill their rather unpleasant lives with idle chatter and aimless bustle. Professor Rose described the paradigmatic character in the hands of both playwrights, in linear terms that emanated from the pen of Isaac Sterne; in every case the principal persona is

> smug, self-proclaimed, and hence, suspect, sincerity, a touted trust in free association. . . . The very fact that these "I's" protest so much is a cue which discredits them. But they want to sound as if beset by a hyperscrupulous intention to say whatever comes into their heads.[90]

And the subject matter of their hyperscrupulousness?—the foibles of everyday life: all man-made systems of logic, philosophy, rhetoric, fashion, sex, decrepitude, and death. Even the simplest of tasks overwhelms the principal characters of Beckett's plays—from *Godot* to *Act without Words*, from *Play* to *Catastrophe*. Rose extended her analysis to include Jack Yeats. Neither in the prose works of Beckett nor in the plays of Jack Yeats are the solutions any better:

> In every anecdote agent X fails in his attempt to perform task Y. The impossible task always seems quite simple. Beckett's Molloy ought to be able to reach his mother's home. Yeats's cast in *La La Noo* should be able to dry out a rain-drenched garment or drive a lorry.[91]

They cannot, of course. And the comic implications of each character's plight provides the artist with a context in which the physical, external realm is seen as merely one more plausible but inadequate expression of reality superimposed on a less-conscious presence that is the real subject of the work.

Facing the void in this strange, haunting world of the unself, Beckett

fashioned his dramaticules at the edge of an abyss that he summarized in
No's Knife:

> Kinds of things still, all at once, all going, until nothing, there was
> never anything, never can be, life and death all nothing, that kind of
> thing, only a voice dreaming and droning on all around, that is
> something, the voice that was once in your mouth.[92]

This presence that describes, that bears witness to life, that is no longer a
subjectivity, is one justification for art.

The question of presence and of images of a schismatic self, within
which a narrative can be constructed, can be traced back to Beckett's
earliest writings. Martin Esslin, for example, noted:

> There can be no doubt that the flight from self perception is one of
> the recurring themes of [Beckett's] writing from *Murphy* to *The Un-
> namable* and beyond, and that the nature of the self, its split into
> perceiver and perceived, an ear that listens and a voice that issues
> forth from the depths, is another.[93]

The concern for this "other" that emanates from sources beyond the ken
of consciousness troubles the figures of many of Beckett's plays: in *Play,*
M expresses cognition of another: "Mere eye. No mind. Opening and
closing on me. Am I as much as being seen?"[94] In *Happy Days,* Winnie
tries to make the best of her situation: "Strange feeling that someone is
looking at me. I am clear, then dim, then gone, then dim again, in and
out of someone's eye."[95] Winnie's feeling persists in act 2: "Someone is
looking at me still. *(Pause.)* Caring for me still. *(Pause.)* That is what I find
so wonderful. *(Pause.)* Eyes on my eyes. *(Pause.)*" (49–50). In *Waiting for
Godot,* Beckett's first published play, the stage is set in act 2 as Estragon
falls asleep and Vladimir watches, knowing that another watches him:

> Was I sleeping, while others suffered? Am I sleeping now? To-mor-
> row, when I wake, or think I do, what shall I say of today?. . . *(He looks
> again at Estragon.)* At me too someone is looking, of me too someone is
> saying, He is sleeping, he knows nothing, let him sleep on. *(Pause.)* I
> can't go on! *(Pause.)* What have I said?
>
> (58A, B)

A decade later, in *Film,* the eye of the camera becomes the eye of the
object perceiving itself, thereby creating the ironic posture (now so
familiar in Beckett's work) summarized in Gontarski's epigram for the
play: "One striving to see one striving not to be seen."[96]

In this regard, *Film* was a distant echo of *Murphy,* and the chess game
with Mr. Endon, the apneic who, after forty-three moves of his chess

pieces, is restored to his original position. The debacle leads Murphy to exclaim: "Mr. Murphy is a speck in Mr. Endon's unseen":

> The relation between Mr. Murphy and Mr. Endon could not have been better summed up than by the former's sorrow at seeing himself in the latter's immunity from seeing anything but himself.[97]

The only reality that Murphy can bear witness to is the presence of absence. In an instant he retreats to his rocking chair, the gas turns on in the w.c., and Murphy is consumed in the ensuing chaos secure in the happy knowledge that Mr. Endon's "unseen" exemplifies the "little world" of Murphy's mind. Nirvana can be reached not only via the contrivance of seven scarves and a rocking chair:

> Most things under the moon got slower and slower and then stopped, a rock got faster and faster and then stopped. Soon his body would be quiet, soon he would be free.[98]

These lines are repeated verbatim after Murphy's first session in the chair, and as he is consumed by the explosion of the gas heater.

In *Rockaby*, Beckett expanded the image of Murphy's rocking chair to include the relation of the image of the real and of discourse to self-perception. Beckett took particular care with the stage directions governing the lighting of the image onstage: first the light on the face of the Woman in the chair; then the chair. At the end of the play, the lighting is reversed: fade-out of the chair, then fade-out of the light on the woman's head. Soon the rocking image fades, soon the woman will be free—of the light and of the probing eyes, "all sides, high and low."[99]

At the opening of *Rockaby*, the other is silent; W says "More," and the voice begins to speak in concert with the mechanical rocking of the chair. In terms of structural tectonics, the sequence of mechanical repeats is as follows (a distant parallel to Mr. Endon's chess game):

> section 1. 2 repeats and echo: "time she stopped."
> section 2. 2 repeats and echo: "living soul."
> section 3. 1 repeat and echo: "time she stopped."
> section 4. No repeats; echo: "rock her off."

The decreasing frequency of repeats signals either an editing process or, at the very least, a disintegration process of consciousness of a physical realm. But the sense of presence with which Beckett imbued the play appears most clearly in the repeats within each section:

V. all eyes

all sides
high and low (9, 10, 11, repeat)

which refer not only to the woman's supposed actions in her life and in the life she narrates through the other voice, but also as they are repeated in the spectator's mind's eye.

Just as in *Film* the eye of the camera becomes the eye perceiving itself, in his metatheatrical *Rockaby* Beckett created the spectator's eye perceiving itself in an act of perception, by watching the stage action from positions "high and low, all sides." The nature of "otherness" in Beckett's theatrical equation in *Rockaby* includes the viewer's imagination and its own echoes as an integral part of the stage picture. At a deeper level, the voice describes the woman listening to the voice of the other describe W's movements as she searches for another companion, or even for the identity of the voice itself that speaks of itself as it uses the words of another—or vice versa—as it speaks of the woman who uses her own words to describe the voice. The sense of presence pervades all inquiry of the *within* (less conscious) or the *in* (consciousness) dichotomy that is the terrain of Beckett's art. At the end of *Rockaby* the image of the woman is finally transferred from the stage to the mind's eye alone, in the slow fade into darkness and oblivion, accompanied by the double entendre "rock her off, rock her off" echoing in the dying light. The rhythmical blackness moving in the light, the jet sequins glittering in the spotlights, the frivolous headdress, the highly polished rocking chair, all emphasize the mechanical and hypnotic mood of the piece:

V. Dead one night
   in the rocker
   in her best black
   head fallen
   and the rocker rocking
   rocking away

(19)

The ending develops its hypnotic effects in a series of repetitions that parallel the movement of the image from light into blackness and return, and that emphasize the echoing rejoinders of the woman in the chair. In the end the spectator is confronted with an image that grows as the piece concludes—of the figure and voice and presence of an illusion—almost a trope, of forms moving into darkness, of light reflecting shadow, and the absence of an afterimage, as the echo and the light fade out for the last time.

In Beckett's review of Jack Yeats's *The Amaranthers* in 1936, he noted: "There is no allegory . . . no symbol . . . but stages of an image."[100] In

Rockaby, Beckett found a means of bringing that same sensibility to the theater. For the woman seated in the rocking chair, alone at last: "Her own other/own other living soul," as the rocking subsides, parallels the spectator's experience in the theater, who must take the image and relinquish it to his or her imagination as the stage light fails.

Beckett invoked the same metatheatrical experience for the spectator in *That Time,* in which the neo-baroque sensational image (the Caravaggio effect) invades the observer's private space. Enoch Brater described the situation precisely:

> As the lighting shifts its focus to work subtle changes of tone and angularity on the spectral flesh of Beckett's visionary head, the image is touched with an ominous foreboding, becoming as shifting and changing as the subject of our dreams. . . . Beckett makes us enter a new world instead of remaining within the theatrical modifications of this one. For in *That Time* Beckett gives visual existence to inner experience.[101]

The image of a suspended head without a body, an old white face with long flowing white hair floating about ten feet above the stage, recalled Beckett's own experience of Caravaggio's *The Beheading of John the Baptist* in a Rome Cathedral, where the playwright "saw" the face of the painter watching him view the scene of execution.[102] That horrific feeling of being observed in the act of participating in an act of savagery—even if only in the role of a passive observor—had a lasting effect on Beckett. It certainly contributed to the metatheatrical context of his art and laid a foundation for the visual images that dominate his later works, *Film* and *Eh Joe* in particular. The dual quality of the eye—its piercing inner and outer world dimensions—collectively symbolized by light and by darkness, can be traced back to *Murphy.* Light, however, is an outer dimension of torment in Beckett's cosmos, while darkness is a respite from the probes of intellectual comprehension—the gaze of the other— that afflicts many of Beckett's creatures. The only salvation from this intolerable tug-of-war between an inner-directed salvation and an outer-directed purgatory is found in art, where the two impulses mingle in the passage from light to darkness, or vice versa, and the sense of presence pervades the image, imbuing it with mythic meaning for which even an echo of discourse is an inadequate medium. In this circumstance, the modernist "semi-transparent envelope" described by Woolf and company is dissolved completely in Beckett's art, replaced by everything that is alien and external to objective reality. In this collapse of the picture plane of modernist art, Beckett found his way, back to a less conscious art that expressed his deepest feeling about the world.

In his notes for *Krapp's Last Tape* Beckett explicated the sense of light as antipathic to true enlightenment. The playwright's production notes were a complete reversal of expectations customarily associated with light and with knowledge:

> The light is thought of anti-mind constituent of mind, the duty of reason being the deliverance of imprisoned light, an error for which Krapp is punished by the eons. The dark is fact of anti-mind alien to mind.[103]

Embracing the modernist envelope, Krapp struggles to keep the dark under as he passes through a succession of selves. But the effectiveness of this communication depends on an external device—the introduction of a tape recorder. The Proustian multiplicity of selves that Beckett explored in *Krapp* is awkwardly limited by mechanical means. In *Ohio Impromptu,* however, Beckett accomplished probes into the schismatic self without any external devices except the introduction of narrative as a dramatic medium. The stage props (bananas, bottles, spools, desk, and drawers) become simply a deal table and a solitary hat. Most important, the sense of presence of the spectator within a metatheatrical setting in which the mind's eye recognizes itself in the act of cognition is a distinct advance over the achievement of *Krapp's Last Tape,* in which the spectator is left to be an interested observer.

In *Ohio Impromptu,* the Listener and the Reader represent not simply the Cartesian mind-body dualism of Krapp's incompatible sense and spirit, but the schismatic inner self, the objective and subjective self that constitutes a single consciousness—symbolized by the black, wide-brimmed hat at the center of the table. The sum of the discourse comes to nothing more than "profounds of mind, where no light penetrates."[104] At the end the figures remain, staring, unblinking, expressionless. The image remains with the audience of a narrative other who speaks while a counterpart listens. On occasion the listener knocks on the table, signaling the speaker to retrace the words, or to advance the text that is—appropriately following the pattern of *Not I*—spoken in the third person. The sense that these figures are shades of an afterlife, or of a representation of the inner halves of Murphy's less conscious world that derives from Jack Yeats's own investigations, is emphasized by the closing lines of the play. "Nothing is left to tell" is literally true for the work. But also there is nothing left to tell in discourse when the subject is so completely foreign to an objective interpretation. The story of the Swans Island and of the hours spent on the islet, are merely artistic license. Krapp's memorable March Equinox and his moments spent drifting in among the flags with a childhood sweetheart are no more relevant to the questions of light and truth and darkness than the story of "he" who appears to R and reads the sad tale through once again. The unique inquisitor in *Play,* and the tape recorder in *Krapp's Last Tape,* perform the same mechanical function as the speaker in *Ohio Impromptu.* Beckett presents a vision of the narrator as the audience member's own voice, a presence without essential discourse since the image communicated lies on the margins of consciousness.

Similarly, *Catastrophe,* Beckett's political commentary on Vaclav Havel, presents an image of P, a protagonist, that is clearly meant to be seen in the best light—literally.[105] The Director and Assistant rework the lighting and costume of the figure until they are satisfied. As the technical rehearsal is completed, the performance begins and the lights are brought up on P's head. A distant storm of applause is now audible. But as P raises his head the applause dies away, and the light glows mysteriously from beneath his head. The spectator is suddenly made aware that the light/dark dichotomy and its attendant values of intellect/mindlessness, are reversed in *Catastrophe* as in Beckett's other works. P's image presents one more example of Beckettian perspective and the collapse of the customary picture plane. One can know nothing from examining external values or postures that are dependent upon intellectual precepts that ignore the Krapp conundrum:

> Light is thought of anti-mind constituent of mind; dark is fact of antimind alien to mind.[106]

To show the mind, one must show the darkness of the presence of the mind, in its own light. In the absence of a grammar of images (for conventional language is functionally nonmetaphorical in its headlong rush towards clarity of expression), the only hope of communicating the sense of humaneness and of a reduced consciousness that precedes these articulating deserts (for some) of consciousness lies in art.

It is undeniable that Beckett shared many of the same concerns as W. B. Yeats, and used the elder Yeats brother as a resource in many of his plays, as numerous commentators have noted. But Beckett found his strongest inspiration in the later novels and artworks of Jack Yeats, where the stages of an image built toward their final expression. With regard to the paintings of the younger Yeats brother, Beckett professed that he could submit "in trembling to the unmasterable"[107] images that his Irish compatriot asembled on canvas. The plays following *Not I,* in which discourse and image united with the spectator in the collapse of rational perspective, to produce a truly metatheatrical, mythical experience, were a final acknowledgment and tribute of Samuel Beckett to the works of Jack Yeats.

PART II
W. B. Yeats and Samuel Beckett

3

The Geography of the Mind's Eye

THE notion of a symbol system as a basis for creating a drama of the self was almost exclusively a preoccupation of W. B. Yeats, who believed that the archetypal connotations of symbols, which have universal significations through their associations with the great religions of the world, could lead the playwright to finite truths about the self. In a highly conscious manner Yeats deliberately fashioned his plays after fifteenth-century Noh drama, but added to them elements derived from Egyptology, Neoplatonism, the Upanishads, medieval alchemy, and contemporary heterodox religious circles.[1] Beckett's conception of drama, on the other hand, was almost diametrically opposite to Yeats's formulations. Everything in Beckett's long search for artistic truth was contained in his assertion that no communication—even symbolic—was possible because there are no vehicles of communication. The artist can only celebrate his helplessness by observing an event, sketching its outline, witnessing its actions. But never could an author declare a fulfilled moment. "I am only a sensibility," suggested Beckett. "Let others declare their absolute convictions."[2]

The Irish sources for these two playwrights' work were similar, and occasionally identical. But where W. B. Yeats's dramas found their critical acclaim in the libraries and drawing rooms of select and adoring coteries of spectators, Beckett's dramas found their fullest expression in public performances that provided a genuine test of his dramatic materials.

In the beginning, W. B. Yeats had great hopes for his Irish literary theater. Support for his burgeoning Irish National Theater Company came from many sources. In April 1904, Yeats received a letter from Miss A. E. F. Horniman that promised to fulfill all the young playwright's dreams. Miss Horniman wrote:

April, 1904

Dear Mr. Yeats,

I have a great sympathy with the artistic and dramatic aims of the Irish National Theatre Company, as publicly explained by you on various occasions. . . . I am taking the Hall of the Mechanic's Institute in

> Abbey Street . . . which I propose to turn into a small Theatre, with a proper Entrance Hall, Green-room, and Dressing-rooms. . . . The Company can have the building rent free whenever they want it, for rehearsals and performances, except when it is let.[3]

Yeats was overjoyed at this news—it was the foundation of the Abbey Theater: it meant that he had acquired artistic control of a national Irish theater. He had spent a decade developing plans for an Irish renaissance. He had recruited the best Irish minds he could find who supported the free Irish cause.[4] In 1891 he had founded the Irish Literary Society of London. The following year in Dublin the National Society of Ireland came into being. In 1896 he joined the Irish Republican Brotherhood, but soon after gave up his active role in political affairs for a role that promised more spiritual reward—that of developer of a mystical national theater. W. B. Yeats, Lady Gregory, John Millington Synge, George Moore, and Edward Martyn, among others, worked together to create a national Irish theater for a small group of actors led by Maud Gonne and the brothers Frank and William Fay.[5]

They did not realize Yeats's dual purpose in pursuing the theater—to explore the unseen reality of dreamscapes of the mind as well as to found a national Irish theater. In its early years Yeats dominated the Abbey Theatre Society with the force of his personality, but his influence did not last. The reasons for Yeats's descent into disfavor should have been evident as early as 1892, when he began to write *The Countess Cathleen* which he finally completed in 1899.

Peter Ure noted that in early versions of *The Countess Cathleen,* Yeats stressed the desperate struggle in the Countess's soul, a struggle between her dreams and her responsibilities.[6] In later versions, Yeats developed the dramatic tension between the two principal characters, Aleel the Poet and Cathleen the Countess:

> This is because Yeats [was] trying to show, in Cathleen and Aleel, what he was later to call Artist and Saint confronting each other upon the stage. . . . [They appeared] more fully conceived when they [were] rendered as two contradictory elements in the same personality.[7]

Yeats's instinct to personify conflict in a single person as two separate characters was sound, and marked his maturation from beginning playwright to experienced man of the stage. In Samuel Beckett's first play, the unpublished "Eleutheria," the principal character, Victor Krap, turns his back to the audience in a mocking gesture of humanity. The play ends at the point where it might well have begun. Only in *En Attendant Godot* was Beckett able to split his central vision into two distinct creatures, Vladimir and Estragon.

The experience of writing and rewriting their plays seemed to sharpen each playwright's theatrical sense. In the case of W. B. Yeats, several scenes in *The Countess Cathleen* suggested his later power. At the beginning of the play the Countess Cathleen searches for her childhood castle in the woods. Accompanying her is Aleel, a poet who plays a stringed instrument to entertain Cathleen, and to prevent her from "pining to her grave." Plague and starvation are on the land. Having accepted money in exchange for their souls, Shemus and his son Teigue—eternal tramps that will be echoed in Vladimir and Estragon—set out for the crossroads of the world. Yeats described the fate of modern Ireland, symbolized by Shemus and Teigue, in the conversation of the soul merchants who come to the Countess Cathleen's castle to barter for her soul:

> *First Merchant.* Some sell because the money gleams, and some
>   Because they are in terror of the grave.
>   And some because their neighbors sold before,
>   And some because there is a kind of joy
>   In casting hope away, in losing joy,
>   In ceasing all resistance, in at last
>   Opening one's arms to the eternal flames,
>   In casting all sails out upon the wind. . . .[8]

Teigue and his father have already lost their souls to greed and the desire for power. Now they attempt to help the devil and his assistants, the soul merchants, to persuade other peasants to give up their souls. Countess Cathleen saves her people by bartering her own soul for theirs. When the immortal transaction has been completed, Cathleen's heart breaks. Twilight falls. The stage gradually darkens until play's end when Oona, the Countess's foster-mother, laments: "O that so many pitchers of rough clay / Should prosper and the porcelain break in two!" (46). A moment later Cathleen dies. Flashes of lightning and thunder announce the arrival of angels. Everything is lost in darkness.

As the sound of horns dies away, a faint light rises over peasants kneeling in supplication, and Oona offers up her sorrowful prayer: "*Oona.* The years like great black oxen tread the world, / And God the herdsman goads them on behind, / And I am broken by their passing feet" (50). The shadows of peasants come and go on the edge of night, like souls on the edge of consciousness. God "the herdsman" drives them into darkness in a scene that anticipates Godot the herdsman. The parallel extends to Teigue and Shemus, son and father, eternal tramps (of whom Beckett's Vladimir and Estragon, with dripping heads and aching feet, are more recent progeny), who venture out on the crossroads of the world, there to meet two merchants with something to sell. It should not be forgotten that in Beckett's play Pozzo is on his way to market to sell Lucky; what could he sell of such a hapless creature but his soul?

Beckett was not adverse to using literary and directorial devices to guide his writings in the 1940s. From W. B. Yeats's plays, Beckett forged into a dramatic technique the sense of interior revelation and of a reality that is in audience members' minds. And Beckett admitted that a production of Strindberg's *The Ghost Sonata*, directed by Roger Blin, played a decisive role in the evolution of *En Attendant Godot*. Beckett also acknowledged that Blin's production led directly to his request that the Frenchman direct the premiere of *Godot*.

The specifics of Beckett's first produced play revealed a dramatic intelligence at once imitative and highly original. Particular notice should be taken of Estragon's feet. Beckett used his character's tired appendages as a device to frame his dreamscape. The two tramps have traveled a considerable distance. Like Teigue and Shemus in *The Countess Cathleen*, Didi and Gogo have a long history of homelessness, and will wait a long time for succor. The play opens with Estragon's swollen feet; he struggles with a boot: "*Estragon. (Giving up again.)* Nothing to be done" (7A). The play, but for Vladimir's final speech and the appearance of Godot's messenger at the end of act two, closes with Gogo's old complaint: "*Estragon.* My feet! *(He sits down again and tries to take off his boots.)* Help me!" (58A). Seated on the edge of consciousness, Didi does not come to Gogo's aid.

> *Didi.* Was I sleeping, while others suffered? Am I sleeping now? To-morrow, when I wake, or think I do, what shall I say of to-day? That with Estragon my friend, at this place, until the fall of night, I waited for Godot? That Pozzo passed, with his carrier, and that he spoke to us? Probably. But in all that what truth will there be? *(Estragon having struggled with his boots in vain, is dozing off again. Vladimir looks at him.)* He'll know nothing. He'll tell me about the blows he received and I'll give him a carrot. *(Pause.)* Astride of a grave and a difficult birth. Down in the hole, lingeringly, the grave-digger puts on the forceps. We have time to grow old. The air is full of our cries. *(He listens.)* But habit is a great deadener. *(He looks again at Estragon.)* At me too someone is looking, of me too someone is saying, He is sleeping, he knows nothing, let him sleep on. *(Pause.)* I can't go on! *(Pause.)* What have I said?
> (58A, B)

As Vladimir watches Gogo sleep a new thought occurs to him. Can the dreamer dream a new reality? And is the reality which we perceive as real not also a dream of reality itself? Beckett leaves nothing to chance:

> *Gogo. (restored to the horror of his situation).*
> I was asleep!

. . . .
 I had a dream.
Didi. Don't tell me!
Gogo. I dreamt that—
Didi. DON'T TELL ME!
Gogo. (*gesture towards the universe*). This one is enough for you?

(11A)

Both Didi and Gogo realize that they are each living out a role in a play of forces from which there is no escape. In *Godot*, the union of theatrical forms, reality and the real, is nearly perfect.

Historical echoes abound in *En Attendant Godot*. The distinguishing moments of Calderon de la Barca's *Life is a Dream*, for example, separate dream from reality through selfless acts of Christian love and generosity. Vladimir and Estragon do no less for each other in *Godot*. But at *this* moment Didi hesitates. For a moment he sees his situation with new eyes, as Beckett would have *us* see it. The moment is paradigmatic: while he watches Estragon sleep, Vladimir *reflects,* and sees an *Other* watching him. It is Vladimir's moment of reflection that promises redemption from the interminable wait for Godot. Conversely, the spectators are observed in the act of observation. An idea is born in his mind's eye—"We have time to grow old." Time is the gravedigger, but it is also the agent that makes one aware of his or her past (and the knowledge of Yeats's Red Man, in *The Green Helmet*). How much better to leave that racial consciousness undisturbed! How much kinder not to awaken Vladimir and Estragon to the nightmare of history! How much quicker will the play end if the audience leave the theater!

Didi puzzles over his insight, and the moment passes. The Boy appears, signaling the end of another round. The image of a child symbolizes tomorrow's hope; there is no reason why this promise should be denied to the creatures of Beckett's moving tableau.

W. B. Yeats learned early to develop the dramatic tension of his principal argument between two characters, but it took him almost ten years to find suitable subject and setting for his mystical plays. In 1899 he voiced a concern not so much with character as with place:

Our legends are always associated with places, and not merely every mountain and valley, but every strange stone and coppice, has its legend, preserved in written or unwritten tradition. Our Irish romantic movement has arisen out of this tradition, and should always, even when it makes new legends about traditional people and things, be haunted by places.[9]

Yeats's need for a sense of place that would evoke tragic revery, a neutral landscape in which he could depict the dream of reality in the mind's

eye—one similar to that which Beckett later used so masterfully in
Godot—eventually led him in 1915 to Japanese Noh drama. Before Yeats
turned eastward to find a sense of place, he found and developed a
subject matter that focused on the glories of ancient Irish myths. During
his composition of *On Baile's Strand* (1904), Yeats wrote a letter to T.
Sturgis Moore:

> I am starting a little heroical play about Cuchulain and am curious to
> see how my recent poetical experience of the stage will effect my
> work.[10]

Yeats's experiment was the most productive of his career in the theater.
His creation of Cuchulain plays continued throughout the period from
1901 to 1938, with only a brief hiatus between *The Green Helmet* (1910)
and *At the Hawk's Well* (1916).

The poet's retelling of the Cuchulain legends was not simply his effort
to recapitulate the legendary prowess of a figure contemporary with
classical Greek folklore. Yeats brought to the myth something of his own
experience of the Irish people, the trials of their self-determination, and
the bitterness and rancor of their patriots, who were unable to find a
consensus to govern the Irish spirit. More important, the Cuchulain
myth was really a universalized statement of Yeats's search for the integrated self, a very personal statement of which Cuchulain (Everyman)
represented an idealized image. Yeats believed, as F. A. C. Wilson
pointed out very clearly, that all religions were one, and that there was, in
fact, a subjective convention of symbolism and belief extending from
ancient Egypt through Neoplatonism and medieval alchemy to contemporary religious practises.[11] Subjective religious faiths particularly appealed to W. B. Yeats because they exalted the notion of the self. And they
seemed to support his contention that the present "objective age," which
he abhorred, was moving toward universal anarchy. The Easter Rebellion (1916) was the Irish portent of the coming chaos.

Using symbols in the search for an integrated self gave W. B. Yeats two
advantages. On the one hand, it allowed the poet to express himself
simultaneously on two levels: on the surface, the narrative tells the story
in familiar terms; at a deeper, archetypal level, the connotations and
patterns established by the symbols create a universal truth.[12] Yeats also
found that his layered approach to drama accorded with his theory of
the self, which fortuitously contained two analogous psychological types.
The objective temperament, in essence the surface narrative, can be
characterized as the contemporary Christian, one who tends to regard
his or her own personality as imperfect or even valueless. The objective
self depends on salvation by means of appeals to an external savior God;

he or she seeks union with that God by means of mortification, self-denial, or other expiatory rites. Yeats's subjective self, based on the archetypal patterns of universal religions, is by nature aware that he or she carries God within; as a consequence, the subjective personality is boundless, infinitely resourceful, and in fact divine. Salvation is attained by cultivating the subjective self or a higher personality. According to Yeats's analysis of history, both the subjective and the objective types continually interact, and all human personality can be assigned to one or another of the molds. Hence, the union of the integrated self (the goal of Cuchulain), or the exchange of the objective for the subjective selves—dramatically portrayed onstage in the adoption of a mask by a character in the middle of a play—fascinated Yeats, who depicted Cuchulain as an Everyman disillusioned with the modern, externally oriented world.

In Yeats's retelling of ancient Irish legends, the poet replaced the old romantic idealization of character and spirit with his own oblique vision, one that allowed a continuous interplay of ironic meanings. Peter Ure noted that the tragic power of Cuchulain and Conchubar (among others in *On Baile's Strand*) derived from their context, one that proved tragic "because of some element which [was] thwarting and contradictory in the nature of heroic acts."[13] Barton Friedman thought that this aspect of Yeats's work in the theater was particularly important because it represented a paradigm of the poet's struggle to find a "genuinely dramatic mode adequate to his aspirations for the stage."[14] These aspirations, according to Friedman, were nothing less than the prospect of awakening from the nightmare of history that was bequeathed by the Renaissance.[15] Yeats would ask his reader/spectator to once again grasp the simplicity and the unity of the self in the mask—the artist projected into his opposite. This was heady stuff indeed. Yeats did not succeed completely. His principal difficulties lay in his theory of tragedy, his belief in systems of symbols and his theory of the stage. The conceptual model of theater that supposes actors to be agents of action describes the work of the principal dramatists of the twentieth century, including Samuel Beckett. But Yeats was a stubborn exception who insisted on using his marionette-like actors, who issued from the acting theories of Edward Gordon Craig. The geography of the stage was Ireland, but the actors were in straitjackets.

Where W. B. Yeats struggled, Samuel Beckett excelled—in adapting subject matter to the stage. Nowhere was this more evident than in the geography he declared to be the province of his drama. For Beckett, the stage is the reality of the mind's eye, in which no symbols intervene. In *En Attendant Godot* Didi and Gogo play out a dream of reality for which there is no escape. The play is not only a representation of past values that have been lost, in the manner of Yeats's *The Countess Cathleen*, but of the living myth of the twentieth century, which seems—at times—to have lost its way in disquisition. Yeats's romantic dreamscape of the early 1900s became Beckett's realistic dreamscape of the 1950s; in the later playwright's work, symbol becomes stage fact, stripped of pretensions. The fact that the mid-century dream is a nightmare supplies an additional dramatic fillip.

In the composition of *On Baile's Strand,* Yeats showed considerable expertise and dramatic sense in his construction of a plot based on the living myth of the Irish people. The play takes place at the threshold of consciousness. The door at the back of the set, through which the Fool and the Blind Man enter, symbolizes man's access to his unconscious. Yeats housed all his dreams in the imagination, his expression of the poet's right to recover what he believed modern civilization to have lost (Beckett was, no doubt, quick to agree):

> We cannot doubt that barbaric people received such influences . . . more easily and fully then we do, for our life in cities, which deafens or kills the passive meditative life, and our education that enlarges the separated, self-moving mind, have made our souls less sensitive. Our souls that were once naked to the winds of heaven are now thickly clad, and have learned to build a house and light a fire upon its hearth, and shut-to the doors and windows.[16]

In Yeats's view, modern Ireland had lost a great deal of substance. In *On Baile's Strand* he introduced a blind man as a symbol of the world's decline, Conchubar as a representative of the decadence of a modern world that plays tricks on its ancient heroes, and Cuchulain as a representative of fallen greatness and a tarnished heroic myth that must accommodate itself to the modern condition.

In *En Attendant Godot,* Beckett depicted a world not unlike Yeats's disquieting picture of twentieth-century civilization. In Beckett's play two tramps find themselves on a road bordering the property of a decadent landowner, Pozzo, who (in act 2) is blind. They tell each other stories to pass the time, as do the Blind Man and the Fool in *On Baile's Strand.* The Blind Man helps the Fool to steal food so that they both survive:

> *Fool.* You have eaten it! you have told me lies. . . .
> *Blind Man.* What would have happened to you but for me, and you without your wits? If I did not take care of you, what would you do for food and warmth?[17]

The quarrel over the chicken in the Yeats play is transposed into a fight between Estragon and Lucky over Pozzo's chicken bones in *Godot:*

"(Estragon approaches Lucky and makes to wipe his eyes. Lucky kicks him violently in the shins . . .)" (21B). The parallel between the Fool and the Blind Man in *On Baile's Strand* and Vladimir and Estragon in *Godot* is even more apparent in Didi's speech: *"Vladimir.* When I think of it . . . all these years . . . but for me . . . where would you be . . . (Decisively.) You'd be nothing more than a little heap of bones at the present minute, no doubt about it" (7B). In *En Attendant Godot,* to paraphrase the Old Woman's speech in *On Baile's Strand,* life for Vladimir and Estragon drifts between Lucky, the fool, and Pozzo, the blind man. Pozzo describes the beauty of the twilight, the edge of consciousness, and Lucky describes, in his tirade, the state of Everyman's sporting activities. Life does drift between twilight and bodily processes—Beckett's explicit message in *Godot,* but only an implied meaning in Yeats's *On Baile's Strand.*

Yeats protested "tainted" continental influences on the great Elizabethan playwrights, but he was not above making use of their borrowed techniques to suit his own purposes. He presented an Elizabethan dumb show in *On Baile's Strand.*

Outside the door in the blue light of the sea-mist are many old and young Kings; amongst them are three women, two of whom carry a bowl of fire. The third, in what follows, puts from time to time fragrant herbs into the fire so that it flickers up into brighter flame.

(260)

In the same play even the quarrel between the Fool and the Blind Man over the chicken that parallels the deadly quarrel between Cuchulain and his illegitimate son—an example of double plotting—reverberates with the echo of Shakespeare's *King Lear* or Marlowe's *Dr. Faustus.* However, Yeats's Fool and Blind Man lead Cuchulain to self-knowledge, madness, and drowning; in Shakespeare's play, a fool and mock-madman restore a king to his greatness.

Yeats handled the irony of the final moments of *On Baile's Strand* brilliantly. He allowed Cuchulain's agony to be seen through the eyes of the common folk. The main action takes place offstage, and the poet presents the spectator with Cuchulain's ordeal as an image from the Fool's mind. When an unaware Cuchulain goes out to meet his own son in mortal combat, the father is the blind man meeting the fool of a son who would challenge his authority. Cuchulain's story is also the story of a blind man who reports the story of a fool. The play's double perspective represents the best of Yeats's early work in the theater, and his most successful attempt to present a reality that had meaning for the mind's eye of his contemporary audiences and for Irish people attuned to ancient Irish mythology.

Yeats incorporated the ancient device of the chorus in *Deirdre,* which he began to write in 1904 and completed in 1907. In the play a group of maenads with stringed instruments and no home "but the roads of the world" warn Deirdre's husband, Naoise, that Conchubar, the male symbol of a decadent, voyeuristic society of the modern era, wants to steal his bride. Deirdre bids her husband farewell:

> *Deirdre.* Bend and kiss me now,
>   For it may be the last before our death.
>   And when that's over, we'll be different;
>   Imperishable things, a cloud or a fire.
>   And I know nothing but this body, nothing
>   But that old vehement, bewildering kiss.[18]

A moment later Conchubar's hired dark-faced Executioner captures Naoise in a net and slaughters him. Deirdre cheats Conchubar of his intended concubine by taking her own life. The play ends as Conchubar screams defiance at a mob of Deirdre's avengers, who represented for Yeats a return to a society that was spirited, honorable, and noble-minded.

Yeats expressed his concern for the state of modern Ireland in *Deirdre* and *On Baile's Strand,* but he saved his most vitriolic remarks for *The Green Helmet* (1910), a scathing indictment of the internecine conflict that he felt repudiated all the goals and frustrated all Yeats's efforts to mold an ideal society. Yeats described the play as a "heroic farce," in which characters and settings were to be painted in shades of green, purple, and black to contrast with the Red Man in the green helmet. In *The Green Helmet* two Irishmen, Conall and Laegaire, are trapped in a game from which they cannot extricate themselves. They spend their days drinking and complaining of their fellow countrymen:

> *Conall.* Here neighbour wars on neighbour, and
>   why there is no man knows,
>   And if a man is lucky all wish his luck away,
>   And take his good name from him between a
>   day and a day.[19]

Yeats's opinion of his fractious countrymen would scarcely improve in the next eighteen years.

The play begins in a familiar setting: misty moonlight shines in a doorway at the back of the stage, through which the audience sees a reflection of the sea. Yeats contained his drama in the space set by the boundaries of the unconscious. In this schemata, the sea represented the Anima Mundi, the consciousness of the race that lies just beyond the constraints of Yeats's dramas. Within the space Conall and Laegaire wait (as Vladimir and Estragon in *Godot* will wait) for a mysterious visitor, the Red Man, who allowed his head to be "whipped off" the previous year, and who demanded the same sacrifices from one of them.

A year has passed since the demand was made. The debt is due. The men are terrified. Cuchulain appears, and forces his way into their house:

Cuchulain. . . . .
　You are waiting for some message to bring you
　to war or love
　In that old secret country beyond the wool-white waves. . . .

(227)

Laegaire and Conall agree to tell Cuchulain for whom they are waiting. A year earlier the two old cronies had been drinking:

Conall. . . . . We were
　there and the ale-cup full.
　We were half drunk and merry, and midnight on
　the stroke
　When a wide, high man came in with a red foxy
　cloak. . . .

(228)

They asked the Red Man, symbol of Ireland's roistering past, what game he would play with them:

Conall. . . . .
　"Why, whip off my head!
　Then one of you stoop down, and I'll
　whip off his," he said.
　"A head for a head," he said, "that is
　the game that I play."

(229)

The Red Man laughed at the befuddled Irishmen until, in a moment of frustration, Conall whipped off the head of the Red Man:

Conall. And there on the ground where it fell
　it went on
　laughing at me
Laegaire. Till he took it up in his hands—
Conall. And splashed himself into the sea.

(229)

The earthy wildness of the tale impresses even Cuchulain, who recalls occasions for his companions when he was also "deep in the cup" and believed every minute in the life of his drunken imagination.

Yeats's tale of Irish drinking stories and songs, told among friends who have drained many ale cups together, finally follows them to the day of reckoning. The mocking of ancient heroes, the symbolic "whipping off" of their heads, demands retribution in kind. The Red Man reappeared, his head on his shoulders, and declared that he would return to the house in exactly twelve months and claim his due. Laegaire declares: "Twelve months are up to-day" (230). Conall thinks their plight is hopeless. How can he fight a figure that laughs "when you whip off his head?" He might well ask "How do you recall words that have been written on the wind?" Cuchulain attempts to intervene, in effect, to return Ireland to its ancient noble sovereignty. The Red Man meets his challenge with a surprising response: the bravest man in Ireland can have the privilege of wearing the green helmet.

The Red Man departs, and immediately quarreling begins. Cuchulain stops the fighting, but the subsequent truce is only momentary. As each man's charioteers, stable boys, and kitchen helpers begin to take sides, Conall comments on the scene:

> *Conall.* And there's not a man in the house that will
>   close his eye to-night,
>   Or be able to keep them from it, or know what
>   set them to fight.
>
> (234)

Yeats saves one of his most bitter indictments of his countrymen for the next line:

> *Conall.* . . . . (*A noise of horns without.*)
>   There, do you hear them now? Such hatred has
>   each for each.
>   They have taken the hunting-horns to drown
>   one another's speech
>   For fear the truth may prevail. . . .
>
> (234)

Hunting horns, symbols of heroic deeds and battle, are reduced to noisemakers. The farce of heroic courage continues, as one charioteer challenges another:

> *Another Charioteer.*
>   It is Laegaire that is best,
>   For he fought with cats in
>   Connacht while Conall

took his rest
And drained his ale-pot.

(235)

The arguments and challenges go on, as the disputes that appear to be tempests in an ale-pot grow more menacing every minute. It seems likely that the Red Man will win not one head, but many.

When Conall's and Laegaire's wives begin to fight over which husband is "the better to look at," or "the better born," the victory of the Red Man seems complete. Cuchulain persuades the wives to enter jointly, and the husbands to break down the walls of the house so each of their spouses can enter at the same moment "each one the wife of a king." Cuchulain takes up the helmet and laments:

> *Cuchulain.* Townland may
>   rail at townland till all have gone to wrack,
>   The very straws may wrangle till they've thrown
>   down the stack;
>   The very door-posts bicker till they've pulled
>   in the door,
>   The very ale-jar jostle till all the ale is on
>   the floor,
>   But this shall help no further.

(240)

Thereupon he throws the helmet into the sea. The Red Man has won. All the combatants turn on Cuchulain, as each believes his side was cheated of the right to wear the crown. In the midst of this flurry of insults the Red Man returns with his black Cat-Men to demand payment of the debt of a head. The symbolic loss is complemented by the Red Man's demand for a comparable real loss.

No one but Cuchulain has the courage to match his words with his head. The Red Man accepts his offer. But instead of whipping off Cuchulain's head, the figure of the Anima Mundi places the helmet on Cuchulain's brow. The Red Man, "Rector of this land," ends the farce with his statement of hope for future Irish generations. Their only hope will be to stop bickering and to learn to live together:

> *Red Man.* . . . . And I choose the laughing lip
>   That shall not turn from laughing, whatever rise or
>   fall;
>   The heart that grows no bitterer although betrayed
>   by all;
>   The hand that loves to scatter; the life like a
>   gambler's throw;
>   And these things I make prosper, till a day come that
>   I know,

When heart and mind shall darken that the weak
may end the strong,
And the long-remembering harpers have matter for
their song.

(243)

Yeats minces no words in his indictment of Ireland's internal strife. "Who is willing to pay the debt of the Red Man now?" he asks. Cuchulain did once, the poet says. Presumably, the challenge remains for each succeeding generation to overcome family conflicts that undermine the greatness of a country. Laegaire and Conall wait in fear and trembling for their destiny; Vladimir and Estragon wait, in similar circumstances, for Godot.

In the Beckett play all vestiges of the original "contract" with Godot have vanished. Didi and Gogo only know they are to "wait for" Godot. Why or for what purpose are forgotten; even the place and date are now obscure:

> Gogo. Let's go.
> Didi. We can't.
> Gogo. Why not?
> Didi. We're waiting for Godot.
> Gogo. (despairingly). Ah! (Pause.) You're sure it was here?

(10A)

Nothing is quite certain. They have met him, they believe. He told them to meet him, they think, at this place, they hope. What Godot looks like, they are not sure:

> Didi. Oh he's a . . . he's a kind of acquaintance.
> Gogo. Nothing of the kind, we hardly know him.
> Didi. True . . . we don't know him very well . . . but all the same . . .
> Gogo. Personally I wouldn't even know him if I saw him.

(16A)

The internal evidence of the play strongly suggests an interpretation in which Vladimir and Estragon perpetually relive the nightmare of history. Each evening of performance the characters are offered an opportunity to recognize their situation:

> Gogo. In my opinion we were here.
> Didi. (looking round). You recognize the place?

(10B)

Each night the tramps fail:

> Didi. All the same . . . that tree . . . (turning towards auditorium) that bog . . .

(10B)

The play resumes its circular plot. The living dream world, within which the characters function in the margins of awareness, remains intact:

> *Gogo.* Well, shall we go?
> *Didi.* Yes, let's go.
>   *They do not move.*

(35B)

and,

> *Didi.* Well? Shall we go?
> *Gogo.* Yes, let's go.
>   *They do not move.*

(60B)

The promise that Godot will come, the champion of a changed land, remains an uncertain promise. In *Godot* the green helmet is a top hat that everyone wears.

If the dreamworld is confirmed, what place does Godot play in the lives of Didi and Gogo? The possibilities seem endless: an offer? a prayer? a supplication? an agreement? Of what sort? He did not say. He would consult his friends, his acquaintances, his books, his bank accounts, before making a decision. Nothing is certain, except for one fact, surprising, particularly in a comedy:

> *Didi.* You'd make me laugh if it wasn't prohibited.
> *Gogo.* We've lost our rights?
> *Didi. (distinctly).* We got rid of them. *Silence. They remain motionless, arms dangling, heads sunk, sagging at the knees.*

(13B)

The image the tramps portray is that of Christ sacrificed on the cross. The compassion so universally noted by commentators on this play is bereft of laughter. The tramps have lost their right to express themselves with genuine mirth. That joy was lost in the battle for the green helmet. Vladimir and Estragon have not heeded the prescription of the Red Man:

> *Red Man.* I choose the laughing lip
>   That shall not turn from laughing, whatever rise or fall. . . .

(243)

Until Cuchulain or his substitute champion offers to match the Red Man, head for head, the little men of the world like Estragon and

Vladimir will wait for Godot, with sunken hopes (Gogo's swollen feet) and feeble understanding (Didi's dripping head). The Boy's descriptions of Godot do not provide much more information. Pozzo is unable to enlighten the tramps on anything but twilights, and Lucky, for whom he claims superior powers, is a fountain of misinformation:

> *Pozzo.* But for him all my thoughts, all my feelings, would have been of common things. *(Pause. With extraordinary vehemence.)* Professional worries! *(Calmer)* Beauty, grace, truth of the first water, I knew they were all beyond me. So I took a knook.
>
> (22B)

When Lucky speaks, we expect to hear jewels of conversation, eloquently set in impeccable stanzas, that contain all the wisdom of the Ark of the Covenant or the Sermon on the Mount. Instead, we are treated to an issuance from the Tower of Babel:

> *Lucky.* Given the existence as uttered forth in the public works of Puncher and Wattmann of a personal God quaquaquaqua with a white beard quaquaquaqua . . .

But Beckett never cheats his spectator. Buried within the profounds of mind that emanate from Lucky is the wisdom of the play: man wastes and pines. He processes food and pines (waits) for change, for novelty, for Godot in the case of Didi and Gogo, until the sum of existence is the waiting.

This play, unlike Yeats's *The Green Helmet,* is not a farce. Lucky's speech only *appears* to be nonsense. To quote Lucky once again:

> *Lucky.* . . . that man . . . in spite of the strides of alimentation and defecation wastes and pines. . . .
>
> (29A)

The fact that man "wastes and pines" is as true in Beckett's play as it is in Yeats's. Laegaire and Conall waste through their drinking, and pine for release from the Red Man's bond. That is the spirit of *The Green Helmet;* that is at least one message of *En Attendant Godot.*

Reading the Cuchulain myth and the Irish countryside into *En Attendant Godot* suggests one interpretation of the nature of Godot. All of the tramps' attempts to define their situation are frustrated. Each of their questions reaffirms Didi's and Gogo's deepest fears. They live in a dreamworld of everyday reality from which there is only one escape. The date of their meeting with Godot is uncertain:

> *Didi.* He said Saturday. *(Pause.)* I think. . . .

Gogo. (very insidious). But what Saturday? And is it Saturday? Is it not rather Sunday? *(Pause.)* Or Monday? *(Pause.)* Or Friday?
Didi. (looking wildly about him, as though the date was inscribed in the landscape). It's not possible!
Gogo. Or Thursday?
Didi. What'll we do?

(10B–11A)

An attempt to discuss the problem rationally only plunges Didi into a deeper gloom:

Gogo. If he came yesterday and we weren't here you may be sure he won't come again to-day.
Didi. But you say we were here yesterday.
Gogo. I may be mistaken.

(11A)

The more each tries to unravel the mystery, the more confused the dream becomes. Beckett does not undercut the message, as does Yeats; Estragon and Vladimir are wrapped in a dream that completes the dramatic statement of life in contemporary times.

In *Godot,* even the nature of the landscape in which Didi and Gogo stand, the geography of the country in which they find themselves, and the season of the year during which they travel are not clear. Didi and Gogo wait by a tree. But even that is not certain:

Gogo. What is it?
Didi. I don't know. A willow.
Gogo. Where are the leaves?
Didi. It must be dead.
Gogo. No more weeping.

(10A)

This is a moment of dramatic irony. The Kabbalistic tree of life is also a symbol of psychic growth. In act 1 the power of the imagination to recall the circumstances surrounding Godot is dead. Without memory no sorrow can intrude. Didi and Gogo have forgotten their heritage. Only a habit of being, not its purpose, remains to them. The situation is tragic in its infinite loss of purpose and comic in its absurdity. By the beginning of act 2, the tree has four or five leaves, but the movement of the play is still circular, emphasizing again the particular hell these two travelers must cross each time they enter the spectator's imagination.

The second act of *Godot* allows not only for a new Godot, or Pozzo, or Lucky, to arrive, but also for a different Vladimir and Estragon to appear. Gogo prepares the stage at the end of act 1:

Gogo. (turning to look at the boots). I'm leaving them there. *(Pause.)* Another will come, just as . . . as . . . as me but with smaller feet, and they'll make him happy.

(34B)

In act 2 another generation of tramps will discover a theater of the imagination where—if only through force of habit—a tree of hope and of comprehension will blossom with four or five leaves. Vladimir's imperfect memory of a quotation from the King James Bible—"*Didi*. Hope deferred maketh the something sick, who said that?" (8A)—recalls a sentence from Proverbs 13.12: "Hope deferred maketh the heart sick; but when desire cometh it is a tree of life." Hope deferred continues the nightmare. But each new generation promises hope that the impasse will be broken; the "window" is open to fresh desire for a moment, "then it's night once more." In *Godot* twilight signals the possibility of change from hope deferred to desire reborn. Beckett discussed this notion in detail in *Comment C'est.* Endless generations unite in the wrong interests,

> and these same couples that eternally form and form again all along this immense circuit that the millionth time that's conceivable is as the inconceivable first and always two strangers uniting in the interests of torment.[20]

Where is the Red Man now that he is needed? One must at least hope (with Mr. Beckett) that the old Irish sow might stop eating her farrow.

The lessons Beckett took from Yeats's *The Green Helmet,* important as they were, scarcely compared with the usefulness of the material Beckett found in Yeats's first major success, *At the Hawk's Well* (1917). *Hawk's Well* was an early experiment in developing a Celtic form of Japanese Noh drama. Yeats deliberately set out to find a balance between competing interests of narrative, dance and music that could communicate at an archetypal level. The play celebrated Yeats's profound spiritual despair; on a personal level, Yeats was admitting his final failure to win the love of Maud Gonne; on a more philosophical level, *Hawk's Well* represented his belief that the search for unity of being in a higher self was inevitably doomed to failure.[21]

The first version of *At the Hawk's Well,* published by *Harper's Bazaar* in March 1917, ended Yeats's dramatic interregnum of six years (1910–16). The playwright announced his venture in a series of essays advertising his "small, unpopular theatre":

> I have written a little play that can be played in a room for so little money that forty or fifty readers of poetry can pay the price. There will be no scenery, for three musicians, whose seeming sunburned

faces will, I hope, suggest that they have wandered from village to village in some country of our dreams. . . .[22]

After six years of preparation, W. B. Yeats was finally prepared to lead his countrymen into a new literary age. But he was still protective of his work: only "readers of poetry," and not the general public, would be expected to attend performances.

The action of the play begins on a bare stage on which a drum, a gong, and a zither are discovered upstage near a patterned screen. The time of the play, according to Yeats's stage directions, is *"The Irish Heroic Age."*[23] As the Musicians unfold a black cloth emblazoned with the image of a hawk, they begin to chant:

> I call to the eye of the mind
> A well long choked up and dry
> And boughs long stripped by the wind,
>
> . . . .
> A man climbing up to a place
> The salt sea wind has swept bare.[24]

The First Musician is masked in face paint, as are the other Musicians and the Guardian of the Well. The Old Man and the Young Man wear real masks. But Yeats christens the play's chorus of Musicians, the principal antagonists of the action, "ideal spectators" in his symbology.[25] They are the actors, their faces made up to resemble masks, who carry what Nietzsche called the "mythic knowledge" that is communicated in a state of revery:

> I sometimes fence for half an hour at the day's end, and when I close my eyes upon the pillow I see a foil playing before me, the button to my face. We meet always in the deep of the mind, whatever our work, wherever our reveries carries us, that other Will.[26]

In the Noh drama of Japan, Yeats discovered a new way to combine the binary association of the world of play with the mythic material of Ireland's heroic past. He had used musicians before: *Deirdre* (1907) begins with a speech by the First Musician. Yeats had also used masks in his earlier plays. The revised version of *On Baile's Strand* (1904), for example, describes the faces of the Fool and the Blind Man enclosed in "Grotesque and extravagant masks." But in none of his plays did Yeats have his character's faces "made up to resemble masks" until he staged *Hawk's Well* in 1917 at the Abbey Theater. Two years later he produced *The Only Jealousy of Emer.* Its characters included three Musicians, their faces "made up to resemble masks."[27] In Noh drama, Yeats discovered a way to display both myth and story in plots that occurred, as Barton Friedman termed it, in the deep of the mind.

Yeats's theory of the self suggested to him the use of masks to represent the image of the integrated personality, achieved by the union of the self and the antiself. Cuchulain could have renounced the objective temperament and earned deliverance from the wheel of becoming by developing a spiritual life within. Instead, Cuchulain follows his nature to be a man of violent and meaningless actions. At the other extreme, the Old Man, embodying the subjective, passive self, fails not in his devotion to the affort, but because the mystery of the higher self has repudiated him. This latter situation is passive, intellectual in nature. Yeats's use of two figures to suggest a split focus of the integrated personality, was also adopted by Beckett in *Waiting for Godot*. Estragon and Vladimir perform without masks their double *dramatic* functions: as agents of the action they wait; as carriers of mythic knowledge, *they have "forgotten their way": Didi Gogo. Let's go. They do not move* (35B, 60B).

Whether approached from the perspective of formal criticism—Aristotelian or not—or from the simple pragmatism of stage dynamics, the inescapable conclusion is that Yeats tended to suspend his images from a skeletal plot, like wash from a clothesline. In the right psychic wind there is a grand unfurling of suggestive forms. Yeats's fabrics gleam in the reflection of their sun. But his symbols from borrowed cultures have no life of their own. If the wind does not blow across Ireland's ancient memories and the sun does not shine, there is no movement, no reflection. Without structural integrity, the symbols appear to be simply soggy appendages, waiting for an agency to give them direction.

If Yeats's success was not complete, his courage to experiment and his insight into problems in his plays remained formidable. Friedman saw Yeats's full dramatic development in this play:

> At the Hawk's Well and the rest of the cycle to which it belongs are—like its models from *Noh* and the cycles to which they belong—kinds of historical drama, attempts to capture the ambiance, as Yeats imagined it, of Ireland's heroic age. . . . To the degree that these plays concern not only crises in their lives but also the playwright's way of thinking about them, they show how, for Yeats, heroic and aesthetic experience merge.[28]

Yeats bitterly denounced his countrymen for their theater of commerce in his 1910 production of *The Green Helmet*. The long dry spell that followed signaled Yeats's own search for a more effective form of poetic drama. The new, disillusioned dramas—beginning with *Hawk's Well*—that followed had nothing to do with a theater of commerce, but everything to do with Yeats's theater of art: a theater of ritual that recalled words "to their ancient sovereignty."[29] Even this formulation had great problems.

Yeats's interest in Noh drama can be traced to a series of translations of Japanese plays edited by Ezra Pound in 1913 and 1914. Richard Ellmann analyzed the playwright's discovery:

> In Asian convention he [Yeats] found a sense of life as ceremonial and ritual, and of drama as august, formal, traditional. But his own plays were adaptations, not copies, and attempted to infuse Western passion into the narrow frame.[30]

Yeats confirmed the later critic's impression in his publication of "Swedenborg, Mediums, Desolate Places," in which he suggested that the year of his discovery was 1913:

> Last winter Mr. Ezra Pound was editing the late Professor Fenellosa's translations of the Noh Drama of Japan, and read me a great deal of what he was doing. Nearly all that my fat old woman in Soho learns from her familiars is there in an unsurpassed lyric poetry and in strange and poignant fables once danced or sung in the houses of nobles.[31]

Yeats instantly translated his rapture over the possibilities of the Noh, for his own writing into words and scenes for a new vision of the Cuchulain legend. Five years had passed since the poet had last chastised his people for their intransigent bickering. As Yeats perceived it, his adaptation of Noh drama to Irish mythology was one way that he could distance himself from the immediacy of his own anguish. It also served to universalize his new set for *At the Hawk's Well*—a bare stage, *"in a high windy place,"* set with only the emblems of a tree, a rock, and a hawk—a stark contrast to his setting for *The Countess Cathleen*, with its *"room with lighted fire . . .* [in which] *Mary, a woman of forty years or so, is grinding a quern."* The specificity and arcaneness of the early play lay in sharp contrast to the neutrality of the later symbolic works.

Yeats's discovery of Noh drama was fortunate for his career, but not necessary in the least. Had Pound not visited Yeats during the period when he was working on Professor Fenellosa's translations, the poet-playwright would have undoubtedly used another source—the Upanishads or the Vedas, perhaps. Yeats was an incessant experimenter, constantly adapting form to Irish substance.

Yeats's early criticism of Shakespeare's dramaturgy, in essays that sprang from his visit to Stratford-on-Avon in April 1901, rebuked the bard for the same offenses that Yeats would later commit.[32] The fact that Yeats, the eager young poet, advertised himself at the bard's expense, in no way relegated Yeats to the ranks of similarly disposed but lesser luminaries. Shaw did the same, with astonishing success, as did Brecht, although for other reasons. Yeats really does not deserve the opprobrium that Richard Ellmann served up:

> Though he [Yeats] never ceases to regard himself as a rebel whom society has imprisoned, he builds his own jails, escapes from them, then builds others; or, to put it another way, Yeats hides in the center of the city and emblazons his name on his hiding place and equips it with a public address system.[33]

Yeats followed a historic precedent in sharpening his dramatic tools in the forge of Shakespeare's reputation, an activity that neither began nor ended with the Irish poet. His justification of his interpretations of dreams, seances, and other occult matters left him more open to criticism than others might have been, however, and undermined his genuine contribution to dramatic literature. Part of the difficulty lay in Yeats's claims for the artist's unrestricted passions:

> I think that we who are poets and artists, not being permitted to shoot beyond the tangible, must go from desire to weariness and so to desire again, and live but for the moment when vision comes to our weariness like terrible lightning, in the humility of the brutes.[34]

But even Shakespeare's forge and the inspiration of Ireland's mythical past could not open the hearts of Yeats's countrymen to his new drama.

A poet's inspiration, which Beckett described in *Proust* as a "delicious deflagration," is a precious commodity whose moments should be sought out and treasured (even to the point of binding Murphy with seven scarves to a rocking chair). No limits should be placed on the sources for such inspiration—Murphy finds his life's goal in the genethliac of Ramiswani Suk's Nativity; Yeats finds his dramaturgy in the symbolism of Japanese Noh plays:

> It is not permitted to a man who takes up pen or chisel, to seek originality, for passion is his only business. . . . He is like those phantom lovers in the Japanese play who, compelled to wander side by side and never mingle, cry: "we neither wake nor sleep and, passing our nights in a sorrow which is in the end a vision, what are these scenes of spring to us?"[35]

The problem was not in Yeats's search for the unself, which absorbed Beckett for decades, but in Yeats's attempt to make the Japanese Noh do the work of the unself, as a symbol system.

From thought to inspiration to symbol, Yeats's system had its own internal consistency. But the relationships between his symbols and his dramatic contexts were somewhat tentative. Ellmann was on substantial ground on this point in his critique of Yeats.

Ellmann's summary was long, but important, for it focused on a crucial distinction between the work of Yeats and Beckett—the passions of the writer as they are translated into vehicles for the theater:

> All the time that he [Yeats] plays with reality he seeks confirmation of his dreams; he haunts like a nostalgic ghost all the seances in London to try to prove that the miraculous, with which he associates the dream, is not uncommon and that all men who are willing to look with an eye unpolluted by scientific incredulity can see it. . . . At last, in marriage, [to Georgie Hyde-Lees] Yeats secures, if not entire confirmation of the supernatural, a dream so large and yet so manipulatable as to give him almost miraculous control over reality. . . . But now his dream is more than a dream, it is a symbol. . . . He must make his dream impregnable by relating it to everything that happens. . . .[36]

Yeats's uncertainty was doubly unfortunate, since it locked him into a system of symbols that he should have used as an intermediate step to the creation of dramatic situations. Ann Saddlemyer's comment that Gordon Craig's influence on Yeats should not be underestimated was never more prophetic than on this point. Ellmann, in his special style, found the personal source of Yeats's choice:

> Symbolism became Yeats's method because he could not otherwise have written; the symbol enabled him to escape uncertainty, to partake of the advantages of both dream and reality. Drawing himself into the symbol he was protected against the sceptic with his direct arguments and the realist with his collections of disturbing facts; he was committed to no literalist belief which he did not feel; he was unified and liberated.[37]

Ellmann's critique made short shrift of Yeats's integrity as a poet. Yeats was sincere in his efforts to mold a new drama, without regard to any "escapist" or "protectionist" motives, as Ellmann alluded to in his summary. But the final effect, the dramas that Yeats staged in the Abbey Theatre, suffered defects and endured criticism, regardless of the causes.

Yeats was more than prepared to defend his work, however, and was capable of mounting a sturdy offensive. Speaking of his innovative importation of Noh scenic techniques to Irish methology, Yeats acknowledged his own success:

> I do not think of my discovery as mere economy, for it has been a great

gain to get rid of scenery, to substitute for a crude landscape painted
upon canvas three performers who, sitting before the wall or a patterned screen, describe landscape or event, and accompany movement
with drum and gong, or deepen the emotion of the words with zither
or flute.[38]

What Yeats failed to do was acknowledge the "strangeness" of Japanese
Noh scenery to the Western eye of a rigorously traditional non-Western
art form that had very specific means of presenting ghost plays. Instead,
Yeats attempted to substitute classical Noh scenic techniques for all
manner of Irish mystical traditions, without regard for the reality of
either Noh drama substance or of Irish mythological context.

Yeats found the reality of his dream images in archetypal connotations
and patterns derived from the world's great religions. He believed that
symbols related to these archetypal forces retained forever their means
of communication. Hence it is easy to understand Yeats's attraction to
Noh drama, based as it was on song and dance representation called
sarugaku, which originated in pantomimic dances performed at ancient
Shinto and Buddhist festivals. W. B. Yeats manipulated the subject matter of these traditional Nohs—the journey, the quest, the communion
with a god or ghost—to provide arbitrary justifications from another
culture for everything that he sought in his own.

M. C. Stopes described the typical scenario of a Japanese Noh drama:

> The hero or heroine, or the secondary character, sets out upon a
> journey, generally in search of some person or to fulfill some duty or
> religious object, and on this journey passes some famous spot. In the
> course of long and generally wearying wanderings, a recital of which
> gives an opportunity for the description of natural beauties, this living
> person meets some god, or the ghost or reincarnated spirit of some
> person of note, or perhaps the altered and melancholy wreck of some
> person of former grand estate. . . . Often a priest forms one of the
> characters, then the ghost may be soothed by his prayers and exhorta-
> tions.[39]

This relatively straightforward description of Noh drama helps to explain W. B. Yeats's adaption of Noh dramatic techniques to his own
purposes, but there is considerably more to Noh. Professor Tatsuro Ishii
described some basic precepts of Noh, citing the writings of Zeami
(1363–1443), the great fifteenth-century Noh actor and dramatist. Commenting on the concept of *shiore* as the "withering of a flower," considered to be the highest attainment of Noh actors, Ishii suggested that the
term refers to an internal, almost subliminal communication between
performer and audience.[40] Furthermore, in *Kakyō,* Zeami's later treatise
on acting, *yūgen* is described as the ultimate state of attainment in all the

arts, consisting of elements of dance, music, imitation, *and the state of the mind of the performer.*

In this age of realistic drama, W. B. Yeats has been roundly chastised for his symbolic representations onstage. But his instincts for Noh drama were, in this regard, infallible: Ishii noted that "imitation" in Noh is neither "imitation" or "realism" in the Western sense of the word, but a totally stylized, symbolic representation of the essence and substance of the human experience, realized through the use of dance, music, and extremely simplified, abstract movement.[41] What W. B. Yeats did not assess, however, was the importance of the relationship between audience and performers, as described in *shiore* and in *yūgen.* Zeami was more specific in his concept of *riken no ken,* "the sight of remote sight," which is the sense of the performer adopting the same perspective of the performance as the audience. In addition, there is the concept of *gaken no ken,* "the sight of self sight," or the sense by which the performer sees himself from his own viewpoint. In other words, the performer must see himself from both objective and subjective viewpoints of the performer's self:

> When a performer is able to see himself with the audience's eyes, so to speak, he has not only the same visual image as they do, but also the audience's mind and awareness. If a performer is able to see all aspects of his body from every perspective—as the audience sees it—by means of *riken no ken,* he will realize an aesthetic ideal on stage which in its balance and harmony approaches perfection.[42]

W. B. Yeats was accurate in his assessment of the symbolic nature of Noh drama. But he did not focus sufficiently on the idea of the spectator as the central component of the actor's art. In this regard, Noh drama presents a kind of ritualistic space for the audience, where both the performer and the spectator share the theatrical event equally. W. B. Yeats, to the contrary, moved his symbols toward a distant trysting space, far removed from reality. Beckett, in such works as *Not I* and *Ohio Impromptu,* worked very much in the tradition of the dehiscent self of the performer that the audience must reassemble.

One major distinction in the structure of Noh drama and its presentation to spectators and the abstraction that Yeats created for his own purposes concerns the division of Noh plays into three parts: *jo, ha,* and *kyū:* "introduction," "development," and "denouement," or "climax." This is the sequential ordering of plays on any given evening. In addition, each play can be divided into segments according to the same principals, with the central division further subdivided into its three constituent elements, in accordance with the overall design:

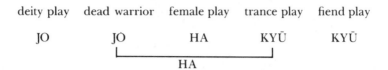

This ritual development of the jo-ha-kyū sequence on a given occasion created an audience expectation of developments within the drama, and a sense of fulfillment when the dramatic design was completed. The bond between actor and spectator was restored with each performance. W. B. Yeats, to the contrary, had no grand design in common with his audiences. Rather than follow a scheme, Yeats took as a model for his theater the dead warrior play (the "jo" of the central "ha" sequence) and made it into *The Dreaming of the Bones.* Yeats's *At the Hawk's Well* resembled the "jo" deity plays and the "kyū" trance play, assembled as a double plot. In the process, something was lost in translation into Irish culture. Where W. B. Yeats searched for universal archetypal symbols of communication, Zeami sought an intimate theatrical experience that depended on both performer and spectator. The goal of Noh performance, according to Professor Ishii's reading of Zeami's confessional on acting, was:

> one that is always accompanied by human intention and consciousness, which nevertheless goes beyond the boundaries of human intention and consciousness and comes closer to accord with the perfect order of nature by means of life long training and discipline [which almost reaches] a religious experience in the esthetics of performance for both the performers and audiences.[43]

Faced with Zeami's lifetime dedication to art, it is little wonder that Yeats failed to grasp the extensive dramaturgy and the intimate knowledge of Japanese theatrical convention that were necessary to comprehend and appreciate the full truth of Noh drama, to his great artistic loss.

At the Hawk's Well took as its theme Yeats's belief that the search for a higher self is doomed to failure. Nothing is worth the hard pain of childbirth. The old man has been wasting his entire life beside a dry well, enduring a fifty-year rite in vain. Peter Ure noted the Musicians' opening song not only sets the action in the "eye of the mind," but also takes the form of a conjuration: "its singers calling forth from the void . . . Cuchulain, the Old Man, and the mountainside with its rocks, choked well and bare trees."[44] The image of the dry well and the bare tree are images of the dark night of the soul. The rocky terrain suggests man's own spiritual failure. The Old Man represents the vain attempt by inept human spirits to reach the goal of an integrated spiritual self, even though their quest has been lifelong. Cuchulain, the active conquerer, cannot attain the state of contemplation because of his violent nature. Cuchulain's tragic situation reflects W. B. Yeats's deepest convictions.[45] Behind this vision lay the artist, wrestling with his own omen of imaginative and physical decay. Yeats the poet, seizing the symbol as a unifying archetypal force for his writing; Yeats the mystic, linking the beliefs of his fat old woman in Soho with the ghosts of the Japanese Noh; Yeats the man, joining life and dream into one composite whole—all failed Yeats the dramatist, who, in abstracting the life of theater into symbols for the mind's eye, abandoned the perspective of the audience. More important, he abandoned the actor's self-perspective.

His abstraction was, of course, intentional. Ezra Pound recorded that the Noh drama was composed for the nobility, a select coterie who might appreciate a drama of masks, "of which both Mr. Yeats and Mr. Craig may approve."[46] With regard to his theater, W. B. Yeats suffered a long spell of little popular success. It did not take long for his personal pique to develop all the intensity of prophetic fever; his limitations became a virtue; the "chosen few" who understood the "art of illusion of Noh drama" (in Pound's words) became a "secret society" that admired Yeats's antitheater or his theater's antiself, depicted in *At the Hawk's Well*.

Despite the limitations already noted, *At the Hawk's Well* is a drama not without poetic power to stir the soul. It was among Samuel Beckett's favorites of W. B. Yeats's plays (as is *The Countess Cathleen*.) In *Hawk's Well*, scene painting is replaced by choric description; props are replaced by geometric shapes; language is restored to its ancient sovereignty; the dancer becomes "the dance," a spiritual figure that mocks humanity with every step.

Yeats had difficulty with the mask symbol in his early years, since his own worldview fluctuated between extremes. But *At the Hawk's Well* represents, in his mature years, "the uncreative ordinary self which has so often accommodated itself to the demands of convention."[47] Seen in this light, the masks of *Hawk's Well* present an interesting display: the Old Man and the Young Man, each wearing a mask, are symbols of humanity engaged in a journey that is life itself. The holy place to which they come is the point of intersection of human and divine worlds. Both seek the properties of the well, which is symbolic of the integrated personality, the unity of Being of the lower self (in Yeats's estimation) that couples to the higher self of the soul. The dry well and the dry tree are symbolic of the dark night of the soul. The three Musicians and the Guardian of the Well, their faces made up to resemble masks, represent the mythic world as it assumes a mantle of convention for ordinary mortals. The goal of the play is to lift the masks from both man and myth, and to perceive the world of the real.[48] But the search for a higher self is not achieved by the living, as the Dancers, symbolizing the presence of a Spiritual World, mockingly remind the audience. Yeats perceived that life, as it is normally lived, is incomplete. On occasion, reality transcends itself and yields moments of completeness or near-completeness, when the real becomes visible, in a moment that he visualized as twilight. *Hawk's Well* takes place at nightfall. *En Attendant Godot* also takes place at nightfall, the time of day-night that is the subject of Pozzo's extended apostrophe on change. Twilight plays an important part in the canons of both Beckett and W. B. Yeats, symbolizing for the environment what a slipping mask represents for a character in a play. Note should also be taken of the rocky terrain and the dessicated tree in each work, the wasteland symbol of man's spiritual poverty.

As *Hawk's Well* begins, Yeats, through the mouth of the First Musician, speaks of his anguished hopes for Ireland. The futility of the moment also expresses the cyclical movement of the play, in which the Old Man has been unable to reach his goal after fifty years of waiting. The prize for Ireland will not come automatically, in the course of time. If there is no talent, there is no grail at the end of the quest, no matter how urgent or lengthy the wait:

> *First Musician.* What were his life soon done!
>   Would he lose by that or win?
>   A mother that saw her son
>   Doubled over a speckled shin,
>   Gross-grained with ninety years,
>   Would cry, "How little worth
>   Were all my hopes and fears
>   And the hard pain of his birth!"[49]

The Musicians unfold and fold the black cloth, on which is painted the likeness of a hawk, as the Guardian of the Well enters and lays a blue cloth on the ground to suggest a well. The mind's eye is awakened, and as twilight falls, the Old Man enters through the audience (symbolizing the spectators' collective mind's eye that is now alerted). As the Old Man moves, the First Musician speaks in the manner of a medium conducting a séance. Each of his movements is accompanied by commentary, song and drum taps.

Yeats's stage directions for the actors in *At the Hawk's Well* are significant: "*His movements, like those of the other persons of the play, suggest a marionette*" (210). Craig's dictates for his "über-marionettes," which forbade the emotions of the actor to interfere with the scheme of the playwright/designer, are the basis of Yeats's Noh dramas. Nothing must intervene between the playwright and the spectator of a drama whose coordinates are framed by the space and time of the imagination, and whose specificity is lost in revery.

Yeats redeemed the play with immediacy of detail in his language:

> *First Musician.* He lays the dry sticks on the leaves
>   And, shivering with cold, he has taken up
>   The fire-stick and socket from its hole.
>   He whirls it round to get a flame. . . .
>
> (210)

The First Musician speaks of mundane things, but his description serves to anchor Yeats's prose to reality.

The Old Man waits by the fairies' well, whose Hawk is the guardian of Ireland's precious past. The Old Man seeks immortality in a place "where nothing thrives" (Yeats's bitter commentary on his Ireland). The landscape is as dessicated as the later set for *Godot*. Beckett dealt with the same theatrical terrain as Yeats. *Godot* begins: "*A country road. A tree. Evening*" (6B). Instead of Yeats's one man doubled with age, standing among old thorn trees and a mound of dry leaves that chokes a well, Beckett's play begins with two old men, one with sore feet, the other with a drip in his head, a mound of earth, and a withered tree. Vladimir and Estragon have been waiting in the dusk. As night falls in *Godot* a Young Boy arrives; in *Hawk's Well* the twilight ends, signaling the arrival of a Young Man:

> *Young Man.* You can, it may be,
>   Lead me to what I seek, a well wherein
>   Three hazels drop their nuts and withered leaves,
>   And where a solitary girl keeps watch
>   Among grey boulders. He who drinks, they say,
>   Of that miraculous water lives for ever
>
> (212)

The Old Man arrived as a young man; the story is about to be repeated. But the round is broken.

The Young Man is Cuchulain, who has saved Ireland in the past and will attempt that impossible task again. Each time the water flows the Old Man is lulled to sleep by the dancer. The warnings of the water's impending flow are the hawk's cry and her shivering dance that none can resist. Ure commented that the water of the well represents "wisdom or immortality (either or both) or love unmixed with hatred."[50] But there is much more here than mere symbolism; the well represents a mysterious gift that liberates the Old Man from the processes of decay, and the son of Sualtim from his heroic fate; the hawk is a release from history. Those who follow the hawk are victims of deceit and illusion.

The pendulum of fate swings constantly between hope and disillusion; the young man arrives full of confidence, and leaves a broken old man. Yeats's ironic statement—the mother's comment were she able to see her child at the age of ninety years—sets the stage for Cuchulain's failure at the hawk's well. Cuchulain defies the Old Man's warning not to look into the Hawk's eyes. Suddenly the bird throws off her cloak and begins her dance. As the Old Man sleeps, Cuchulain crosses to the blue cloth, the well. The dancer leaves the stage; the Young Man drops his spear and, *"as if in a dream . . . goes out"* (217). The Guardian of the Well, possessed of a fierce attraction that overcomes all earthly desire, has captured Cuchulain with a vision of the real. Of the two men on the stage, one sleeps, the other does not, but leaves:

> *Musicians. (singing)* He has lost what may not be found
>   Till men heap his burial-mound
>   And all the history ends.
>   He might have lived at his ease,
>   An old dog's head on his knees,
>   Among his children and friends.

(217)

Using language and images that Beckett will explore in *Krapp's Last Tape*, W. B. Yeats defines both the urgency and the uncertainty of any quest in life, beyond the comforts of the hearth and kin.

Another echo of the Old Man sleeping and the Young Man exiting the stage "as if in a dream" appeared at the end of *En attendant Godot*. In Beckett's play, Vladimir and Estragon are left alone on the stage; one sleeps, the other does not. But Vladimir does not leave the stage, as does Cuchulain (the Young Man in *Hawk's Well*). There is no exit from the dream of *Godot*. External reality is a nightmare. The masks have been removed from Beckett's creatures, and the characters have arrived at the right site. But their purpose has been lost in disquisition along the way. Didi and Gogo have each other for surety, they play games for amusement, they entertain of necessity, they dream in terror, they make up stories to prove their existence, but they wait for nothing.

Beckett identified the top-hatted and hygienic ministers who ride the pendulum of artistic creation in *Proust*. The poet-creator begins in hope. At the moment of the hawk's cry, to use Yeats's symbolism, underlying reality exposes the artist to intense Suffering, which continues unabated until Boredom sets in, as the Habit of Being regains control:

> If there were no such thing as Habit, Life would of necessity appear delicious to all those whom Death would threaten at every moment, that is to say, to all Mankind.[51]

Beckett was exceedingly generous to his characters in *Godot*. Mr. Godot will come not today "but surely to-morrow" (59B). The principal characters are left with great hopes. Indeed, at the end all they have is the habit of hope. W. B. Yeats, on the contrary, displayed a dark spirit in *Hawk's Well*. His first lines in the initial draft of the latter play contained lines that revealed the bitter autobiographical nature of his play:

> Accursed the life of man—between passion and emptiness what he longs for never comes. All his days are a preparation for what never comes.[52]

Where Yeats negates life, Beckett's *En Attendant Godot* might be seen as an affirmation of life despite its nightmarish qualities. In Vladimir's final speech, before the Boy enters for the last time, there is a hint of reconciliation.

Hawk's Well ends on an ironic note. Life may be difficult. If Ireland does not pay attention to her past, nor endure the pain necessary to recover her spirit, her land will remain barren. The tree of psychic growth will not flourish. The Musicians conclude the play:

> "The man that I praise,"
> Cries out the empty well,
> "Lives out his days
> Where a hand on the bell
> Can call the milch cows
> To the comfortable door of his house.
> Who but an idiot would praise
> Dry stones in a well?"
> "The man that I praise,"
> Cries out the leafless tree,
> "Has Married and stays
> By an old hearth, and he,
> On naught has set store
> But children and dogs on the floor
> Who but an idiot would praise
> A withered tree?"
>
> (219–20)

The leafless tree is a symbol of the corrupt lives led by men of Yeats's generation, who ignored the heroic past. As he did so often in his writings Yeats once again appealed to his countrymen to leave the cities (and the academies) and return to the completeness, the roundness, of a pastoral life, there to rediscover ancient truths. Passions, the poet suggested, are the angels of God, just as feeling is "the child of all past ages."[53] No one is exempt from the unmoistened gaze of the hawk's eye. If Cuchulain fails in his vigil, even to the point of piercing his own foot to

stay awake, what prospect is there for an ordinary man—for a man like
Estragon, who also has a sore (pierced) foot?

Yeats admonished the Irish: stay at home, do not struggle with adversity, raise your families! He told them: if you challenge the guardian of
the well, the curse may descend on your head:

> Never to win a woman's love and keep it;
> Or always to mix hatred in the love;
> Or it may be that she will kill your children,
> That you will find them, their throats torn and bloody,
> Or you will be so maddened that you kill them with your own hand.
>
> (215)

Cuchulain's fate combines all the evils mentioned here. Here also is
something of Yeats's unrequited love for Maud Gonne, and his unrequited love for a country that did not heed his words.

At the end of the play, Cuchulain goes out to face the Guardian of the
Well and the furies she has aroused, *"no longer as if in a dream, but
shouldering his spear . . ."* (218). A life spent in preparation for something
that never comes is a dream-life. The Old Man curses the well that has
deluded him for a lifetime and, in effect, stolen his life from him. He is
unable to strip the mask from his face and see the truth of the well's
secrets. But if the Old Man's struggle is successful, and he overcomes
adversity, the Guardian of the Well will no longer be the fearsome hawk.
When that day comes the tree will bear leaves and fruit, the well will flow,
and man will be at peace with both his inner and his outer being.

The well is also a symbol of unconscious creation. It can only flow
when the Old Man is asleep, not conscious of the manifestation of
creative process in external reality. There is no need to seek out the
waters of the well. The stream will "plash" of its own accord, the Musicians seem to say, if you can "hear" the well of your own unconscious.

Samuel Beckett claimed no less for his own work, and made a pointed
analogy between his plays and the paintings of Jack Yeats: "Less . . .*(long
pause)* . . . conscious." W. B. Yeats, adapting a foreign symbol system for
his Irish dramas, also set his plays in the mind's eye. But Yeats's notion of
versimilitude, the specificity of time, place, and action, is lost in revery.
This lessens the dramatic impact since it offers a virtual aspect, but no
actual presence, of human beings engaged in the manipulation of illusion. What Yeats made new was the union of the spectator's mind's eye,
the actual imagination used as imagination, with the actor's virtual presence, used as symbol for the eye of the imagination. Little wonder that in
Yeats's drama the actor is a puppet, since virtual drama depends exclusively on the mind's eye for its emotional context. The actor is a

mediating point in the chain of communication, wherein character, in the traditional sense of western theater, is unknown.

In its premiere production, *At the Hawk's Well* featured the dancing of Michio Ito. Friedman quoted Yeats's excitement in watching Michio dance the Guardian of the Well's role as if he were receding from the audience to inhabit "as it were the deeps of the mind."[54] The transmission of images from the stage to the mind's eye, begun with the Musicians' summons to the Old Man and the Young Man, concluded with the hypnotic dance of the hawk:

> He [Michio] was able, as he rose from the floor, where he had been sitting cross-legged, or as he threw out an arm, to recede from us into some more powerful life.[55]

Cuchulain awakens from his revery and goes out to fight Aoife and the fierce women of the hills. That is his mistake. The man of contemplation rather than the man of action will find the road to contemplation.[56] To imagine heroism is to become a hero, and approaches the condition of the antiself:

> I call to the mysterious one who yet
> Shall walk the wet sand by the edge of the stream
> And look most like me, being indeed my double,
> And prove of all imaginable things
> The most unlike, being my anti-self.[57]

The virtual act of perceiving the images of *At the Hawk's Well* as if they are images in the mind's eye is the moment of possibility. The late plays of W. B. Yeats provide a frail but nonetheless supportive foundation for the early works of Samuel Beckett.

Yeats's Old Man turns inward to become a paradigm of subjectivity who progressively denies the world outside his own being.[58] Like Beckett's Krapp, in *Krapp's Last Tape,* the Old Man represents the conflict between the fixed, palpable world of human affairs, described by Tom Parkinson as "the world of passion and aspiration, which [is] beyond reason, system or office."[59] During rehearsals for a 1977 production of *Krapp's Last Tape* that Beckett directed in Berlin, the playwright gave the following instructions to the actor playing Krapp: "Make the thing your own in terms of incarceration, for example, incarceration in self. He escapes from the trap of the other only to be trapped in self."[60] Rick Cluchey quoted Beckett's 1977 rehearsal period remarks extensively in his later article on Beckett. They give a rare insight into the playwright's own thoughts about Krapp.

The conflict between the world of external affairs and the world of internal passions Yeats dealt with in his work was also very much a concern of Samuel Beckett. He spoke of the recording Krapp makes on his thirty-ninth birthday:

> "It is his critical age." In this year of "profound gloom and indigence" he had a vision "at the end of the jetty, in the howling wind." Under its influence, he made a decision of grave consequence: "a farewell to love," and he resolved to turn away from "the life of the body, the sexual life," and to turn towards "the life of the mind, an intellectual life. . . ." Thirty years later, the old Krapp recognizes that he was wrong. He is an "arch dreamer"; now he knows that he became "the victim of his dreams"—"they were his ruin. . . ." The fire filling the younger Krapp was "the fire of the vision, the magnum opus." The 69-year-old Krapp feels a fire burning in him too, "but it is a different one, the old Krapp is 'burning to be gone.'" Maybe because he knows: "whichever decision he might have taken, he would have failed."[61]

Beckett's words recall the speech of the Old Man in *At the Hawk's Well:* "Accursed dancers, you have stolen my life . . . you have deluded me my whole life through!" (218); the words might as well come from the mouth of Beckett's supporter of Manichaean destinies. Krapp makes the choice to struggle to bring forth his magnum opus, which lies (he believes) within his dark inner nature. Krapp's thought processes are simplistic, either a product of his own naïveté or the *reducto ad absurdum* of his years of concerted effort to codify his being. Either the life of the body or the life of the mind—light or dark—must be chosen. When the life of the mind fails to reward him with the world's accolades, Krapp feels cheated: "Krapp: Seventeen copies sold, of which eleven at trade price to free circulating libraries beyond the seas. Getting known."[62] Sales of "seventeen copies," of which only six were retail, is hardly solid evidence of imminent literary success and economic independence. But Krapp has made his choice, and it is now too late for him to change. Krapp's other option, to embrace the world about him—"Bianca in Kedar Street," or the woman in the punt on the river and all she implies—is equally futile. Cluchey recounted an anecdote of Beckett directing the 1977 production of *Krapp* that says it all:

> During a relaxed break, Beckett depicts with a smile the image of an old Krapp who had made the opposite decision: surrounded by an aged wife and many, many children . . . "good God!"[63]

Yeats argued for the same principles in his work. The *completeness* of man is to be found neither in the intellect nor in the external world, but in the act of reflection which is "less conscious," in a symbol system that might take a lifetime to master.

The similarity between Yeats's treatment of the Cuchulain legend in his cycle of plays and Beckett's use of the two tramps in *En Attendant Godot* has been noted by at least one other commentator. Barton Friedman looked at similarities of staging and dialogue in *At the Hawk's Well* and *En Attendant Godot:*

> Yet intellect, as the state of the Old Man and the landscape denote, is ultimately barren: it desires the wrong kind of immortality. The dancers have not, as the Old Man thinks, stolen his life. Having imposed on himself a passivity strikingly like the paralysis of Vladimir and Estragon in *Godot,* he has wasted it. In resisting the temptation to this passivity Cuchulain must leave intellect behind.[64]

Turning to *The Green Helmet,* Friedman made a further comparison:

> *Laegaire.* But twelve months upon the clock—
> *Conall.* A twelve month from the first time—
> *Laegaire.* And the jug full up to the brim:
>   For we had been put from our drinking by the very thought of him—
> *Conall.* We stood as we're standing now—
> *Laegaire.* The hours were as empty—
> *Conall.* when
> *Laegaire.* He ran up out of the sea with his head on his shoulders again.
>
> (93–97)

This dialogue, with its syncopation, looks forward to some of the parody vaudeville in Beckett.[65]

Without analyzing the philosophical considerations that underlay Beckett's works, Friedman made valid contributions to the understanding of the "Irishness" of both writers' concerns. Pure intellect and pure emotion are, separately, barren of possibility. Vladimir and Estragon embody, separately, each of these conditions as surely as Krapp embodies the intellectual precepts as a means of conquering the world. Until each is able to move beyond mind/body dualism, the Manichaean torment syndrome, life can be no more than a dream of reality, its entertainments provided by the unreality of the circus or the music hall.

Richard Ellmann provided a deeper analysis of the dream that was the basis of Yeats's adapted Noh drama. Ellmann described the Fool character as the "detached spokesman" for Yeats.

> The peasant who has successfully avoided cities and science and education—and because he was supposed to know nothing, in fact knew everything. His wisdom would not be reduced to reason, nor his instinct to emotion.[66]

Beckett's fool is Lucky, who supplies much of the wisdom of *En Attendant*

Godot: "*Lucky.* . . . that man in brief in spite of the strides of alimentation and defecation wastes and pines . . ." (29A). The play makes precisely that statement. In spite of all the efforts of Vladimir and Estragon, with an assist from Pozzo and the Boy, the tramps begin and end their pilgrimage in the same place, in the same condition, with the same effective knowledge of their situation as Lucky presents in his monologue. In an article for *New Yeats Papers,* Kathleen Raine cited Yeats's unpublished notes on the Tarot "Key of Death," in which he spoke of the skeletal reaper accompanied by the symbolic figure of a newborn child: "because for every death from one world there is birth into another."[67] Pozzo also alludes to this principle in *Godot:* "*Pozzo.* The tears of the world are a constant quantity. For each one who begins to weep somewhere else another stops" (22A). A Boy appears at the end of each act, signifying birth into another world. " 'Let's go.' *They do not move*" is a precise stage direction because movement in the other world is not physical, nor is it intellectual, as Yeats and Beckett never tired of telling the attentive spectator (35B, 60B).

Perhaps the most spectacular example in Beckett's writing of the fool as the detached spokesman who has avoided cities and science and education is Mr. Nackybal in *Watt.* Mr. Nackybal is examined on his method of deriving the cube root of a number of six figures "in the short space of thirty-five or forty seconds."[68] The confused agitation of the examiners and the examinee raises farce to new heights, as the committee proceeds, through endless machinations, to focus their attention on everything but the subject at hand. "Not this evening" is Mr. Nackybal's final answer to seven pages of inquisition. The committee disperses, in a disquietude that takes an additional three pages of testimony to relate:

> But hardly had Mr. O'Meldon, ceasing to greet Mr. MacStern, ceasing to brood, moved on, accompanied by Mr. O'Meldon, towards Mr. de Baker. But hardly had Mr. O'Meldon, then Mr. MacStern, the first to greet, the second to brood, moved on together towards Mr. de Baker, when Mr. de Baker, ceasing to kneel, moved on, accompanied by Mr. O'Meldon and Mr. MacStern, towards Mr. Magershon. . . .[69]

The words of the fool take on new meaning as the proceedings drag on to their conclusion—not this evening, nor any evening, will this committee function.

Yeats's vision of mankind did not noticeably brighten as he developed his Cuchulain cycle of plays. A year after the first production of *At the Hawk's Well,* Yeats was at work on *The Only Jealousy of Emer.* In the later play Cuchulain is an old man, consumed, as Beckett's Krapp would be consumed, by memories of the past. In *The Only Jealousy of Emer,* Yeats made the implied moral of *Hawk's Well* explicit: knowledge of the Higher Self is not necessarily granted, even to heroic individuals. He developed this same theme further in *Calvary* (1920), and wrote a stunning indictment of the conventional Christian faith in an everlasting life. In the play Jesus Christ, promising to deliver man from death, succeeds only in depriving man of his sanctity and his solitude for the rest of time. Lazarus, a subjective "white heron" who is born "out of phase" in a dark, objective age, is denied the opportunity to achieve his Higher Self; he is even denied the benefits of salvation offered by an external Savior. Salvation and damnation are interchangeable in the modern era.

Beckett also dealt with the theme of damnation and salvation as it related to his particular perception of heaven and hell. The familiar pairings of "damnation/hell" and salvation/heaven" were reversed. In *The Chelsea Review,* Alan Schneider supplied a relevant quote from Beckett:

> There is a wonderful sentence in Augustine: "Do not despair; one of the thieves was saved. Do not presume; one of the thieves was damned." That sentence has a wonderful shape. It is the shape that matters.[70]

The shape does matter. But there is a great deal more of importance, particularly if the working of *Godot's* plot is examined. In *En Attendant Godot,* Estragon and Vladimir discuss interpretations of the New Testament:

> *Didi.* . . . how is it that of the four Evangelists only one speaks of a thief being saved. . . . One out of four. Of the others three don't mention any thieves at all and the third says that both of them abused him.
>
> . . . .
> *Gogo.* What's all this about? Abused who?
> *Didi.* The Saviour.
> *Gogo.* Why?
> *Didi.* Because he wouldn't save them.
> *Gogo.* From Hell?
> *Didi.* Imbecile! From death.
> *Gogo.* I thought you said hell.
> *Didi.* From death, from death.
>
> (9B)

Their discussion seems to focus on logistics. If only one of the four Evangelists speaks of a thief being saved, why believe him and not the majority, who say nothing at all. The quality of mercy is not strained, even for the figure of Christ dying on the cross. St. Augustine's warning to mankind, not to adopt extreme positions in the matter of salvation, is exemplified in the moment. Conventional wisdom would indicate that a thief saved from death would also be saved from hell. Estragon seems to misunderstand this proposition. In fact, that is not the situation in *Godot;* that is also not the situation in Yeats's *Calvary,* from which Beckett took his cue.

Calvary mocks the Christian notion of salvation, in favor of an elaborate process of purification the soul undertakes if it chooses to return to this time-world. In a letter to Olivia Shakespear, written in 1932, the poet discussed the matter:

> "Only two topics can be of the least interest to a serious and studious mind—sex and the dead." For generation and death are the gates between worlds.[71]

The gates of generation and death, represented by the form of a doorway leading to a misty seacoast, signaled Yeats's preoccupation "not with death as such but with that other life to which death is the gate."[72] Kathleen Raine went even further in making Yeats's point clear:

> To say merely that he "believed" in the soul's immortality is not even to indicate the complexity of Yeats's thought, the passion of his searchings for knowledge of the state of the discarnate. . . . Not the fact, but the nature of our immortality, was his concern.[73]

There could be no salvation in a world based on the concept of an objective God figure, and certainly no salvation based on treatises from the last three hundred "provincial years." Salvation is based on a religion of the self—from within.

Calvary begins with a familiar setting: Three Musicians appear, their faces made up to resemble masks, images of external man. They are accompanied by three Roman Soldiers, also in painted faces. Christ, Lazarus, and Judas appear in masks. Yeats begins the play with an image of subjective, contemplative man, symbolized as a white heron. His words are bitter:

Second Musician. God has not died for the white heron.[74]

Man does not find immortality from an external source. Even Christ's passion is powerless to help. The Christ figure, alone and helpless as he makes his way to Calvary, is mocked on all sides by jeering citizens.

As the Savior dreams his passion anew, on Good Friday, Lazarus appears in a discomfited state:

Lazarus. For four whole days

I have been dead and I was lying still
In an old comfortable mountain covern. . . .

(451)

Christ performs a miracle and saves Lazarus, by dragging him "to the light." The situation is replete with dramatic irony. Lazarus wants his death back, but Christ has robbed him of it and substituted his own in its stead. (Echoes of this situation can be seen in Beckett's *Play*, where M, W1, and W2 are dragged from their funeral urns into the light of a temporal world.)

Lazarus. But death is what I ask

. . . .
But now you will blind with light the solitude
That death has made; you will disturb that corner
Where I had thought I might lie safe for ever.

(452)

Lazarus will have no death, but a condemnation to serve an external God, to live where they are, in Yeats's view, an endless succession of howling winds, solitary birds, dry wells, and rocky terrains. Hell is not an afterlife nightmare, but the reality of life on earth for those who are denied the opportunity of achieving a Higher Self (universal Christian man) through analyses of their subjective Selves: an old man at a hawk's well is one possibility.

Vladimir is correct. Hell and death are not the same thing. Hell is life on earth, without death, if you are part of a dream of redemption. In the spirit of *Godot*'s humanism, Christ, at one stroke, saves a thief from death and ironically condemns him to hell everlasting. St. Augustine's words are refuted, or seen through a mirror darkly depending on the interpretation: to be "saved" is to die, and to be "damned" is to live. The Christian doctrine of salvation poses equally grave difficulties for the minds of a Yeatsian Neoplatonic humanist. The Roman soldiers are exempt from influence because they are not believers. They maintain their freedom precisely because they are not even aware of a fall from grace.

Yeats concluded *Calvary* with the same bitter indictment of Christian salvation as he began: "*First Musician*. What can a swan need but a swan? *Second Musician*. God has not appeared to the birds" (457). The swan, Yeats's symbol of subjective man, or of self-sufficient man, stands outside the vile modern age.[75] What hope can there be for self-sufficiency in Ireland, a land disrupted by conflicting factions of Christian theology for centuries?

A year before completing *Calvary*, and two years after *Hawk's Well*, Yeats attempted to come to final terms with his Cuchulain cycle and his distress over Ireland's internecine conflicts by completing *The Only Jealousy of Emer* (1919). In *Emer,* Yeats dealt with the legendary Cuchulain as a pitiable old man on the brink of death, who is watched over by Emer, his wife, and Eithne Inguba, his mistress. Cuchulain is plagued by memories he will not release, and blessed by a wife who forswears her own memories. Eithne Inguba kisses Cuchulain's still figure shortly before Bricriu, the god of discord—disguised as *the figure of Cuchulain—* sits up and demands that Emer renounce her rights to her husband in return for Bricriu's sparing his life. At first Emer refuses. But Bricriu is persuasive:

> *Figure.* He'll never sit beside you at the hearth
>   Or make old bones, but die of wounds and toil
>   On some far shore or mountain, a strange Woman
>   Beside his mattress.[76]

Emer is resolute. When the Woman of the Sidhe (or fairyworld) appears, Yeats takes the opportunity to speak of a world beyond immediate consciousness. Memories, he says, possess the shades of life after death, drag on for centuries, and pull the head down to the knees with old guilt. Memories, he says, are the things that hurt, after death, in the first stage of the world of shades:

> *Ghost.*   Old memories:
>   A woman in her happy youth
>   Before her man had broken troth,
>   Dead men and women. Memories
>   Have pulled my head upon my knees.
>
> (291)

The Woman of the Sidhe promises to free the ghost of Cuchulain from all past memories, but at the last moment he calls out to his wife: "O Emer, Emer!" and refuses the Woman of the Sidhe's kiss of oblivion. Memory has made Cuchulain "impure." He will be swept away by the Sidhe in a moment, if Emer does not save him by renouncing him. At the last moment she does; Cuchulain awakens from a death-swoon, and Inguba, his mistress, embraces him. Emer is silent. She has saved the life of her husband, whom she will never enjoy again. More important, she has saved the memory of a dream, which is also a body, that moves "ever towards a dreamless youth."

There are reverberations of the thought processes W. B. Yeats introduced in *The Only Jealousy of Emer* in at least two works by Samuel Beckett. *Imagination Dead Imagine* deals with an image remarkably similar to that of the Ghost of Cuchulain and to that of the Woman of the Sidhe:

within the circumference of a circle three feet in diameter lie two white bodies, that of a man and that of a woman:

> On their right sides therefore both and back to back head to arse. Hold a mirror to their lips, it mists. With their left hands they hold their left legs a little below the knee, with their right hands their left arms a little above the elbow. . . .[77]

Absolute stillness prevails, except for brief moments when everything vibrates, and brief moments when their two left eyes open and gaze unblinkingly: "Never the two gazes together except once, when the beginning of one overlapped the end of the other, for about ten seconds" (13). The "overlap" allows time to renounce memories, and to accept the oblivion of the Sidhe. But the imagination is not dead; the figures remain in the mind's eye of the reader, as he or she re-creates the image. Beckett's final sentence is inquisitive and full of dramatic irony:

> No, life ends and no, there is nothing elsewhere, and no question now of ever finding again that white speck lost in whiteness, to see if they still lie still in the stress of that storm, or of a worse storm, or in the black dark for good, or the great whiteness unchanging, and if not what they are doing. (14)

The thought of lying "in the black dark for good" recalls the hope of Lazarus, in Yeats's *Calvary*, who is blinded by light. The figures in the text of *Imagination Dead Imagine* will also live when the reader's eye resurrects them from their solitude. Their redemption depends completely on the receptivity of imagination, which, coupled with the memory of similar figures, brings the pair back to life.

Play invokes a similar memory process. The play's events are dredged up by the Light, a "unique inquisitor," who extracts responses from the characters by beaming the light on each of them simultaneously, or in succession. This editing process is cyclical: repeats are indicated in the script. Furthermore, examination of the text reveals that the cycle diminishes in the accelerated repeat. Progress in the editing? Elimination of superfluities? Beckett never commented.

The mind's eye—and its relation to memory, light, and darkness in *Imagination Dead Imagine*—is also manifest in a physical state in *Play*. M, W1, and W2 are a play of the imagination, as well as a play of light, in a play that is a stage production. Within the context of production, the actors play roles, the characters play with each other's emotions, and, of course, love is play, as much as play is love when the other cheats. Finally the play winds down; it is no longer the play it once was. In the first run-through, the concluding stage directions read:

M. Am I as much as . . . being seen? *Spots off M. Blackout. Five seconds. Faint spots simultaneously on three faces. Three seconds. Voices faint, largely unintelligible.*
W1)   (Yes, strange, etc.)
W2) Together (Yes, perhaps, etc.)
M)   (Yes, peace, etc.)
   Repeat play.[78]

At the conclusion of the repeat there is a change in light cues. M's words are the same, but the Light beams a *strong spot* on the three faces, indicating perhaps a moment of intense examination by the Light in its editing function. Beckett seems to be describing a methodology whereby forms of the imagination are brought to the light of consciousness and then revised or edited to conform to the play he has in mind.

The result of the editing is a shortening of the dialogue. As the characters resume, the first "tri-ologue" is dropped from the script. Then a second change occurs. The stage directions should read: *"Spots off. Blackout. Five seconds. Spots on W1"* (10); instead, the stage directions read: *"Spots off. Blackout. Five seconds. Spot on M."* (22). The Light has edited out a cue and focused on M, rather than on W1. M speaks, beginning his next recital, but he is cut off by the blackout before he can conclude. Two speeches of W1 and W2 have been eliminated. There are no more changes; no more needs to be said. The script does not resume, but instead there is a *curtain,* a final editing play on play as theater.

What is of particular interest in this work, besides the technical aspects of play that are incorporated into the script, is the pivotal role of memory and imagination derived from Yeats's formulas. The principal event of the play evolves from the disaffection of M for his wife, W1, and the establishment of W2, his mistress, as the center of attention. The relationships between the characters can be characterized as hostile; each serves as victim and tormentor of the other in scenes pulled from memory by the light. The figures, encased in funeral urns, are quite clearly Yeats's shades, suffering from old memories that have drawn them to the light:

> Old memories:
> A woman in her happy youth
> Before her man had broken troth. . . .
>
> (291)

Beckett's figures wanted their peace and solitude as well. They plead with the Light, the mind's eye dramatized, for release:

> *W1*. It is that I do not tell the truth, is that it, that some day somehow I may tell the truth at last and then no more light at last, for the truth?
>
> (16)

W2. Are you listening to me? Is anyone listening to me? Is anyone looking at me? Is anyone bothering about me at all?

(17)

M. Am I as much as . . . being seen?

(22)

No character speaks to another. Each is lost in the memories summoned by the light, and wishes to be done with the "hellish" recollections. If only the Light will recognize them, and give them a life of their own, they will be content. But the Light's commitment is to an overall plan. The editing function follows creation. The tension between the two creates the dramatic illusion of real life in the theater. Once again, as in *Godot*, Beckett has found a way of dramatizing an intellectual precept of W. B. Yeats's dramaturgy. The landscape of Yeats's imaginings in the Cuchulain plays becomes the stagescape in Beckett's plays, as symbol becomes dramatic image.

Yeats's symbol system was a complex one, and many authors have applied time and expertise to dissipate its complexity. To approach the meaning of *The Dreaming of the Bones*, it is necessary to examine only an aspect of Yeats's symbol system, that of discarnate beings. Yeats described the first stages of the discarnate being in the final edition of *A Vision* (1937). He called the first stage *The Vision of the Blood Kindred,* and included in it "all apparitions seen at the moment of death."[79] He noted the second stage consisted, in part, of *The Dreaming Back* and *The Return:*

> In *The Dreaming Back,* the *Spirit* is compelled to live over and over again the events that had most moved it; there can be nothing new, but the old events stand forth in a light which is dim or bright according to the intensity of the passion that accompanied them. . . . In *The Return,* upon the other hand, the *Spirit* must live through past events in the order of their occurrence, because it is compelled . . . to trace every passionate event to its cause until all are related and understood, turned into knowledge, made a part of itself (226).

The discarnate being lives the life of the mind, limited to the memories of a physical life, in a state exactly analogous to the life of a character in a play, forced to relive an already written text. Beckett's *Play* is part of this tradition. But Yeats had more to contribute. *The Dreaming of the Bones* (1919) and *Purgatory* (1939) are examples of a third condition of the second stage of the discarnate being:

> . . . which is called the *Phantasmagoria,* which exists to exhaust, not nature, not pain and pleasure, but emotion. . . . The *Phantasmagoria* completes not only life but imagination (230).

In the *Phantasmagoria* objects of hope (life and imagination) are "completed," and then dismissed, a point that Beckett made clear in *Godot*.

Yeats had something very specific in mind for *the Dreaming of the Bones* (1919). In a note for the play he outlined his belief that "the dead dream back, for a certain time, through the more personal thoughts and deeds of life."[80] Peter Ure noted that in one of Yeats's earlier essays the poet's treatment of discarnate beings in *The Dreaming of the Bones* was also similar to his exploration of the subject in *A Vision:*

> The dead, as the passionate necessity wears out, come into a measure of freedom . . . gradually they perceive, although they are still but living in their memories, harmonies, symbols and patterns, as though all were being refashioned by an artist, and they are moved by emotions, sweet for no imagined good but in themselves, like those of children dancing in a ring; and I do not doubt that they make love in that union which Swedenborg has said is of the whole body and seems from far off an incandescence.[81]

In this passage the poet describes another version of the *Phantasmagoria*, the third stage of the second phase of discarnate being, and the phase in which Diarmuid and Dervorgilla of *The Dreaming of the Bones* seem to belong. Peter Ure saw the play as the one "whose form most resembles the traditional *Noh* of the ghosts," and presaged Yeats's *Purgatory:* "perhaps his greatest play, and certainly his most profoundly human treatment of this subject."[82]

The Dreaming of the Bones takes place in Yeats's present. The time is 1916, a year of insurrection and revolution in Ireland, punctuated by the Easter Rebellion and the Sinn Fein movement's declaration that Ireland must have complete independence from England. The Irish land question (the understated summation of nine centuries of anguish and frustration) dominated Irish politics from the twelfth-century English invasion to the twentieth-century Irish rebellion. Yeats makes that quite clear in his play. The setting for the play is a screen covered with a pattern of mountains and sky that only symbolizes or suggests a reality. *The Dreaming of the Bones* begins with the entrance of three Musicians (as does *At the Hawk's Well*), whose song transports their listeners into the mind's eye:

> *First Musician.* Have not old writers said
>   That dizzy dreams can spring
>   From the dry bones of the dead?
>   And many a night it seems
>   That all the valley fills
>   With those fantastic dreams.[83]

The time is after midnight, the hour before dawn, and the moon is covered by clouds. A Young Man enters, praying in Irish. The next moment a Stranger and a Young Girl enter. The latter two characters wear heroic masks and costumes of the past. Their dialogue discloses the information that the Young Man has been at the Dublin Post Office during the Easter Rebellion, and will be shot if he is captured. The two ghost figures offer to counsel the fugitive, and secure a hiding place where he can stay until he can escape to the Aran Islands. The trio follow their path to safety by traversing the stage three times in a symbolic journey to the ruins of the Abbey of Corcomroe.

On a hill above the ruins, the Young Man waits for daylight while the Young Girl tells the story of Diarmuid and Dervorgilla, a ghost story that is the tale of her own life. The Young Man questions her about angry ghosts who wander the hills in restless solitude. She speaks of Donough O'Brien and the other rebels who sided with the Anglo-Normans in their overthrow of a legitimate Irish King: *"Young Girl.* They and their enemies of Thomond's party / Mix in brief dream-battle above their bones. . ." (439). The cause of the insurrection was the illicit love affair of Diarmuid and Dervorgilla. Diarmuid, King of Leinster, unmindful of his duties toward his subjects, abducted Dervorgilla from her husband's house. Her wronged husband, the King of Thomond, vowed vengeance, raised an army that included High King Rory O'Connor, and challenged Diarmuid:

> *Young Girl.* Her king and lover
>   Was overthrown in battle by her husband,
>   And for her sake and for his own, being blind
>   And bitter and bitterly in love, he brought
>   A foreign army from across the sea.
>
> (442)

The play repeats the story of Dervorgilla and Diarmuid, or Dermot McMurrough (or Diarmuid Mac Murchada, King of Leinster, 1110–71), who, following his defeat of 1166 at the hands of the King of Thomond and High King Rory O'Connor, asked Henry II of England for help. Henry's answer was to send Richard de Clare, second earl of Pembroke, to invade Ireland some time between 1168 and 1170. By late 1170 he had conquered much of the country. Shortly thereafter Pembroke married Diarmuid's daughter, finally securing his succession, gained by fiat and force of arms, to an Irish "throne." The long conquest and subjugation of Ireland by English kings dates from these twelfth-century battles.

The punishment that Yeats accords to Diarmuid and Dervorgilla in *The Dreaming of the Bones* is a mockery of the passion they once shared:

Young Girl. Though eyes can meet, their lips can never meet.
  . . . but when he has bent his head
  Close to her head, or hand would slip in hand,
  The memory of their crime flows up between
  And drives them apart.

(441)

As shades they are condemned to the eternal torment of never consummating their lovers' kiss. The situation is analogous to that of Beckett's couple in *Imagination Dead Imagine.* The punishment of Diarmuid and Dervorgilla in Yeats's play will continue until one member of their race will forgive them for having sold their country into slavery. At that moment, "Lip would be pressed on lip," and Diarmuid and Dervorgilla would be freed from their agonies. Three times the Young Woman asks her young Irish patriot for forgiveness; three times he replies: *"Young Man. . . .*—never, never / Shall Diarmuid and Dervorgilla be forgiven" (442, 444). The shades depart, a cloud floats up, and in a moment the Young Girl and the Stranger are swept away (444). A moment of temptation has passed. The suffering that has afflicted Ireland for nine centuries as a result of the theft of a neighbor's wife continues in both carnate and incarnate beings. Peter Ure accurately described the play as one in which "nothing is done or undone, and scarcely anything disturbs the intensity with which suffering winds in upon itself."[84]

In *The Dreaming of the Bones,* written in 1919 at the height of Yeats's inspiration, the playwright evinced support for more pastoral settings, away from the playwright's disillusionment with popular politics. The play lent strength to Irish aspiration for freedom. For Yeats, equally important was the question he posed for himself: whether sexual loss—specifically, the loss of Maud Gonne's love—is final and irrevocable, or whether the lover may hope to find the peace and fulfillment that had been denied him, either beyond the grave or in a subsequent incarnation.[85] In a period of dreaming back, according to F. A. C. Wilson's interpretation, "the Shade constantly relives all the actions and emotions of the past existence, until it is able to purge itself equally of joy and pain."[86] At that moment the Shade returns to a state of prenatal intelligence, and presumably enters heaven.

This admixture of early-twentieth-century Irish politics, mystical revelations, and historic Irish folklore typified W. B. Yeats's dramaturgy. In Beckett's *Imagination Dead Imagine,* on the other hand, the playwright made no claim to proselytize social or political revolution. Only with some difficulty does the analogy with Yeats's drama clarify the later work of art that needs no clarification. If that analogy is pursued, it might be reasonable to make the assumption that the man and the woman of

Imagination Dead Imagine are figures or Shades of Diarmuid and Dervorgilla:

> No, life ends and no, there is nothing elsewhere, and no question now of ever finding again that white speck lost in whiteness . . . and if not what they are doing, (14)

If the imagination is dead, and the memories of Ireland's past are gone, the answer is: "Yes, life has ended, and the two Shades are at peace at last." The entwined figures in Beckett's dramaticule can return to a state of beatitude, or consummate their love in a subsequent incarnation. But that is also the signal for the end of art, an impossible art, that denies itself to save itself. If there is no imagination, the question is moot. If there *is* imagination, and the drama is reborn in every generation, Diarmuid and Dervorgilla will never rest. They will supply poetic license for future playwrights. In Beckett's case, apolitical in the realm of art at least, that search for stillness within, beyond the actions and emotions of a past existence, remains the core of his art. Poetic license remains—as their bones remain—in a vault, "a ring as in the imagination the ring of bone" (8). Heady stuff indeed.

4

"The Painter's Brush Consumes His Dreams"

THE last years of W. B. Yeats's life were marred by frustrations and bitterness. Twenty-two years after completing *The Deaming of the Bones* Yeats had changed dramatically. His depiction of the poetic process, the poetic mind, the picturesque statement, were replaced by spare, relentless prose, caustic cries of despair, and rage at an Ireland that had failed to heed his vision. I. A. Richards partially summarized the Yeatsean dilemma:

> After a drawn battle with the drama, Mr. Yeats made a violent repudiation, not merely of current civilization but of life itself, in favor of a supernatural world. But the world of the "eternal moods," of supernal essences and immortal beings is not, like the Irish peasant stories and the Irish landscape, part of his natural and familiar experience. Now he turns to a world of symbolic phantasmagoria about which he is desperately uncertain. He is uncertain because he had adopted as a technique of inspiration the use of trance, of dissociated phases of consciousness, and the revelations given in these dissociated states are insufficiently connected with normal experience.[1]

Of more serious concern, however, was the failure of W. B. Yeats to develop a dramatic technique for dealing with dissociated phases of consciousness as they are, or can be, connected with normal experience. His failure, in short, was not only one of judgment but one of art as well.

Yeats wrote *Purgatory* in 1938. The play was his bitter commentary on the collapse of aristocratic Ireland and his hatred of the new Ireland. In a letter to Alan Wade, Yeats explained his intentions for the work:

> I have put nothing into the play because it seemed picturesque; I have put there my own conviction about this world and the next.[2]

In *Purgatory* there are no masks and no backdrops, symbolic or otherwise; there are only a Boy, an Old Man, a ruined house, and a bare tree. Yeats has not discarded his symbols, but he has greatly simplified them.

According to Ellmann, the Boy represents both folly and strength, and the Old Man represents both wisdom and debility.[3] Comparing the contraries that represent body and mind, the poet offers contradiction: wisdom is paired with folly, strength with debility.[4] Yeats integrates the semiotics of this model into the background of a ruined house—the state of Ireland—and a bare tree—the infertility of the land.

Yeats's poetry of the 1930s is equally despairing; "The Statues" speak of the Irish nation "thrown upon this filthy modern tide." His poetic "celebration" of the Irish revolution is markedly acerbic:

> Hurrah for revolution and more cannon-shot!
> A beggar upon horseback lashes a beggar on foot.
> Hurrah for revolution and cannon come again!
> The beggars have changed places, but the lash goes on.[5]

The hope Yeats invested in the young revolutionary of *The Dreaming of the Bones* is nowhere evident in *Purgatory*, which John Rees Moore described as a play "of unredeemed and apparently unredeemable blackness."[6]

The punishment in *Purgatory* is the same as that in *The Dreaming of the Bones:* a spirit must relive a moment of shame that has brought down the "house":

> *Old Man.* . . . she must live
>   Through everything in exact detail,
>   Driven to it by remorse, and yet
>   Can she renew the sexual act
>   And find no pleasure in it. . . .[7]

The situation is not unlike that in Strindberg's *Miss Julie.* In *Purgatory* the father of the Old Man is a groom who marries a wealthy woman and proceeds to squander the family fortune. On the sixteenth anniversary of their wedding night (when the Old Man was conceived), the Old Man murders his father and burns their house. The mother had already died giving birth to him. The son is accused of his father's murder, but he escapes, becomes a peddler, and fathers a son upon a tinker's daughter. Sixteen more years pass. It is the anniversary of both the father's and the grandfather's wedding night, and of the sixteenth year of the son's (grandson's) age. As the light rises in the window of their former home, now a shell, someone appears to be standing there:

> *Old Man.* Look at the window; she stands there
>   Listening, the servants are all in bed,
>   . . . my father

Has come to find a glass for his whiskey.
He leans there like some tired beast.

(685, 687)

Rather than offering the Shades, who intercede on behalf of the people and pray for an end to their torment as in *The Dreaming of the Bones,* in *Purgatory* Yeats offers the Old Man who tells the tale. Father and son quarrel over the father's money. The retribution of the son on the father has the inevitability of a Greek drama: "*Boy.* What if I kill you? You killed my grand-dad./ Because you were young and he was old./ Now I am young and you are old" (687). The father's answer to the son's question is sudden and simple. He stabs his son, believing that in so doing he can end the curse on their house. The light in the window goes out. The Old Man picks up the money and prepares to depart, carrying with him the burden of his son's murder. The Old Man has not dissolved the pollution, but has doubled it: his mother's spirit now bears the sorrow of both her husband's and her grandson's death:

> *Old Man.* Twice a murderer and all for nothing,
>   And she must animate that dead night
>   Not once but many times!
>   O God,
>   Release my mother's soul from its dream!

(689)

The revolution has begun to claim its own children as victims. Yeats's *Purgatory* depicts hell on earth, not only for the Shades, as in *The Dreaming of the Bones,* but for all who share a heritage that has been abused.

A "hell on earth" that reflects Yeats's *Purgatory* appeared in Samuel Beckett's notes for his 1971 German production of *Krapp's Last Tape:* "Man created by Satan. Cain and Abel sons not of Adam but of Satan and Eve."[8]

A brief structural analysis of *Purgatory* can be diagrammed as follows, using a "culture/nature" axis:

OLD MAN

Permitted relations	S	Unacceptable relations
(Culture)		(Nature)
"Mind" relations		"Abnormal body" relations
(Prescribed)		(Forbidden)
[Wisdom] sl	◄ ·· (contraries) ···► s2	[Debility]
[Strength] s̄2	◄ ················· ► s̄1	[Folly]
"Body" relations		"Non-mind" relations
(Not forbidden)	S	(Not prescribed)

The dotted lines indicate contraries; the solid lines indicate contradictories. By substituting A, B, C, and D for s1, s2, š2, and š1, any number of relations can be articulated along either axis of contradictory or contrary relations. Similarly, any form of semantic substitution, whereby the values obtained are greater than or equal to the substitute forms of s1 and š2, will contribute to Yeats's notion of purgatory on earth. A comparison of the relations between wisdom and folly (s1–š1), debility and strength (s2–š2), folly and strength (š1–š2), or debility and wisdom (s2–s1), in terms of sexual relations, social expectations, economic opportunities, or even relations with the shades of an afterlife, provides various modes of semantic articulation. The possibilities are endless.

Beckett explored this articulation in an unpublished outline for a play tentatively titled *J. M. Mime*.[9] He identified his characters as:

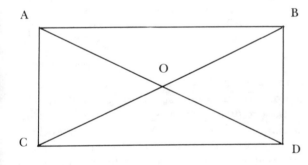

2 players: Son and father)
                          ?
             Son and mother)

paths: OA, OB, OC
         OD
         AB, AC, BD,
         DC

Although he uses other terms to describe the same articulations as Yeats, Beckett's model is identical to that of *Purgatory*, except for his addition of a core point. The defining terms—son and father, son and mother—are the same as the characters of *Purgatory*. Beckett's development of the play's possible relationships covers two pages of handwritten script, on which he explores each of the variations of the possibilities available to him: "Starting from O, return to O by greatest number of paths (one way)"; then "2 ways" including errors; and finally, "complicate if necessary" with the addition of an intermediate line EH, which bisects lines AB and CD, and FG, which bisects lines AC and BD. The rat's maze Beckett constructs is evidence of a very early form, one that precedes his investment of the structure with emotional components to give meaning to his enterprise. The project seems to have remained unfinished. The subject evidently fascinated Beckett, who saw a number of possibilities in the model.

Purgatory offers the spectator a number of options, but no escape from the modern condition, as Moore pointed out:

> By killing his son, the Old Man hopes to escape from the cage of "mythical" time in which he is trapped, to awake from the nightmare of history, and to return to the normal world of eating and sleeping, of making a living and telling jokes. The climactic revelation of the play is that there is no escape from the greater reality once the inner eye has had a vision of it.[10]

Yeats's finest drama is his most austere; Beckett may have abandoned his own project with good reason. What makes *Purgatory* particularly effective is its subject, one grounded in a reality that does not depend on the operation of the mind's eye for at least one level of meaning. Yeats saw its application in his immediate surroundings:

> In my play, a spirit suffers because of its share, when alive, in the destruction of an honored house; that destruction is taking place all over Ireland today. Sometimes it is the result of poverty, but more often because a new individualistic generation has lost interest in the ancient sanctities.[11]

But Ireland was no longer listening. In the academies critics like R. P. Blackmur rejected all notions of the supernatural in Yeats's works, the "mumbo-jumbo" (to use George Orwell's words) of a man who put his faith in Swedenborg, mediums, and desolate places.[12] The Abbey Theatre had long since rejected his ideas for a mystical theater, and was producing realistic drama. Yeats's interest in politics, which had induced him to serve six years in the Irish Senate, had ended, as he explained in a letter to Ethel Mannin and Ernst Töller:

> Do not try to make a politician of me, even in Ireland I shall never I think be that again—as my sense of reality deepens, & I think it does with age, my horror at the cruelty of governments grows greater. . . . I am not callous, every nerve trembles with horror at what is happening in Europe "the ceremony of innocence is drowned."[13]

As a last act in defiance of the secular, clerical, and mystical worlds that denied him, Yeats wrote *The Death of Cuchulain* in 1938.

Forty years earlier, in May 1899, he had declared his opposition to the "theatre of commerce" that stupefied memory; in its place would be, he said, a poetic drama of plays that were, for the most part, "remote, spiritual, and ideal."[14] The prologue to *The Death of Cuchulain* has as its narrator an Old Man (Yeats himself), who rails at the age with all the savage indignation of a Swift:

> Old Man. . . . I have been selected because I am out of fashion and out of date like the antiquated romantic stuff the thing is made of. . . . I am sure that as I am producing a play for people I like, it is not probable, in this vile age, that they will be more in number than those who listened to the first performance of Milton's *Comus*.[15]

The play was, as Friedman noted, Yeats's epitaph for the theater. He had stopped writing plays for his Abbey Theatre in 1910; in 1939, he stopped writing plays for anyone.

Sparsity of language and simplicity of setting were goals toward which Yeats had worked for almost a quarter century, and he reached them in *The Death of Cuchulain*. He also neutralized the period of the play. The time is no longer "a distant past" or "1916," but "any period." In this play Yeats even rejected the need for masks, a basic ingredient of the "Ideal spectator" in his earlier Noh-drama adaptations. In *The Death of Cuchulain* masks are reduced to severed heads about which Emer will dance, in memory of a past for which the aging author-poet has no words, or at least no words for his contemporary audience. In this play he hints at the limitations of words in the realm of the imagination, where there are no words, but only translations and symbols that stand for emotional constructs. Unfortunately, the poet never had an opportunity to develop this topic:

> Old Man. . . . I promise a dance. I wanted a dance because where there are no words there is less to spoil. Emer must dance, there must be severed heads—I am old, I belong to mythology—severed heads for her to dance before. . . . I could have got such a dancer once, but she has gone; the tragi-comedian dancer, the tragic dancer, upon the same neck love and loathing, life and death.
>
> (694)

But Yeats's instinct for a primary theater of visual images remained sound and unfulfilled.

The dance was a symbol for all Yeats's actors, whose movements were choreographed to reflect the playwright's thought and Gordon Craig's dramatic theories, both of which neutralized the actors' stage spaces and emotional responses. What more perfect symbol of the dancer could the poet have chosen than Isadora Duncan, the San Francisco dancer who captured the fancy of Gordon Craig and the attention of the courts of Europe. She was a "tragic dancer," whose own symbol, a flowing scarf worn at her neck, caught in the wheel of an open touring car and ended her life. *The Death of Cuchulain* might be considered a memorial to Craig and Duncan, and to the hopes the young playwright once held for an Irish renaissance, captured in the image of an artist and a dancer, both of whom had held so much early promise. In 1939, Yeats had moved beyond his own early promise, his literary fame assured. But he sensed that he was a creature of the past. He wrote himself out of the present: "*Cuchulain*. I make the truth!" (698). Yeats's knowledge of truth, a portent of the future, is restored to the serenity of a dream, simultaneously past, present, and future. In this kind of emotional landscape, a neutral playing area of timeless dimension was a necessity.

In *The Death of Cuchulain* the Old Man exits as the stage darkens, the curtain falls (although it did not rise at the opening), and it is clear to the spectator that the conventional theater fare for the evening is over. Pipe and drum supply musical entertainment until the curtain rises on a bare stage. The music stops. There is silence. There is not a voice to evoke the "eye of the mind" for the spectator, as in *At the Hawk's Well*, nor even a setting of a room with a lighted fire *"and a door into the open air, through which [he can] see, perhaps, the trees of a wood,"* as in *The Countess Cathleen* (3). Yeats makes the spectator wait for half a minute before Eithne Inguba enters to begin the dream of the poet, now an old man.

Cuchulain enters from the back—the familiar entrance from the threshold of consciousness—to confront Eithne. Yeats makes Cuchulain a Cassandra figure who possesses "the agony of true vision." Not only is he aware of his fate, which he will play out, but he is also the author of his myth, on which he comments, in scenes replete with dramatic irony:

> *Cuchulain*. This letter is from Emer,
>   It tells a different story. . . .
> *Eithne*. I do not understand.
>   Who can have put that letter in my hand?
> *Cuchulain*. . . . you are sent
>   To be my bedfellow, but have no fear,
>   All that is written, but I much prefer
>   Your own unwritten words.
>
> (695–96)

The mystery of the letter in Eithne's hands, of which she apparently has no knowledge, may be the poet's ironic commentary on the superfluous requirements of realistic drama, Yeats's particular *bête noire*. The reality of this play is still the mind's eye of *At The Hawk's Well*, a play of the imagination, in which no magic is required. The letter episode also allows the poet to display Eithne's treachery, and Cuchulain's heroic qualities, as he is both the creator and the embodiment of his own myth.

Yeats summons all the principals of the Cuchulain cycle of plays to appear in this, the last and most important play of the cycle. Each of them plays a part in the old warrior's death throes. As Cuchulain leaves the stage to fight for his life, the set darkens in symbolic tribute to the agonies he is to endure. The lights of the set restored, he reenters, followed by Aoife, the woman who conceived his child after he had subdued her in pitched battle. The child grew to manhood, but died at the hands of his father in *On Baile's Strand*. Aoife and her fierce women of the hills challenged Cuchulain in *At the Hawk's Well*. Their battle was inconclusive. In *The Death of Cuchulain*, the estranged parents meet for the third and last time:

> *Aoife.* Am I recognized, Cuchulain?
> *Cuchulain.*   You fought with a sword,
>   It seemed that we should kill each other, then
>   Your body wearied and I took your sword.

                                                        (699)

The scene is that of *Purgatory:* a wandering man seduces a queen of a realm, and she bears him a son whom he subsequently kills. This time, the queen, Aoife, will have her revenge. But she is cheated, for Cuchulain has already sustained mortal wounds. Yeats's instinctive disappointment in his countrymen, first evident in *On Baile's Strand*—"Life drifts between a fool and a blind man/To the end, and nobody can know his end"—is resolved in *The Death of Cuchulain* (271). The fool is an intellectual dolt, and the blind man suffers a physical handicap. Together they struggle to survive, symbolizing a modern world slipping into decadence and decay.

Beckett's Hamm and Clov, in *Fin de Partie*, similarly represent a universe of zero scope. Hamm depends on Clov for mobility; Clov needs Hamm for sustenance; until the end, when the games of external reality are over, Clov waits by the door:

> *Hamm.* Clov!
> *(Long pause.)*
> No? Good.
> *(He takes out the handkerchief.)*
> Since that's the way we're playing it . . .
> *(he unfolds handkerchief)*
> . . . let's play it that way . . .
> *(he unfolds)*
> . . . and speak no more about it . . .
> *(he finishes unfolding)*
> . . . speak no more.
> *(He holds handkerchief spread out before him.)*
> Old stancher!

(Pause.)
You . . . remain.
(Pause. He covers his face with handkerchief,
lowers his arms to armrests, remains motionless.)
(Brief tableau.)
                                        Curtain.[16]

Clov may stay or leave, and it makes no difference to Hamm, engaged in his play of the imagination. There is no need of the other in a physical world that *keys* on the imagination for its value systems. At the end Hamm is bloodied, but unbeaten; Cuchulain is wounded, but similarly unbeaten by his foes. Yeats, the artist-hero, dreams the protagonist back, thereby allowing him to become his own myth. In *On Baile's Strand*, there is a moment, before Cuchulain charges at the waves in savage indignation, when he senses his betrayal and becomes embodied in the myth: the play ends in a tragic revery of inescapable reality. *The Death of Cuchulain*, on the contrary, seems full of ironic commentary. Cuchulain partakes of his fate, but also stands aside to comment on it. Yeats deliberately destroys his creation; denied the plaudits of the crowd, he goes elsewhere to confront the darkness that marks the close of his life.

Aoife winds her veil about Cuchulain, as Clytemnestra had a net wound about Agamemnon, and as Isadora wound a kerchief about her dancer's neck. Those tokens of love are symbols of death's embrace. A few moments of tenderness—when Aoife asks if her son was an able man, and fought well—are broken by the Blind Man's entrance. Aoife repeats Eithne Inguba's message that Cuchulain is about to die, and exits. The Blind Man, the symbol of fallen humanity, will kill the mortally wounded Cuchulain, bound and helpless, for twelve pennies. This is Yeats's final curse on mankind, his final ironic statement: "*Cuchulain.* Twelve pennies! What better reason for killing a man?" (702). The Blind Man feels his way up Cuchulain's body. He comes to the old man's bound throat: "*Old Man.* This is your neck. Ah!Ah! Are you ready, Cuchulain! *Cuchulain.* I say it is about to sing" (703). Cuchulain dies, not at the hands of a victor in battle, but at the hands of a petty blind mercenary.

As the curtain rises, again on a bare stage, seven parallelograms are visible on the set. They represent Cuchulain and the six warriors (who slew him in battle) in the first phase after death. No words are exchanged between the shapes and the form of Emer that moves in the image of a famous dancer: "*There is silence, and in the silence a few faint bird notes*" (704). Words are audible only to mortals, beggar-men and harlots who sell their souls for a few pennies. The play concludes with a song sung by the harlot to the beggar-man:

Singer. No body like his body

Has modern woman borne,
But an old man looking on life
Imagines it in scorn.
A statue's there to mark the place,
By Oliver Sheppard done.
So ends the tale that the harlot
Sang to the beggar-man.

(705)

The man is Cuchulain—whose statue stands in the Dublin Post Office to commemorate those who fought there in 1916—the only living memory of an ancient Irish hero whom Yeats feels his own people have betrayed. So the poet returned Cuchulain to the imagination and to the shades of another generation who would do honor to Conall, Cuchulain, and Usna's boys.

Samuel Beckett also paid homage to Cuchulain, but in quite a different way. Professor A. J. Leventhal described his receipt of an urgent postcard from Beckett in the 1930s:

> Would I betake me to the Dublin Post Office and measure the height from the ground of Cuchulain's arse? . . . A crowd gathered round as I knelt with a tape measure to carry out my task and I was lucky to get away without arrest.[17]

The reason for the urgency of the message is clear in chapter 4 of *Murphy,* where the earliest of Murphy's antagonists, Neary, ". . . minus his whiskers was recognized by a former pupil called Wylie, in the General Post Office contemplating from behind the statue of Cuchulain."[18] Neary's homage consists in his running at the statue from behind, ramming his head against the buttocks of Cuchulain, in a gesture of questionable devotion.

On the death of Cuchulain, Yeats was left with neither a subject nor a legend to develop. Time was running out, in fact had run out, for the poet of the Celtic Revival. His long struggle to maintain an aristocratic stance in an increasingly proletarian and sectarian state might well have ended during the Irish Revolution. In 1936 Yeats was, as Friedman so aptly put it, "a man out of phase . . . rendered futile by history."[19]

Just how far W. B. Yeats was out of step with his time, even at the beginning of his career, can be seen in his general approach to the theater, and to his sympathies with the emerging Symbolist theater movement. Symbolist playwrights at the turn of the century dramatized man's inner spiritual existence in short dramaticules composed of highly stylized, incantatory idioms, frequent pauses, segments of silence, hypnotic repetitions of words, phrases, and lines, and carefully orchestrated sound and meter. W. B. Yeats and fellow Symbolists Hauptmann,

Maeterlinck, and Viliers de l'Isle Adam among others, carefully preserved the stage's aesthetic distance in direct contradiction to both the
new techniques of expressionism, rooted in Strindberg's later works, and
in the avant-garde drama in general. Yeats sought out the novel and
accommodated the measured new in his work. Truly experimental theater confused him.

W. B. Yeats's visit to the Théâtre Nouveau in Paris, on 1 December
1896, to see the premiere performance of Alfred Jarry's *Uba Roi* revealed the Irish playwright's conservative approach to theater. *Ubu Roi*
was considered by many to be the progenitor of avant-garde drama in
the twentieth century. Michael Benedikt described the work as "among
the most important theatrical developments of the late nineteenth and
twentieth centuries."[20] Apollinaire, the protosurrealistic playwright,
who would be tragically dead of war wounds within a decade, paid
tribute to Jarry in a posthumous essay in 1907: Apollinaire's words gave
a sense of Jarry's theatrical style in particular.

> Someone once said within earshot of me that Jarry was our last author
> of burlesque. An error! . . . We don't even possess terms adequate to
> describe his peculiar kind of liveliness in which lyricism becomes
> satiric, or where satire in its operation upon reality surpasses the object
> so totally that it completely destroys it and then climbs so high that
> Poetry itself can hardly keep up with it. . . . Jarry was the last of our
> sublime debauches.[21]

But when W. B. Yeats and friends visited the theater to see *Ubu,* they
viewed the work of the "sublime debaucher" with considerable alarm.
Instead of rendering applause for the militantly antirealistic devices that
Jarry employed, devices no less strange but as compelling as Japanese
Noh drama, Yeats saw only chaos and literalness:

> . . . The players are supposed to be dolls, toys, marionettes, and now
> they are all hopping like wooden frogs, and I can see for myself that
> the chief personage, who is some kind of king, carries for a sceptre a
> brush of the kind that we use to clean a closet.[22]

How different W. B. Yeats's reputation would be if scholars and critics
interpreted his plays with the same literalness! To be fair, Yeats's knowledge of French was not perfect. But his failure to comprehend the
energy and vitality of a symbol system outside his immediate interests, or
to appreciate the satiric depths of Jarry's mock epic, revealed more about
W. B. Yeats and his coterie drama than almost anything else he ever did:

> . . . That night at the Hotel Corneille I am very sad, for comedy,

objectivity, has displayed its growing power once more. I say, "After Stephen Mallarmé, after Paul Verlain, after Gustave Moreau, after Puves de Chavannes, after our own verse, after all our subtle colour and nervous rhythm, after the faint mixed tints of Conder, what more is possible? After us the Savage God."[23]

Where W. B. Yeats saw only uncouth gestures and scatalogical devices of an entire generation, Apollinaire, Cocteau, Artaud, and the playwrights of the theater of the absurd found inspiration and light to guide their way through the twentieth century.

By the time W. B. Yeats reached his mature years the temper of the times scarcely coincided with his vision. As a consequence of his increasing frustration with a seemingly uncaring world, Yeats buried the dreams of his youth in vitriolic attacks on the country that would not sustain his idealistic goals. The brush of reality consumed the dreams of Yeats's youth: what had begun in the last decades of the nineteenth century as a mythic vision for Ireland ended in the 1930s as an embittered nightmarish image, wrung from a poet totally out of phase and sympathy with his modern world.

To be "out of phase" was, for Yeats, an end, and for Beckett, a beginning. *Company* represents Beckett's creation and degradation of a personal memory, much as the Cuchulain cycle of plays represents Yeats's lifelong exploration and glorification of a historical memory. Yeats denounced his world in *The Death of Cuchulain;* Beckett celebrated his inviolable aloneness in *Company.* The dichotomy could not be more precise.

Beckett's *Company* contains, as do most of his works, an impossible compromise. "A voice comes to one in the dark, Imagine."[24] Whose voice is it? By what name can it be described or known? Beckett supplies no answers: "You will end as you now are. And in another dark or in the same another devising it all for company" (8). Neither does he raise expectations by alluding to symbol systems that anchor images to language, nor can he speak "to and of whom the voice speaks" in his imagination. But the idea of this communication is rational, hence the impossible compromise of communicating the speech that is not speaking, of a voice that is not "I," when he speaks.

In *Company,* a man on his back, in the dark, imagines scenes from his early life. He is a small boy again, looking at a blue sky that seems very near. He asks his mother if it is not much closer than it appears. Her reply is a "cutting retort . . . never forgotten" (11). The biography is irrelevant. What is important is the identity of the voice. Beckett prepares the reader very carefully:

Who asks, Whose voice asking this? And answers, His soever who devises it all.

In the same dark as his creature or in another. For company. And in the end
answers as above? And adds long after to himself, Unless another still. Nowhere to be found. Nowhere to be sought. The unthinkable last of all.
Unnamable. Last person. I (24).

Let him be again as he was. The hearer. Unnamable. You (32).

The Unnamable ("I" and "you") is the third novel of the trilogy that
Beckett wrote between 1947 and 1949, the same time during which he
composed *En Attendant Godot.*[25] In *The Unnamable,* the author poses the
question of identity with the same predictable results:

You must say words, as long as there are any, until they find me, until
they say me, strange pain, strange sin, you must go on . . . I can't go
on, I'll go on.[26]

In his earlier work Beckett used the first person singular to identify the
speaker, an unnamable speaker of subjective nature; but beginning with
Not I, he changed his method.

Because using the second person singular (or plural, if there are
voices) distanced the source, Beckett situated the voice, vis-à-vis the
sensibility, in an objective sphere that he called "reason-ridden imagination" (33). Rational thought guides the reader to focus instinctively on
the source of the voice. But Beckett's voice is "less conscious" than that.
Its origin lies at the edge of language, in spatial constructs and images
that free the mind from the limitations of verbal substance. The process
of discovery is the discovery, acknowledged or not; the unwilling reader
of *Company* is overcome with answers:

Bloom of adulthood. Imagine a whiff of that. On your back in the dark you
remember. Ah you you remember. Cloudless May day. She joins you in the
little summerhouse. . . . All dead still. The ruby lips do not return your smile.
Your gaze descends to the breasts. You do not remember them so big. To the
abdomen. Same impression. Dissolve to your father's straining against the
unbuttoned waistband. Can it be she is with child without your having asked
for as much as her hand? You go back into your mind. She too did you but
know it has closed her eyes (38, 42).

As he paints this picture from his mind's eye, Beckett chooses images that
are hard, precise, selective, as a painter might sketch and lay in a
landscape. There are no Yeatsean symbol systems in the later works of
Beckett.

Beckett's technique is cinematic, cries out for pictorial expression, and
breaks images into split-screen segments that coalesce on a level at which
imagination must intuit meaning. Professor Leventhal, who succeeded
Beckett as a lecturer at Trinity College in 1931, and who remained his

lifelong friend, lamented that there was no great illustrator who would interpret Beckett's work, as Blake and Dali interpreted Dante's: "it would require a mixture of both their qualities, a power of illumination plus magic."[27] Beckett's work answers Leventhal's concern. The man on his back, imagining scenes from his past, *is* a pictorial artist. One of his brushes certainly belonged to Jack Yeats, whom Beckett adopted as an artistic "father-figure." His other tools were those of other artists, from Arikha to Giacometti, Bram van Velde to Caravaggio. The Irish landscape, seen in his mind's eye, was the canvas Samuel Beckett shared with W. B. Yeats. But only Beckett treated the canvas as an "in-scape" (Hopkins's term), thereby raising his art above pedantry. However, as he developed a schemata of signs and symbols (a veritable "house of Knott"), Beckett never forgot that unknowable man stood at its center.

Beckett's *Company* is objective, "reason-ridden;" even in fantasy he imagines a creature who, crawling, imagines him. Mirror after mirror reflects mirror, but not substance. The author "reasons" forth another possibility:

> Why crawl at all? Why not just lie in the dark with closed eyes and give up? Give up all. Have done with all. With bootless crawl and figments comfortless (55).

But as silence falls, a new longing for the old company arises. The operation is automatic. Language is automatic, like the voices in *Play*, who are edited to speak at the insistence of their unique tormentor, the light. From the perspective of the urn people, the sense of their language is incidental. In the light, the voices sound; in the dark, the voices are still, always subject to the demands of the light. In fact, the voices are a need; what sense they display is quite incidental. The light as a psychic entity reflects the spectator's habitual pose—a member of the audience anticipating a text with substance. "Meaning" is a glaze whose transparent nature Beckett exposes in *Play* and in *Company:*

> The need to hear that voice again. If only saying again, You are on your back in the dark. Or if only, You first saw the light and cried at the close of the day when in darkness Christ died at the ninth hour cried and died (55).

The biographical material—Samuel Beckett, born 13 April 1906, Good Friday—merges with Christ's image and a voice that dies, in order to live as the *other*. It is all a fable, told to give the impression that people exist, in a world where there is no issue: "And you as you always were. Alone" (63).

Man's power of reflection, his most ancient attribute, is said to have been acquired ten thousand years ago, in the Pleistocene era. At some moment in that time man crossed what has been called "the Threshold of Reflection." John McPhee described man's thought, a revolution:

> Outwardly, almost nothing in the organs had changed. But in depth, a great revolution had taken place: consciousness was now leaping and boiling in a space of super-sensory relationships and representations; and simultaneously consciousness was capable of perceiving itself in the concentrated simplicity of its faculties.[28]

The art of reflection was the first work of art. Succeeding generations of artists discovered the vitality of this primary source. That this act has been restored to something of its original wonder and power is first a tribute to W. B. Yeats, who called attention to the errors of three hundred years of rational thought; that it has been developed, even expanded in scope, is a tribute to Samuel Beckett.

The crucial disparity between the plays of W. B. Yeats and those of Samuel Beckett is not in subject but in sense of space, within which they both display forms of the imagination. Beckett explained at least once, in unequivocal language, his sense of the real:

Dec. 29, 1957

> . . . My work is a matter of fundamental sounds (no joke intended) made as fully as possible, and I accept responsibility for nothing else. . . . Hamm as stated, and Clov as stated, together as stated, nec tecum, nec sine te, in such a place, and in such a world, that's all I can manage, more than I could.[29]

Yeats took a more deliberately poetic view:

> The actor must also, in order to project the impression that he stands "at the trysting-place" of mortal and immortal, time and eternity, achieve *Marmorean stillness* in imitation of the life beyond rather than that of the chaotic, busy life outside the theatre.[30]

Yeats forsook the theatrical space, as well as the life surrounding it and pressing against it, for a theory of tragedy that reached beyond the boundaries of reason. In doing so, he effectively excluded the theatrical space as a site in which the power of the imagination could create forms of meaning. His plays became symbols of an abstract drama that achieved its effect through ironic posture, an intellectual pursuit that Yeats derided during most of his career in the theater, but preserved in his own writing.

Yeats also created a symbol system that should have been an intermediate step toward the establishment of meaning. For Yeats symbols were a mediating necessity to counter the disastrous Cartesian mind-body dualism Western man had inherited from the seventeenth century. However, Yeats's symbols abstracted life from reality. He allowed his latent energies to be neutralized, rather than universalized, and generations of Irishmen studiously ignored the founder of Ireland's modern theater.

In contrast, there are no symbols in Beckett's work; there are only the objects as seen, as experienced, as heard, however well, by the artist, a sensibility. Indeed, one of the distinguishing features of his writing is his unrelenting stare at the real. In his major plays he reduced sentiment to a minimum, and sometimes less. No tears cloud the eyes of Winnie at the end of her happy days; no sound escapes the lips of Krapp as his last tape drones to a conclusion; no self-identification issues from Mouth as the old woman slips into unconsciousness. Beckett took his experience of the real and celebrated it in theatrical space as no other twentieth-century poet did. His work could be the century's most important legacy. A comparison of the real in W. B. Yeats's poem "The Tower" and Beckett's dramaticule . . . *but the clouds* . . . (the latter play's title a phrase taken from "The Tower") showed startling dissimilarities in the treatment of the topic. Yeats postures before the world; the real is buried in an avalanche of invective, hurled at objective reality; Beckett reaches beneath objective reality; the real seeps through the interstices of the dramatic image. For Beckett, form is a means of communicating a sense of the real; for Yeats, the real is an excuse for whiplashing mankind's indifference.

In "The Tower" (1926) the poet rages to be done with life, indeed rages that such a thing as "life" and "death" are only human attributes of process. He would be done with human philosophies:

> I mock Plotinus' thought
> And cry in Plato's teeth,
> Death and life were not
> Till Man made up the whole.[31]

Once, the pride and glory of knights in arms, "cross-gartered to the knees," ruled Ireland with the values of an aristocratic hierarchy. But now Yeats, embittered and ignored, can only recall the early promise. Where once he sought for truth everywhere, the poet finds himself

> A figure that has grown so fabulous
> There's not a neighbor left to say
> When he finished his dog's day:
> An ancient bankrupt master of this house.

(221)

In old age the imagination seems inversely to be more alive than in youth. But the poet is powerless to change the world; instead, he will compose his soul and study, until the immediacy of the world, ". . . wreck of body, slow decay of blood, / Testy delirium . . . The death of friends. . . ," is seen as ". . . but the clouds of the sky. . ." (224–25). This bitter denunciation of a modern world lies in sharp contrast with Yeats's dream:

> That, being dead, we rise,
> Dream and so create
> Translunar Paradise.
>
> (223)

By substituting one symbol system for another, Yeats continually moved from one eternal verity to another.

Beckett paid W. B. Yeats his highest compliment in dramatizing the final moments of "The Tower." . . . *but the clouds*. . . , a play for television, chronicled the movements of M through three poles of his small world, as he tries to cast off his old feelings for an unrequited love affair:

> one: she appeared and—
> . . . .
> In the same breath was gone. . . . Two: she
> appeared and—
> . . . .
> lingered. . . . With those unseeing eyes I so
> begged when alive to look at me.
> . . . .
> Three: she appeared and—
> . . . .
> After a moment—
> *W's lips move, uttering inaudibly:* ". . . clouds . . . but
> the clouds . . . of the sky. . . ."[32]

M's voice murmurs the last phrase synchronously. There is a fourth case, the last, when M begs to be relieved of old memories. As he disappears into the shadows in the West, there to resume walking the back roads of his life, the voice returns one last time:

> V. ". . . but the clouds of the sky . . . when the horizon fades . . . or a bird's
> sleepy cry . . . among the deepening shades. . . ."
>
> (262)

Yeats's power of invention of language images had a strong impact on Samuel Beckett, who found a way to dramatize dissociated phases of consciousness of the real more simply, more directly, without the strutting and posturing of the older poet.

Despite the limitations in Yeats's plays, there is a unity in his writing that is as impressive as it is comprehensive. Friedman described its length and its depth:

> Yeats insists at the close of his dramatic career, as he had at its opening in plays like *The King's Threshold* and *On Baile's Strand,* that heroic conduct is diametrically opposed to practical wisdom.[33]

Cuchulain is Yeats, the hero-as-artist, making his own myth, transcribing the epics of ancient Ireland from the arabesques of his imagination into everyday art. John Rees Moore pointed out that Yeats's particular virtue was his capacity to use myth as a way of seeing the contemporary world:

> What he [Yeats] did was to conduct a life-long search for a connection between the powerful fantasies that plagued and delighted him in childhood and youth and their source in that greater imagination out of which every man and every civilization has been created.[34]

Yeats never really ended his search. Six days before he died, he wrote: "Man can embody truth but he cannot know it."[35]

Yeats believed that life could only be symbol of some other presence: if the world of the real were a stage, its actors should move slowly and quietly, and not very much, for there should be something in their movements that was "decorative and rhythmical, as if they were figures in a frieze."[36] Yeats treated the reality of the commercial theater, its stress on verisimilitude, and its Ibsenite plots mirroring society, with great disdain. And yet even as he spoke to his countrymen, he felt himself to be an outsider:

> No man can think or write with music and vigor except in his mother tongue. . . . I could not more have written in Gaelic than can those Indians write in English; Gaelic is my national language, but it is not my mother tongue.[37]

Yeats wrote of his countrymen to his countrymen, assailing them with images that were largely unflattering. At no time did he cater to them. In the end, he felt neglected by their indifference. It is doubtful that even Yeats's heroic tales of Cuchulain, performed in Gaelic at the Abbey Theatre, could have changed their minds. The old Symbolist, faced with the "Savage Gods" of Père Ubu's modernism, was writing beyond his time.

Samuel Beckett defied Yeats's injunction not to write in another tongue, and did so with élan. His soft Dublin accent, so apparent in conversation, did not often intrude on his prose. There are portions of his early works that are lyrical at the expense of his narrative. What he began as an exercise in trimming excesses from his youthful style—writing short prose works in French—finally became his distinctive way of translating images from the imagination into the mind. He translated English into French, and French into English.[38]

Beckett did demonstrate Yeats's influence in his composition of *Krapp's Last Tape*. Deirdre Bair made a strong, but errant, claim that Krapp is Beckett.[39] The significance of autobiography in the play is minimal. Gontarski traced the evolution of the play in a thorough study of Beckett's various drafts of the manuscript.[40] The first version contains a passage in which a thirty-one-year-old Krapp records "in the third decade of the Ram." The reference is to Aries, the astrological sign of the Ram, and Beckett's own sign. He evidently wrestled with the image, and finally took it out of the text in typescript three. His wrestling with an image is significant, and shows that he experienced the process Yeats describes in *Per Amica Silentia Lunae:* "We make of the quarrel with others, rhetoric, but of the quarrel with ourselves, poetry."[41]

Unlike Beckett's Krapp, Yeats is the Old Man in *At the Hawk's Well.* The thing he fears most is old age and decrepitude. By putting on the mask of age, the poet creates the dramatic tension between the intellect and the antithetical self, whose only business is passion.[42]

Beckett's Krapp is, without doubt, his antiself: a writer whose lifelong struggle to reconcile the forces of light and darkness, spirit and flesh, has brought its author no awareness of unchanging changes. The man who curses his younger selves for having abandoned love is the man who, as playwright-director, reacts with mock horror at the image of an old Krapp, surrounded by dogs and children.

Yeats's Daimon is a powerful antidote to a writer's prospective failure. Art *is* "the art of failure" for men concerned with their interiorities. Beckett emphasizes this in "Three Dialogues," when he discusses the pictorial work of artists Tal Coat, Masson, and Bram van Velde:

> . . . to be an artist is to fail, as no other dare fail, that failure is his world and the shrink from it desertion, art and craft, good housekeeping, living. . . . I know that all that is required now, in order to bring even this horrible matter to an acceptable conclusion, is to make of this submission, this admission, this fidelity to failure, a new occasion, a new term of relation, and of the act which, unable to act, obliged to act, he makes, an expressive act, even if only of itself, of its impossibility, of its obligation.[43]

According to Beckett, the relationship of the artist to his creation, so long considered a continuum, is in fact no relationship at all. At best the artist serves as a conduit of sensory experience, and should pretend no claim to his work—painting, sculpture, or narrative—as a possession. The proprietary pronoun in "his" painting and "her" poem is meaningless. In the passage from light to dark, when the old woman falls in a cow pasture and hears sounds for the first time, she also recognizes, for the first time, the voice is "not I—she!" The artist's expression of conscience, which Beckett describes as "less conscious," can no longer be deluded to attempt "more authentic, more ample, less exclusive relations between representer and representee, in a kind of tropism towards the light."[44]

Not I is an expression of the continuum Yeats spoke of in his essays and introductions, and Beckett commented on in "Three Dialogues" Yeats cited Maeterlinck's analogy of new drama to old paintings:

> The true artist . . . is well aware that the psychology of victory or murder is but elementary and exceptional, and that the solemn voice of men and things, the voice that issues forth so timidly and hesitatingly, cannot be heard amidst the idle uproar of acts of violence.[45]

The forces of external reality that most readily lend themselves to dramatic interpretation are no longer suitable. What is suitable for the new theater of Maeterlinck, Yeats, and Beckett is a new subjectivity: "And therefore will he place on his canvas a house lost in the heart of the country, a door open at the end of a passage, a face or hands at rest."[46]

From W. B. Yeats, Samuel Beckett inherited an inspiration rich with subjective sources and a rejection of "three provincial centuries" of Cartesian thought that focused on the external, verifiable world. But from Jack Yeats Samuel Beckett inherited a spirit of artistic enterprise and a method to establish his identity as an artist. The "painter-ly brother," Jack Yeats, developed pictorial images on canvas that form the more direct link to Maeterlinck and the subjectivity of the new drama.

Both W. B. Yeats and Richard Ellmann discussed the poet's inspiration and what might be described as the "felicity of expression" in his writings. In *Yeats: The Man and the Masks,* Ellmann concluded:

> Few poets have found mastery of themselves and of their craft so difficult or have sought such mastery, through conflict and struggle, so unflinchingly.[47]

In 1905, Yeats noted that his practice of carefully crafting all his prose was coming unstuck. He had too much to do and too little time in which to do it:

I have had very little to say this year in *Samhain,* and I have said it badly. When I wrote *Ideas of Good and Evil* and *The Celtic Twilight,* I wrote everything very slowly and a great many times over. . . . I did the last *Samhain* this way . . . but this time I am letting the first draft remain with all its carelessness of phrase and rhythm. . . . One casts something away every year, and I shall, I think, have to cast away the hope of ever having a prose style that amounts to anything.[48]

Of course Yeats did develop a prose style of careful phrasing and conscious rhythms, but it was studied. The "felicity of expression" with which a poet "paints a picture" in words eluded him. Despite his desire, his effort, and his interest in Oriental subjects, he never crafted language like that with which the eighth-century Chinese poet Wang-Wei "painted" a picture of his studio:

> I sit alone deep in a bamboo grove,
> Strumming on my lute while singing a song;
> In the deep forest no one knows I am here.
> Only the bright moon comes to shine on me.[49]

W. B.'s brother Jack fully developed his own stunning talent for painting scenes of solitary splendor with oils on canvas. Samuel Beckett did no less, although in another medium:

> *V.* so in the end
>   close of a long day
>   went down
>   in the end went down
>   down the deep stair
>   let down the blind and down
>   right down
>   into the rocker
>   mother rocker
>   where mother sat
>   all the years
>   all in black
>   best black
>   sat and rocked
>   rocked
>   till her end came . . .[50]

The chanting language of a woman, prematurely old, rocking herself into old age and death—strangely un-alone—exudes the same kind of poetic power. The image of rocking onstage becomes an image of black—moving in light, beyond image, beyond symbol, beyond light and shadow—of a world W. B. Yeats could intuit, in his best work; of a realm in which Jack Yeats could always be found, in his least effort.

PART III

Jack B. Yeats and Samuel Beckett

5

"Continuosity, Impetuosity and Exuberance"

No-one creates . . . the artist assembles memories.

—Jack Yeats

WILLIAM Butler Yeats played the role of twentieth-century Ireland's foremost literary figure with natural aplomb, and an air born of practiced self-assurance. There is some question, however, that even within his own family he deserved the honor. White records that "old Mr. Yeats once said that Jack was really the poet of the family."[1] The younger brother was Ireland's national painter, as well as an accomplished playwright and novelist. It is possible that history will credit the more reticent younger brother as the true embodiment, on stage and canvas, of a living Irish mythology.

Jack Yeats did not confine his astonishing facility for painting Irish landscapes to that genre alone. He had a gift for displaying the dramatic. In his early analysis of Yeats's work, Thomas MacGreevy made the point succinctly:

> I do not think I am claiming too much for Jack Yeats when I say that nobody before him had juxtaposed landscape and figure without subduing the character of either to that of the other.[2]

MacGreevy's praise put Yeats in the category of Poussin, Claude, and Constable—artists whose sensibilities captured the mood of a particular moment and environment. Yeats offered even more than captured mood to the perceptive viewer. He did not hesitate to provoke his spectator into making an observation on his painting. Hilary Pyle noted that Yeats was in the habit of talking to his guests about his paintings, "providing a story as a background, with the greatest facility, and charming anecdotes . . . to which he himself attached little importance." When he had completed his tale, he would turn to his listener and say: "Now, *you* tell me what the picture is about!"[3] In this manner the artist made the

159

viewer an active participant in the interpretation of his painting; using his imagination, the spectator was invited to create, or to re-create, the emotional context of the work.

Samuel Beckett made the same command invitation to spectators at performances of his late plays. The summons to participate, for those who dare, is an explicit element of performance of Beckett's works. The provenance of this essential element of both Beckett's dramatic art and Yeats's figural art can be partially attributed to Jack Yeats's development as a mature artist.

Although the richly productive years of Jack Yeats's artistic career covered nearly seven decades, from 1888—when he published his first black-and-white illustration—until his death in 1957, he never formulated an artistic aesthetic in the extravagant style of his brother, W. B. Yeats. In the 1920s Jack Yeats professed great interest in James Joyce. Joyce returned his feelings, and bought two of Yeats's early paintings—*Porter Boats* (of the River Liffey) and *Salmon Leap, Leixlip* (of Dublin Bay)—and declared, at one point, that their creative methods were similar.[4] Jack Yeats's 1920 letter to John Quinn, in which the painter defended George Moore's reputation, revealed a great deal about Jack Yeats as an artist:

> To me, man is only part of a splendor and a memory of it. And if he wants to express his memories well he must know he is only a conduit. It is his work to keep that conduit free from old bird's nests and blowflies.[5]

Jack Yeats and Samuel Beckett first met late in 1930, at a time when Beckett, a recent graduate of Trinity College, Dublin, was serving as *lecteur d'anglais* at L'Ecole Normale Superieure in Paris. Thomas MacGreevy, his predecessor in the prestigious two-year appointment, arranged his introduction to Yeats, and humorously recorded the evident excitement of the young scholar, aged twenty-two, in the following letter to the painter:

> He was completely staggered by the pictures and though he has met many people through me he dismissed them all in his letter with the remark, "and to think I owe meeting Jack Yeats *and* Joyce to you!"[6]

Beckett did not extend the plaudits he reserved for Jack Yeats to his elder brother William. Beckett used the pseudonym Andrew Belis to write his 1934 article in *The Bookman,* in which he chastised the elder Yeats brother for his "flight from self-awareness," in expressing peripheral concerns: "an iridescence of themes . . . segment after segment of cut-and-dried sanctity and loveliness."[7]

W. B. Yeats's symbol systems held no more fascination for Beckett than they had for James Joyce, because they obscured rather than revealed the artist at work. Rather than hiding behind his symbols, as Ellmann claimed Yeats did, Beckett chose to base his own art on "self-perception," which to his mind was the space that intervenes between the artist and the images he creates. As late as 1970 Beckett reaffirmed his choice:

> Self-perception is the most frightening of all human observations . . . when man faces himself he is looking into the abyss.[8]

Jack Yeats had formulated his own approach to the problem of perception, which he published in a 1922 book entitled *Modern Art:*

> True painting is not a trick of juggling; the artist is a person who has developed observation and memory clearly and if his hand is sure, he can give us his vision as it came to him, and painting can reach as high as men can reach.

His formulation was somewhat more oblique than Beckett's, as it dealt with his approach to the pictorial artist's subject matter. But the period around 1922 signaled a change in Yeats's own work: it began to show a painterly quality, a new freedom, and a lyricism that blurred the outlines of the superb draftsman of his early watercolors. He accomplished the transition through the development of his artist's "memory":

> Drawings must not be made as memories of the drawings of others, they must be the memories of the person who makes them. I use the word memory, for all drawing is from memory.[10]

Yeats's concept of memory lay behind his mature paintings, certainly those he painted after 1945. As early as 1920, however, he had begun to inseparably associate memory and dream states.[11] The research had important consequences for paintings completed in the late 1930s and early 1940s.

The basis of much of Jack Yeats's intellectual development lay in his 1900 watercolor entitled *Memory Harbour.* James White described *Memory Harbour* as "Yeats's most important watercolor, a view of Rosses Point in Sligo."[12] Pyle also described its foreshortened peninsula:

> with the long single line of thatched and whitewashed cottages, leading the eye to the rocks of Deadman's Point, and to the Metal Man, the twelve-foot high sailor on his pedestal, clad in white trowsers and royal blue sailor coat and black tie, with hair of upstanding wire.[13]

The figure in the foreground, smoking a cigar, might be a personifica-

Memory Harbour, 1900, watercolor on card, 12½ × 18½. Sen. Michael Yeats. (Photo by John Kellet, 1988)

tion of a returned Irish-American, or Jack Yeats himself, or Bowsie, or the Baron, or Mr. No Matter, in his later novels.

Anne Yeats, Jack's niece, and an accomplished painter, described the relationship between her uncle and the people and the countryside of the West of Ireland, and Sligo in particular:

> Always wherever he lived he remained in love with Sligo, and retained his passionate excitement and childlike curiosity about those travelling people who came and went so freely but so seldom stayed, those people about whom you'd wonder "from whence have they come, and where will they go?"[14]

Jack Yeats's quality of innocence has been noted by other commentators, notably Brian O'Doherty, who stated that, by refusing to grow up, "Yeats preserved his capacity to transform experience into myth and myth into experience."[15] Memories of a childhood spent in Sligo with his grandparents provided the painter with an endless source of material that he could reconstruct, in his mind's eye, in a process he described as "half-memory." Hilary Pyle described the process, whereby Yeats's memory was stimulated and transcended by his imagination:

He was freed from the past. The new state allowed memory to develop and fluctuate after it first gripped the mind, to distort the original experience. It gave license for the inclusion of extraneous forces, or for the addition of detail not necessarily relevant, but carried in by a fresh emotion at the moment of painting. In this way the original experience was translated into a newly created and visionary happening.[16]

Samuel Beckett used the same process in such works as *Imagination Dead Imagine*, the ironic title of which suggests the myth of a sleeping couple (say Diarmuid and Dervorgilla) in the mind's eye:

It is clear however, from a thousand little signs too long to imagine, that they are not sleeping. Only murmur ah, no more, in this silence, and at the same instant for the eye of prey the infinitesimal shudder instantaneously suppressed.[17]

He also used it in *Company,* his own *Memory Harbour:*

A small boy you come out of Connolly's Stores holding your mother by the hand. . . . Looking up at the blue sky and then at your mother's face you break the silence asking her if it is not in reality much more distant than it appears. The sky this is. The blue sky. Receiving no answer you mentally reframe your question and some hundred paces later look up at her face again and ask her if it does not appear much less distant than in reality it is. . . . she shook off your little hand and made you a cutting retort you have never forgotten.[18]

The playwright had good memories, too—diving from the high board, throwing himself onto great pine branches, lying on his back, devising images, for company, and the taste of the bloom of his adulthood—that were material for his process.

In each case, the subject matter, whether of reality or of the mind's eye of the imagination, whether of a historical present or of a mythological past, was only the ground layer on which Beckett laid the pigments, the emotions that were the process. In the process, sensibility was stirred, and elements of the mind were arranged for redistribution, gathered perhaps from fragments of lived life that, until then, lacked their full meaning. The key, of course, was memory, a kind of secondary reality that imploded on the senses in a kind of "delicious deflagration" (as Beckett described the process in *Proust*), from the perspective of both artist and observer, whereby not only the object but the *real*, "the Lazarus that it charmed," was recovered, beyond all measure of familiar, experienced reality.[19]

The pattern of inward development of memory and imagination that

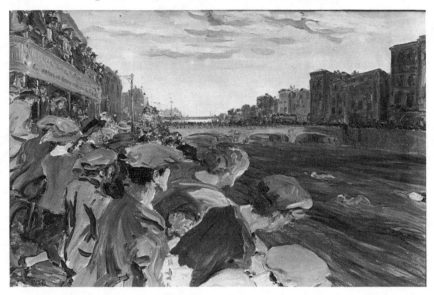

The Liffey Swim, 1923, oil on canvas, 24 × 36. National Gallery of Ireland.

Beckett outlined in *Proust* (1931) appeared in the work of Jack Yeats in 1924 or 1925. James White described the change in the artist who, until that time, had been content to record the ephemeral world about him—gamblers, circuses, boxers, horse races, carnivals, fishermen, tinkers, and travelers—and the environments in which they lived. Some event, or some series of events surrounding the abortive Irish Civil War—which divided the country against itself, and William Butler Yeats against Jack Yeats—signaled a change in the method by which the artist translated his images onto canvas:

> Then the plastic vision of painting incited him to wait for subjects which were inspired by some encounter with real life. This encounter pressed on a nerve . . . and suddenly the subject came clear, the present encounter turned magic by the past illumination, each aspect revealing the other. . . . He could see the figures and the background taking shape in his mind's eye. He did not then have to juggle with words but to reach out for tubes and brush, eagerly to pursue color and texture, air and light and movement.[20]

The Liffey Swim showed the strong, confident, transitional style, no outlines, broad, long brush strokes, rich color: the whole painted with great rapidity.

A year before Beckett wrote *Proust,* he met Jack Yeats. Shortly thereafter, Beckett acquired a painting by Yeats entitled *Regatta Evening on Dublin Bay,* an acquisition that had a devastating effect on the young writer's bank balance. Anne Yeats commented that Beckett and Yeats "were . . . friends for many years and they greatly admired each other's work."[21] There can be no question that the influence of Jack Yeats was important for the development of Samuel Beckett as an artist, particularly as the painter matured as an artist in the 1920s and 1930s.

Jack Yeats's rearrangement of "stages of an image" in the mind's eye gave his late paintings an immediacy and an evocative power that far surpassed his watercolors and the drawings he had done for *Broadside,* published by Dun Emer Press since July 1908. Pyle described Yeats's creative process at this time as "half-memory," one in which the artist was the celebrant of a world reborn. Beckett, whose frame of reference was darker (in 1931 at least, when he came in contact with Jack Yeats's work), saw this recombinant memory and imagination as justification for a view that the life of the body on earth was "defunctus."[23] A half-century later, that view still pertained: in a late theater piece, *Rockaby* (1981), Beckett showed his version of "stages of an image" transitional processes of the mind's eye. *Rockaby* is divided into four sections, each section framed by a single word spoken by the Woman seated in the rocking chair: "More." The play also contains an interesting sequence of decreasing repetitions as W and V intone their lines together:

W. More
  . . .
V. *time she stopped*
  . . .
time she stopped
  . . .
time she stopped
(Together: echo of "time she stopped," coming to rest of rock. faint fade of light.)
  . . .
W. More
  . . .
V. *time she stopped*
  . . .
time she stopped
  . . .
one other living soul
(Together: echo of "living soul," coming to rest of rock, faint fade of light.)
  . . .
W. More
  . . .
V. *Rock her off*
(Together: echo of "rock her off," coming to rest of rock, slow fade out.)[23]

The actress onstage slowly becomes the image of her inner voice, a memory of the event witnessed by the spectators, but now reformed by the eye of the imagination. The repetition of the phrase "time she stopped" in the first three sections is further exaggerated by the echoing effects at the conclusion of all four sections. Language repetition is balanced by visual repetition: the sight of the woman rocking mechanically onstage merges with the sound of language flowing rhythmically—and mechanically—from the voice.

The celebratory process is the same—joyous revelry in Jack Yeats's work, in which the figures burst with life, or scabrous denial of everyday reality in Beckett's works, in which the figures withdraw into another realm—if only the viewer has eyes to see.

The mechanical qualities of language and of onstage visual images transport the spectator beyond the immediate meanings of language and gesture—the mind's eye patterns of an old woman, all eyes, always watching the world from her window—to stages of a developing image, moving in and out of a pool of light. When the evocative power of a rhythmic chant almost transforms V's words into a mantra, the stage image of W, dressed in black and white and rocking back and forth in alternate shades of light and darkness, exerts the effect on the mind.

In this manner the inward qualities of the play, its visionary character, is only completed as the play ends and the fractured images are restored. Beckett develops the central image of the old woman gradually as V narrates the story. The playwright's advice to Hildegarde Schmahl, playing the part of May in *Footfalls* (1976),

"Try gradually, while you speak the words, to see the whole inwardly. . . . It is an image which develops gradually. When you begin to narrate the story, you don't know the end. . . ."[24]

applies equally well to the actress in *Rockaby*. Beckett, of course, did not directly acknowledge his debt to Jack Yeats. But this structural similarity of Samuel Beckett and Jack Yeats in their development of persona as an end-product of discrete stages of an artwork lay in sharp contrast to a conventional dramaturgy that demanded clear character outlines and a clear premise at the outset of the play, with ensuing conflict, crisis, resolution, and character development provided by the dramatist.

Beckett's reconstruction of materials into mythic components, whether of the heroic past of ancient Irish legend, or of living memory, that transcends the immediacy of the moment was defined by Brian O'Doherty as a peculiarly Irish tradition, born of centuries of repression. O'Doherty commented, in particular, on the paintings of Jack Yeats:

The dialectic of his art is promise and regret, both of which have virtuoso traditions. In Ireland the future was full of regret and the past was full of promise.[25]

O'Doherty saw the reversal of expectations as a consequence of a national self-image imposed on Ireland by conquering Englishmen:

> In return for certain flatteries—the Irishman was witty, hard-drinking, outrageous, poetic, capable of wild and impractical gestures, lovable, colorful in speech, picturesque in aspect. . . . He was also, in the twinkling of an eye, moody, cunning, untrustworthy, rebellious, incapable of responsibility.[26]

The only means the Irish found to escape such an oppressive self-image were to focus on the myths of their past, or on the myth of an age to come, or to travel, anywhere, beyond reach of the oppressor. Beckett's tramps, no less than Yeats's Bowsie and the Baron, recover a measure of self-dignity and universal humanity in their travel through the Irish landscape.

There is a great deal more to the Yeats equation that cannot be reduced to political rhetoric, inverted time dimensions, or the celebration of vagabonds who live by moving through the physical and imaginative landscapes of the Irish mind. The mythic components of the Yeats family begin in the family seat. William Murphy, in his discussion of the Yeats family and the Pollexfens of Sligo, noted:

> We cannot understand William Butler Yeats fully unless we know the Pollexfens, as we cannot understand the art of Jack Yeats without knowing Sligo.[27]

Hilary Pyle, in contrast, remarked that the particular traits of the Pollexfens, Jack Yeats's maternal forebears, were clearly visible in their favorite grandson. He had "the silence, the independence, the reserve, the calm elusiveness and puckish humor, the absence of irritabiliy, the love of ceremony, the upright nature, and a definite business acumen . . ." that were their bequest.[28] Certainly the John Butler Yeats–Susan Mary Pollexfen marriage, celebrated on 10 September 1863, promised to be a happy union of a sailing master's daughter and a clergyman's son who was a young lawyer and an authentic Irish landlord. Within three years, John Butler Yeats abandoned the King's Inn of Dublin for an artist's career in London.

The change destroyed Susan's health and dictated young Jack's removal to Sligo for eight years of his education, because his father's income did not permit all the Yeatses to live together in London. Jack lived with his Pollexfen grandparents, who tended to be (in his father's opinion) a "strange people, intense, silent, brooding . . . who rejected the natural impulses their God had given them," and was free to come and go as he pleased, among the Irish of Sligo.[29] According to Lily Yeats, his oldest sister, Jack, "the white-haired boy," was "the only one who ever had talk with Grandpapa" and was therefore accorded special freedoms.[30] Five years after Jack moved in with his grandparents, during the most impressionable period of his life, his father wrote to his friend, the English critic Edward Dowden:

> The Pollexfens were as solid and powerful as the sea-cliffs; but hitherto they are altogether dumb. . . . To give them a voice is like giving a voice to the sea-cliffs, when what wild babblings must break forth.[31]

For many years it was assumed that the eldest grandson, William Butler Yeats, gave tongue to the sea-cliffs; but more sober assessment found W. B. hiding in the caves of the cliff, occasionally emitting an archaic sound, while his younger brother soared from the promontories, on the wings of the seagull that adorned each of his completed paintings.[32]

At a rather early age Jack Yeats found himself in Sligo, a small seaport in the west of Ireland, that provided the impressionable young boy with sights and sounds he never forgot: "the ships loading and unloading, the sight of Ben Bulben and Knocknarea, the stoning of raisins for the Christmas pudding, the Hazelwood Racecourse with the crowds, the smell of bruised grass, the thud of horses over the jumps. . . ."[33] As important as the memories were the opportunities afforded the son of a descendant of Anglo-Irish landed gentry to know the people of Sligo. MacGreevy pointed out, in his decisive, early essay on Jack Yeats, that the child knew the native Irish "from the inside to a degree that very few Anglo-Irishmen before him had known [them]."[34]

From his childhood memories Yeats assembled a lifetime of associations that never left his art—from memories of Grandfather, at breakfast:

> a man of direct action; the tapping of the top of a boiled egg infuriated him. His way was to hold the egg cup firmly on its plate with his left hand, then with a sharp knife in his right hand to behead the egg with one blow. Where the top of the egg went was not his business. It might hit a grandchild or the ceiling. He never looked.

to Jack's doll house, called "The Farm":

> Wherever he [Jack] went his farm had to accompany him. The model later developed into a miniature theater for which he wrote plays and designed scenery.

to the habits and labors of the country folk and fishermen of Western Ireland:

> I think the two most beautiful pieces of man's handiwork are the old-fashioned plough and a sailing ship. In each every curve is there at the command of the elements. . . .[35]

This last subject in particular, the relationship of nature, man, and the elements, consumed the artist's attention. Yeats felt that the urban life of his parents and siblings was false, whereas the rural life, that showed the veil between artist and nature to be transparent, was true. The artist in the country knew

> what is happening every hour; the corn is springing, or a storm is coming and the floating archipelago of clouds are banking together. . . . If he is on the coast he knows the spring-tides from the neap-tides. The other country dwellers feel all these things too, and so he has a greater comradeship.[36]

In 1887, at the age of sixteen, Jack rejoined his parents in London, where he attended art schools and showed great promise as a black-and-white illustrator. He married Mary Cottenham White ("Cottie") in 1897 and had his first one-man show at the Clifford Gallery, London, in 1897.[37] His Pollexfen grandparents remained in Sligo until their deaths in 1892. (They had sold Merville, the family home, when Jack left for London.) But if Jack Yeats's new interests were centered on providing a home and a living for his new wife, his artistic attention remained on Sligo. Whenever possible, he would return to his ancestral village for the centuries-old weekly markets, or the race meetings at Bowmore Racecourse, Rosses Point (known as "four pound nineteens"; since the prizes did not reach the value of five pounds, the meetings were governed by no official rules):

> Jockeys in brilliant striped costumes lined up on their mounts by the flags and sped off around the poles marking the edges of the strand, at times ending in the sea, if one of the great mists arose. On the shore itself were groups of long low tents, made of bent saplings covered with sacking, where poitín, the twenty-four hour whiskey, was consumed in great quantity . . . and ballad singers would give their performances, and sell their printed ware.[38]

On the Old Racecourse, painted in 1922, is a memory picture of Bowmore, and shows Yeats's uncle, George Pollexfen, cane in hand, standing halfway to the strand, a jump to his left, and the mane and head of a spirited

The First Time Around, 1903, watercolor on paper, 35¾ × 53⅝. Sen. Michael Yeats. (Photo by John Kellet, 1988)

race horse in the foreground. But Yeats's paintings of Drumcliffe Strand—*The First Time Around* (1903) and *On Drumcliffe Strand* (1918)—reveal the artist's fascination with the people engaged in activities associated with the races—conversing, drinking, singing, watching, waiting, eyeing suspiciously and ignoring studiously outsiders who posed a threat to the ordinary Irish of Sligo. Circuses and boxing rings, centers of mystery and intrigue, where elemental passions held sway over large assemblages of the Irish people, vied with the sea, and the men of the sea, as depicted in *The Man from Aranmore* (1905), or *The Breaker Out* (1925) and *The Island Funeral* (1923), for the artist's attention. Indeed, during the first twenty years of his artistic career, Jack Yeats established his reputation as a painter of the Irish people, and he was, as MacGreevy pointed out, the first to do so in three hundred years.[39] Conditions were ripe for an Irish renaissance, but not of the kind that inspired Lady Gregory and W. B. Yeats to invoke the gods of Dana, the legends of Cuchulain and Emer, or the stories of Finn and Oisin, Diarmuid and Grania. Their invocation of the past, recalling a dreamy world of symbols that might inspire a new aristocracy in Ireland, led in precisely the

The Island Funeral, **1923, 24 × 36. Sligo County Library and Museum.**

wrong direction for realistic art in the twentieth century. The lyrical, introspective work that W. B. Yeats demanded was replete with ennobled and idealized gestures, and a rhetorical style to match the classical mythology. He summarized it in his preface to Lady Gregory's *Gods and Fighting Men:*

> If we would create a great community—and what other game is so worth the labor?—we must recreate the old foundations of life . . . as they must always exist when the finest minds and Ned the beggar and Sean the fool think about the same thing, although they may not think the same thought about it.[40]

The brothers hardly agreed. W. B.'s epic dreaming was very unlike his brother Jack's extraordinary ordinariness. The trivial happenings and the very banality of the lives of the Irish attracted Jack to celebrate them in painting after painting. In his later years the younger Yeats shifted his treatment of his subjects from a concentration on the objects he represented to a concentration on the manner in which he represented them. But during the early years of his career, he developed his craft to the point where he was *the* national painter of the Irish, a broken nation of disinherited peasants who clung to the land for solace. In *On Another Man's Wound*, Earnan O'Malley described the situation of the Irish:

> There was a strange passionate love of the land amongst the people. Material possessions were low or gone, the arts were a broken tradition, the ideal of beauty had gone into the soil and the physical body. Their eyes had long dwelt on the form, color and structure of the landscape. It had become personal; its praise had been sung by joyous poets or despairing poets, and had been felt by the people. An old soil well loved had given much to them, and they had put much into it. They clung to this last treasure . . . with imagination and with physical senses.[41]

Yeats did not despair; rather, he infused his paintings with a sense of celebration and joyous encounter with life—witness *The Rake* (1901), in which a solitary figure, stopped mid-stride, hat at a classical angle, pointed shoes and checkered vested suit (completely buttoned), shoves his hands into his pockets to effect an air of nonchalance. The same figure might have sat for *The Rogue* (1903), except for the broken nose, the shabby clothing in disrepair, and the glass of poitin sitting on the bench. In his treatment of his subjects, Yeats created movement and drama that reflected his own perception of their daily lives. No better example of the mundaneness of the world, which consumes its inhabitants with passionate intensity, can be found than in Beckett's *Godot*. Taking their cue from Jack Yeats, the principal characters, Didi and Gogo, consume time as they wait for Godot, the absent antagonist of the plot, by telling stories, improvising scenes, abusing one another, taunting, cajoling, pleading, imploring, and castigating Pozzo and Lucky, in turn, for sins of commission and other transgressions. Lucky's monstrous widsom, in his speech on the public works of Puncher and Wattmann, that man "in spite of the strides of alimentation wastes and pines" is, in fact, only an embellishment of the Yeats central vision of the Irish, who clung to a vision as the tramps cling to their wait for Godot. Their verbal celebration of diversions while they wait—

> tennis football running cycling swimming flying floating riding gliding conating camogie skating tennis of all kinds dying flying sport of all sorts autumn summer winter winter tennis of all kinds hockey of all sorts . . .
>
> (29A)

—is only one among the many "sports and games" that Vladimir and Estragon, Pozzo and Lucky, and even the Boy (who arrives at the end of each act), contrive to pass the time. Even Vladimir, who is able to break

The Rogue, 1903, 21 × 14. Municipal Gallery of Modern Art, Dublin.

through the dream of reality and glimpse a moment of truth, cannot help himself:

> *Didi.* We wait, we are bored. *(He throws up his hand.)* No, don't protest, we are bored to death, there's no denying it. . . . Come, let's get to work! *(He advances toward the heap, stops in his stride.)* In an instant all will vanish and we'll be alone once more, in the midst of nothingness!
>
> (52A)

Pozzo's cry follows Didi's moment of brooding reflection, and Didi instantly rejoins the game of staying busy, of profiting from another's misfortune—an endless series of nonevents that defines the nature of existence. The very ordinariness of the lives of Vladimir and Estragon is again emphasized in *Endgame,* where the principal characters, Hamm and Clov, display an unrelieved humanity "of fundamental sounds . . . made as fully as possible . . . in such a place and in such a world. . . ."[42] *Fin de Partie* is a play with hooks that claw at the spectator, impure, like Rodin's *Balzac,* bereft of adornment, as Flaubert's *Madame Bovary.* Conceived as unfinished, created without comment or analysis, Beckett's work ranks with Shakespeare's *King Lear* as a testament to unaccommodated mankind. Beckett's inspiration for *Fin de Partie* belonged to Jack Yeats.

Yeats's artistic career was little influenced by politics, despite the considerable turmoil created by the Irish "Home Rule" question and the demands of the Sinn Fein. From his vantage point in Devon, Jack wrote to his long-time friend, John Quinn, his own unequivocal response to the surge of Irish nationalism:

> If I could live in my own country I would be interested in some kind of politics. But here in England it is so strange to listen to the people getting excited about things that I do not give a thrawneen about.[43]

This paradoxical situation, in which Yeats separated the major subject matter of his drawings and paintings—the Irish people—from the critical issue of their existence—their continued subjugation by foreign rule—provides a clue to his artistic temperament. Unlike his brother W. B., Jack Yeats was unalterably opposed to posturing of any kind. Indeed, the haughtiness and apparent snobbishness of William Butler Yeats was almost universally acknowledged, although Murphy noted that, among the Pollexfens, "he seem[ed] perfectly ordinary."[44] Though he distrusted the self-serving propogandists among the Irish reformers who promoted their cause by sending stories of imaginary outrages to English papers gratis, Yeats remained profoundly influenced by events in Ireland. The source of much of that interest, and the man who, more than any other figure of influence in Yeats's life, focused the artist on the possibilities of depicting Irish life, was John Millington Synge.[45]

Jack Yeats had met Synge at Coole, Lady Gregory's country home and a summer haven for the literati of the Irish artistic set:

> Sarah Purser, Douglas Hyde, Standish O'Grady, the Fays and the Abbey actors . . . Augustus John, Miss Horniman, and Susan Mitchell. . . .[46]

Others went there too; W. B. Yeats, John Masefield, John Quinn, and George Russell (Æ), who took a fancy to Jack Yeats and Cottie and went sketching with Jack. Pyle reported one occasion on which Jack Yeats and Æ sat down to sketch a particularly interesting landscape; after a time, the artist looked over to see how Russell was progressing. Instead of the flora of the countryside that he expected, Yeats was astonished to see Russell's sketch-pad covered with winged creatures.

John Millington Synge was a more rational being who was very concerned with discovering his roots. Anglo-Irish, like the Yeatses, and born near Dublin in 1871, the same year as Jack, of Protestant parents, he shared with Jack many of the problems that distanced them from the Irish of their country. By the age of twenty-five, having taken his degree at Trinity College, Dublin, and studied music in Germany and Racine in Paris, the inveterate traveler wrote in one of his notebooks:

> A human being finds a resting place only where he is in harmony with his surroundings, and is reminded that his soul and the soul of nature are of the same organization.[47]

He soon returned to Ireland, at the instigation of W. B. Yeats, to devote himself to creative work among the natives. John Masefield suggested to Synge that he might write a story of the Aran Islands for *The Manchester Guardian*. But Synge decided instead to visit the west of Ireland—Connemara and North Mayo—and he took Jack Yeats along with him, to be his illustrator. Six months later, on 3 June 1905, Yeats and Synge set out for Galway. From the very beginning it was clear who would be in charge, as Jack Yeats told it:

> When we started on our journey, as the train steamed out of Dublin, Synge said: "Now the elder of us should be in command on this trip!" So we compared notes and I found that he was two months older than myself. So he was the boss and whenever it was a question whether we should take the road to the west or the road to the south, it was Synge who finally decided.[48]

Robin Skelton noted that, whether by design or by accident of birth, Synge was the dominant figure of the duo, and undoubtedly influenced the "younger" man with his campaign against middle-class gentility and propriety, of which he was an inextricable product.[49] Ostensibly the subject matter of his essays, plays, and periodicals related to the people of western Ireland. But his images were refracted by a personal vision that colored all his observations. Synge's refraction may have been the germ of Jack Yeat's own "half-memory pictures" that he developed many years later. Haunted by a sense of guilt at his breech of middle-class propriety in becoming an artist, and faced with the necessity of pacifying an overly protective mother (whom he outlived by only three months), Synge was forced to live on the edge of his inner turmoil. At one point he announced to Padraic Colum that all his work was subjective, "coming out of moods in his own life."[50] He found the solution to his personal problems in his art, and the country people of his childhood. What better way to rediscover the roots of one's soul than to tramp about the land, with a friend at one's side, and listen to and report ancient tales, in an ancient language. In an essay, Synge wrote words that describe all of Yeats wanderers, as well as Beckett's tramps:

> In the middle classes the gifted son of a family is always the poorest— usually a writer or an artist with no sense for speculation—and in a family of peasants, where the average comfort is just over penury, the gifted son sinks also, and is soon a tramp on the roadside.[51]

But the truth was not on the roadside, nor in the villages of the Irish-speaking areas of Connemara, nor in the "congested district" of North Mayo, where the peasants lived out their poverty-stricken lives in a stark landscape bounded by sea and cold mists and driving rainstorms. Synge found truth in the relationships of the people to the uncompromising promise of the land. He communicated his truth to Yeats, who accepted it, rediscovered it, renewed it, and communicated it to Synge. The readers of *The Manchester Guardian,* safely middle class or proletarian intellectual, would scarcely have had any familiarity with the wildness of the adventures that Synge narrated, and Yeats illustrated, for their pleasure. But what appeared to subscribers of Masefield's paper to be exotic tales of a foreign journey was, for Synge and Yeats, a voyage of self-discovery. W. B. Yeats, in a particularly prescient essay, described Synge and his achievement:

> Synge, like all the great kin, sought the race, not through the eyes or in history, or even in the future, but where those monks [of Mont-Saint-Michel] found God, in the depths of the mind. . . .[52]

Almost immediately, W. B. Yeats began his own Noh Drama, in *At the Hawk's Well*, which called out to the eye of the mind. The divergent paths to this conception of art—W. B. Yeats's elaboration of ancient myths in symbol systems, Jack Yeats's simplification of the means of presentation, to the point where the means of presentation became a dominant focus—are a measure of the importance of Synge's work. Unfortunately, Synge's life was cut short by a fatal illness. Jack Yeats visited him for the last time in September 1908. After Synge's death, Yeats wrote a touching tribute to his friend that was much like Yeats's beloved "plays for the miniature theatre":

> If he had lived in the days of piracy he would have been the fiddler in a pirate schooner, him they called "the music."—"The music" looked on at everything with dancing eyes but drew no sword, and when the schooner was taken and the pirates hung at Cape Corso Castle or the Island of Saint Christopher's, "the music" was spared because he *was* "the music."[53]

Synge did play the fiddle, and he gained the trust of the Aran Islanders by playing for them at parties. And he died, in the grand tradition of Captain Carricknagat, a pirate in *The Scourge of the Gulph*, with a question unanswered:

> *Miles.* (. . . holding up skull.) An empty skull, a black box, a dead skipper! Have I done anything or nothing?[54]

The answer must be affirmative. Synge did much for Jack Yeats. His influence is clear in Yeats's later paintings—*Shouting* (1950) or *Left—Left, We left our name, On the Road, On the road, On the famous road, On the famous road, Of fame* (1948)—in which the pure joy of traveling together, one with another, is vividly depicted.

In the 1920s Yeats began to develop the energy and orginality in his paintings that made him Ireland's greatest painter.[55] That decade was a time of great strain for the Irish people, and Yeats's paintings reflected a topicality that Earnan O'Malley described as brooding and introspective:

> His figures now enter a subjective world in which they are related to the loneliness of the individual soul, the vague lack of pattern in living with its sense of inherent tragedy, brooding nostalgia, associated with time as well as variations on the freer moments as of old.[56]

Jack and Cottie Yeats had returned to Ireland in 1910. Suddenly, the distance from the Irish turbulence, which had effectively insulated him in Devon, could not shield the artist from life around him. He responded, not as a fanatic, but as a sensibility. Pyle noted that, at that time,

"a deeper dimension entered [Yeats's art], and the depictions of history
. . . were fortified with a real and powerful emotion."[57] He began to
paint reflections of scenes from the turbulent political and socialist
meetings of the time. Harrowing political events—the 1916 Easter Rebellion and the Sunday, 16 July 1914, massacre at O'Connell Bridge—
captured his imagination. Emotional strain caused by overwork and the
turmoil of the insurrection drained the artist, and he suffered a serious
illness in April 1916 that necessitated a prolonged period of recupera-
tion. Pyle noted that something collapsed inside the artist at the time
when the failure of his nation's half-realized dream became a certainty:

> Jack Yeats's patriotism was intense and of a deeply idealistic nature. To
> him the Free Staters were middle class, while the Republicans repre-
> sented all that was noble and free.[58]

Expectedly, the Irish Civil War divided the Yeatses, brother against
brother. Jack Yeats sided with the Irish peasant class against the North-
ern Free Staters whom W. B. Yeats supported. O'Doherty suggested that
the division was as much a matter of the brothers' personality traits as of
their political beliefs:

> Jack Yeats of course took the outsider, Republican side against the new
> Free Stater. His brother, always well-disposed to the grandeur of
> institutions, became a Free State senator. . . .[59]

The Civil War ended in 1923. In its aftermath, Jack Yeats's work developed an inner power and emotional strength that beggared the line
drawings of the first decades of his artistic career. He was fifty-two years
of age. The events of the preceding eight years had deepened his vision,
and his paintings began to reveal the change: movement and color
dominated form, carefully selected elements of objective reality became
the subject, and draughting technique nearly disappeared. MacGreevy
noted that, by 1924, Yeats's paintings consisted of richer, more delicate
and brilliant color harmonies, while form was "deferred to only in so far
as it [was] congenial to a much more self-consciously fastidious artistic
temperament than of old."[60] The Jack Yeats of 1924 was not the Jack
Yeats of 1900, who meticulously recorded every nuance of line and
surface in his drawings. Interestingly enough, W. B. Yeats had, at precisely the same age, also changed his artistic approach. In 1914, at the
age of fifty, the elder brother began work with Ezra Pound on the
Fenellosa translations of Japanese Noh drama. It would seem that the
artistic reputations of both brothers were destined to accelerate after
mid-life. That was certainly true of Samuel Beckett's reputation: *En
Attendant Godot* was first produced in 1953, when Beckett was forty-

seven; *Fin de Partie* in 1957 (Beckett, fifty-one); *Krapp's Last Tape* in 1958 (Beckett, age fifty-two).

The marked frustrations these artists suffered in their efforts to depict an ordered reality of objective phenomena, which seemed to accrue in their mature years, has not been sufficiently commented upon. Certainly, Jack Yeats, who spent twenty years of his artistic career doing line drawings for the Cuala Press, made an abrupt change in 1925. In a letter to his brother, Jack complained about his publisher's demands:

> The last two or three prints I have given them against my will. These reproductions are a drag, and a loss to me in my reputation.[61]

W. B. Yeats initiated his own change with publication of *At the Hawk's Well* (1917), and his summons to "the eye of the mind." Beckett's first play, "Eleutheria," in which Victor Krap turned his back to the world, was 133 pages long. The entire corpus of Beckett's subsequent works for the theater might have been contained within its pages, as his vision grew more acute, deliberate, unsparing, and sure with each passing decade.

Of course Jack Yeats was aware of the progression of his works from line-drawing illustration to free-form painting, but he saw it as representative of the natural progression of a maturing artist.[62] He opined to his brother that he no longer wished to be known as an illustrator, but as a "living painter":

> You say my painting is now "great." Great is a word that may mean so many different things. But I know I am the first living painter in the world. . . . I have no modesty. I have the immodesty of a spear head.[63]

His profound confidence in his abilities as a painter, rather than an illustrator, shone as he reveled in his new freedom.

For the first time since he had abandoned writing plays for his miniature theater in 1907, Jack Yeats began to produce dramatic pieces and novels. His first such text was about his favorite place, Sligo, as he had depicted it in *Memory Harbor* thirty years earlier. *Sligo* was published in 1930. Three years later *Apparitions*, composed of three plays—*The Old Sea Road, Rattle,* and *Apparitions*—appeared. The first production of one of his plays, *Harlequin's Positions,* opened on 5 June 1939 at the Abbey Experimental Theatre. In the years between 1930 and 1934 Yeats had composed four novels, *Sailing, Sailing Swiftly* (1933), *The Amaranthers* (1936), *The Charmed Life* (1938), and *Ah Well* (1942), which preceded the Abbey Theatre production of his play *La La Noo* on 3 May 1942. He followed two more novels, *And to You Also* (1944) and *The Careless Flower* (1947), with *In Sand,* his last play to premiere during his lifetime, on 19

April 1949. Of the other plays Yeats wrote, *The Deathly Terrace* and *The Silencer* were included in the *Collected Plays of Jack B. Yeats* (1971), edited by Robin Skelton. Altogether, he wrote nine plays and seven novels between 1929 and 1949. His production of paintings was understandably less during this part of his life; it may be concluded that the experiences of his sixty years were gestating, in preparation for the final, great period of his art, the years between 1945 and 1957. For him the thirties were a time of reflection. He made it very clear, in *Sligo*, why he wrote:

> Collectors of curios are an attempt at a manufactured brainfull of memories. The real brain, soaked, indexed and counter-indexed with memories, is handier and can be carried about with you, carried along too much perhaps, and that is why I am writing this book. To jettison some memories.[64]

The inspiration that had brought Jack Yeats to the forefront of Irish painting, through the depiction of the precarious nature of human achievement of the people of Ireland in the face of an intransigent, hostile environment, from sailing ships to ploughing shares, found a whimsical expression in the novels of the 1930s. As the artist suggested, he jettisoned memories; but he did something much more interesting in his work—he allowed the subjective element in his work to become increasingly important. Skelton noted a change in Yeats's sympathies for the peasants, which extended beyond the individual, "to the life-process itself . . . and [to] the rhythm of the universe that contains and comprehends both life and death."[65] Yeats, in effect, cast off the conscious memories that he had advocated for the artist, for himself, in his essay *Modern Art* (1922):

> The artist looks at the object he is painting, and then at the canvas paper, and puts down as much as he remembers of what he saw when looking at the object.[66]

By 1922, Yeats had removed his own objectivity from his painting; by 1936, he had removed his own subjectivity from his painting, and by 1945, he had removed his conscious self from his painting. He had become a sensibility. His work summoned the spectator to re-create his artist's inspiration.

In *Sligo* the first memories he "jettisoned" were remembrances of long ago, and far away. In the novel the speaker sits perched on a bare rocky hill top, and imagines:

I am in deep broad country, with a magnificent sea-coast, and mountains stooping to the beaches, and lakes, and bogs, and Inland Towns; and a fine sea port. Fine to me (8).

There are memories of America, of regattas, of horse races, and of ship's pilots who had been to New York and knew there was a street there called Three Hundred and Sixty-Sixth Street (13). The author recalls memories of the Strand, of Rosses Point's Bowmore Racecourse, and of the pounding hooves of race horses:

> To get the full feeling of a horse-race one should lie on the grass, to get a low horizon and let the horses go thudding by you with their bodies between you and the sky (67).

He recalls memories of Drumcliffe Strand, in Sligo, where ponies sometimes vanished in the sea mists:

> I see races on strands, on the shores of the Atlantic at low spring tide, when there is a flat plain of sand like a country so large it dwarfs the little brown and black turf-colored crowd about the tents and the winning post, with the green flag flapping in the ocean air (16).

Yeats also recalls memories of boxing matches by gaslight, and preferred them to those better lighted, because they appeared "more blood-thirsty, more of action," and the spectators—himself included—joined, in imagination, the action of the fight: "the blows, bobbing up and down, and wincing, and setting my teeth and crushing forward" (22).

He recalls memories of New York, a walk through Woolworth's Store, a visit to Coney Island in Brooklyn, where a life-sized wooden cow gives milk for five cents a glass, and a trip to Central Park, in Manhattan, where he watches a man pet a squirrel:

> A squirrel with his forepaws on the man's necktie, and his hind paws on his chest, nipping a nut from the proud man's lips (140).

He recalls his 1904 visit to New York, where he saw the boroughs' Italian and Sicilian puppet theaters, whose colorful marionettes, "fair-haired ladies and Knights and Saracens," tromped and clashed, banged and died in fighting heaps—much in the manner of Yeats's own Miniature Theatre spectacles (152).

In *Sligo*, Yeats last recalls old memories of the circus, of great processions of bandwagons, and of foals running among the people through the streets of hundreds of country towns. He sees the world through the eyes of the foal, and wonders about the memories of the foal; "knowing green fields and rings and tents in them," and "different sets of memories, memories of sights, of smells, of things they touch with those tender lips of theirs" so at variance with the life, and memories, of a dray, or working horse (155). Jack Yeats brought a perspective to his paintings that allowed him to make the land as important as the figures he set upon it. He applied the same perspective principle to his novels. Not since *Black Beauty* had there been such a celebration of equine sensibility as that in *Sligo*. But Yeats's intention was to communicate the emotional experience of any given moment, in any way he could, whether in writing or in paintings. The glorious excitement of the horse in *Freedom* (1947), its fiery red-orange mane, its high stride across the rich green country, the strand in the background, and Uncle George Pollexfen, cane in hand, looking on, contrasts with another kind of excitement, in *My Beautiful, My Beautiful!* (1953), where the figure of the Arab, distraught at the thought of giving up his most prized possession, seems to merge into the outline of the horse's shoulder. Yeats expresses the same emotional excitement in *Sligo*, in his description of the circus horses with whom he had the greatest sympathy:

> It must be rather dismal for yourself having to make a hearty effort along a broad green Avenue, between two black strips of people, with a ponderous-looking old gentleman, in a kind of a bridecake-top box, the only individual in sight (156).

In "jettisoning" his memories, Yeats freed himself from his past, and restored his creativity.

Yeats's greatest memory of all, though it was inherited, was of a free Ireland. Yeats concludes *Sligo* with a piece of ancient folk wisdom: to forbid the Irish their ancient claim to be free, one might "as well forbid the grasses from growing as they grow" (158). Yeats would not preach liberation for the Irish, but it was in every work of art he ever made, whether he acknowledged it or not. The moral structure of life was important to Yeats, according to Alan Denson, even though he would not preach it, and thought it missing in the work of Samuel Beckett.[67]

Beckett maintained, as late as November 1980, that his work dealt with Ireland and the Irish countryside. And he remained steadfastly loyal to the memory of his long-time friend, Jack Yeats. There was a period of time when Beckett was outraged that his countrymen did not acknowledge Jack Yeats's gifts, and it led Beckett to express sentiments regarding the Irish people that were unflattering (which led Deirdre Bair to conclude, incorrectly, that Beckett was opposed to any notion of being considered an "Irish" writer).[68] In a letter to Thomas MacGreevy, dated 31 January 1938, Beckett, presumably responding to an early draft of

MacGreevy's essay on Jack B. Yeats completed that same month, complained of his

> chronic inability to understand . . . a phrase like "The Irish People" or
> to imagine that it ever gave a fart in its corduroys for any form of art
> whatsoever, whether before the union or after, or that it was ever
> capable of any thought or act other than rudimentary thoughts and
> acts . . . or that it would ever care or know that there was once a
> painter in Ireland called Jack Butler Yeats.[69]

But that did not prevent him from writing about his country, in his first
published novel, *Murphy,* or in subsequent prose pieces and plays that he
produced in the 1940s. He remarked to John Kobler, in September
1971, on the reasons why Ireland had produced so many great writers
since the last half of the nineteenth century: "It's the priests and the
British. They have buggered us into existence. After all, when you are in
the last bloody ditch, there is nothing left but to sing."[70] In a letter of 21
June 1956, written while he was writing *Fin de Partie,* Beckett commented to Alan Schneider: "I'm in a ditch somewhere near the last
stretch and would like to crawl up on it."[71]

The most compelling reason to compare the works of Jack Yeats to
those of Samuel Beckett is the similarity of their treatment of a common
subject matter. The emotional excitement that flows from successive
feasts of old memories has not been sufficiently emphasized in the
production of Beckett's works. In his best works he summons his audience to participate in the excitement of the immediacy of the moment,
coupled to the memory of that experience's structure. In *Not I,* for
example, the playwright offers both an oral and an aural experience of
Mouth, babbling away in torrents of sound (every bit as powerful as
Yeats's "immodest spear heads"), and the silent Auditor, who, in a gesture of helpless compassion, raises and lowers his arms at four intervals.
The integration of form and process in a single work of art became
apparent in Yeats's later work, as it was apparent in Beckett's later work.
But in the 1930s the painter was still struggling for an articulation he
would find toward the end of World War II. In the 1930s he still had
more plays and novels to write to "jettison" the accumulated memories of
his seven decades.

Yeats described the process of understanding what a painting *means* in
his essay *Modern Art,* in 1922. The picture was the medium, through
which the artist communicated to the spectator:

> The artist tells you what the scene he painted looked like to him, also
> he tells you about it through himself, and if he has felt deeply what he

painted he will communicate what he felt to you, and you will stand
before the painted scene as the artist himself stood.[72]

Much less complicated than the printed word, paintings communicated
emotion directly to the viewer. In *Sligo,* Yeats "paints" pictures designed
to stir the memories of readers, in the same way as he stood before his
easel in his studio, and applied color to canvas. A coterie of "memory-
prints" begins with an image of "the Baron leaning out of his window, . . . one summer night," into a churchyard, where a startled black-
bird awakes and sings his song (93). The Baron, one of Yeats's "pseudo-
selves," allowed the artist to objectify himself into a series of "others," in
the same way that Beckett developed the pseudocouple, Mercier and
Camier, prototypes of the couple Molly and Moran, in his next novel,
and of the couple Vladimir and Estragon, in *En Attendant Godot.* In
Yeats's later works, the Baron and Bowsie stand in for their author. In
The Charmed Life, Yeats presents his philosophy of life through the
characters Mr. No Matter, philosopher and man of deep emotion, and
Bowsie, creature of great intuition, as they move through a country in a
manner reminiscent of Baron Munchausen. The tradition of developing
a dialectic of thesis and antithesis, as the basis of a work of art, in which
one creature espouses the emotion of the work, and the second, the
intellect, can be adapted to Beckett as well as to Yeats. Vivian Mercier and
David Hesla each wrote books on Beckett, with the dialectic framework
specifically in mind, and each text is convincing proof that the dialectic is
a sound basis from which to begin.[73] The important thing to note,
however, is what takes place in the interstices of the frame, as the reader/
spectator is summoned to participate in the creative process as the artist
himself did.

A catalog of the pictures in the *Sligo* gallery would fill too many pages
of text; it covers nineteen pages of the 1930 publication, but there is one
image that sticks. Yeats describes a shop window, with the same care as he
detailed his pictures:

> A green glass bottle with half a dozen of peggy's legs in it, three apples,
> and a large-match-box in a very small shop in a narrow street in a
> country town are all in their places from conscious instinct (123).

This is the setting for Beckett's *The Unnamable,* who feels "the cang, the
flies, the sawdust under my stumps, the tarpaulin of my skull . . ." or, is
"stuck like a sheaf of flowers in a deep jar, its neck flush with my mouth,
on the side of a quiet street near the shambles," and knows no one, no I,
no me, but words "I can't go on, I'll go on."[74] The interstices are never
more apparent, in language, than in this work, which Maurice Blanchot

described as not quite a nonbook, but "something more than a book; perhaps . . . a movement from which all books derive, that point which always ruins the work, the point of perpetual unworkableness with which the work must maintain an increasingly *initial* relation or risk becoming nothing at all."[75] The ultimate fact of this creature, the unnamable, composed solely of words, is determined by the reader, who is placed in the position of the creator, the source of words itself:

> I'm in words, made of words, others' words, what others, the place too, the air, the walls, the floor, the ceiling, all words, the whole world is here with me, I'm the air, the walls, the walled-in one, everything yields, opens, ebbs, flows, like flakes . . . wherever I go I find me, leave me, go towards me, come from me, nothing ever but me . . . (386).

Every word is true, if the reader has the eyes to see.

The form of waiting, playing, speaking, conceiving, is the meaning, as Beckett noted in an addendum to *Watt:*

> Who may tell the tale
> . . . .
> of the world's woes?
> Nothingness
> in words enclose?[76]

The trilogy of novels that followed *Watt*—*Molloy, Malone Dies,* and *The Unnamable*—develop Watt's methods of interpreting events, to the point at which there is a complete transformation, not only of the event, but of the seeker of the event itself. As no symbols are involved, the moment is evanescent, as Watt demonstrates in the last moments of the novel:

> The feet, following each other in rapid and impetuous succession, were flung, the right foot to the right, the left foot to the left, as much outwards as forwards, with the result that, for every stride of say three feet in compass, the ground gained did not exceed one (226).

The description is that of Watt's own "headlong tardigrade," the figure of death advancing on the living, or the principle of regeneration, begun anew, as a portion of the old Watt departs. Watt, transformed into Arsene, transformed into Arthur, becomes Moran searching for Malone, searching for Molloy. Somewhere in the moment of transformation, when one image loses identity, and another gains identity, Beckett seeks a trace of the ancient paradox of being that defies encasement, and exists only in form.

The kinship of generation and regeneration in *Molloy* begins as the narrator, in an advanced state of decomposition, speaks from his mother's bed. Images of two men, one tall and the other short—a pseudocouple, in fact, derived from Yeats's work—leave town to advance across the terrain of the narrator's mindscape. Each wears a topcoat. "A" turns back and meets "C" in a dip in the landscape. "A" returns to town, while "C" continues on his way, into the countryside, "like someone trying to fix landmarks in his mind" (9). From this humble beginning near a crumbling cattlemarket, Molloy discovers his name, and begins to relate the "whole ghastly business" of life for what it is, "senseless, speechless, issueless misery" (22, 13). James White noted that Jack Yeats gave more serious thought, in the early thirties, to the idea of the finality of life.[77] As supporting evidence, he cited a passage from *The Deathly Terrace:*

> There is always coming nearer the day, when the last pullable leg will be pulled. A poet has shown us the sadness of the last man, the hangman with no-one in the world left to pull his legs. But I see another picture of the last man looking with desolated eyes searching for the last leg but two, just to pull it, and his mind will be brimming with splendid schemes for leg pulling—too late, and he could not stoop to pull his own leg.[78]

But White did not put the emphasis in the right place. Yeats was not concerned with finality, but with the transitoriness of people's impressions of the finiteness of life. Everything is process and change, or interpretation of the moment. The generation and regeneration of *Molloy* derived from Yeats's work of the twenties and thirties, and found confirmation in Erwin Schrödinger's analysis of the dynamics of life, *What is Life?*, a copy of which Beckett gave to his uncle, Dr. Gerald Beckett, in 1946:

> Everything that is going on in Nature means an increase of the entropy of the part of the world where it is going on. Thus a living organism continually increases its entropy—or, as you may say, produces positive entropy—and thus tends to approach the dangerous state of maximum entropy, which is death.[79]

Life is an expression of relative death. The equilibrium between positive and negative entropy comes into being at the moment of conception. Until the organism ceases to function, entropy accumulates. Nowhere can an individual escape containment by entropy, nor can an individual reside in a virtual realm of the mind that knows no processes but the perpetual rise and fall of forms, except in the re-creation of memory forms. The Baron and Bowsie find joy in memory in the picture gallery in *Sligo;* Molloy and his small coterie of friends, who comprise the nuclear material of regeneration, find the same joy:

> I listen and the voice is of a world collapsing endlessly, a frozen world, under a faint untroubled sky, enough to see by, yes, and frozen too. And I hear it murmur that all wilts and yields, as if loaded down. . . . For what possible end to these wastes where true light never was, nor any upright thing, nor any true foundation . . . a world at an end, in spite of appearances, its end brought it forth, ending it began, is it clear enough? (40)

Beckett's relationship to his work was apparent from the beginning. Jack Yeats and Beckett differ in their emphasis on the interpretation of their continua of forms: Yeats's characters are filled with "splendid schemes" for enduring; Beckett's creatures are aghast at the thought of their "senseless misery." It becomes, in the end, a question of tastes or, as Pim remarks in Beckett's *How It Is,* a question of screams:

> and this business of a procession no answer this business of a procession yes never any procession no nor any journey no never any Pim no nor any Bom no never anyone no only me no answer only me yes so that was true yes it was true about me yes and what's my name no answer WHAT's MY NAME screams good[80]

A note in the *Partisan Review* in 1976 suggested that Beckett's writing created the sensation of entry into "a posthumous universe, in some geography dreamed up by a demon," a world stripped of everything, following the end of some cosmic epoch.[81] In the manner of conventional literary criticism, E. M. Cioran, the reviewer, emphasized the final product of Beckett's writing. But Beckett achieved much more in this work than Cioran allowed in his criticism. The sense of being a "living writer," a student of the creative process, imbued Beckett's best work, as it did Jack Yeats's creations. Nowhere was the "immodest spearhead" of the latter artist more apparent than in his plays of the 1930s.

The Deathly Terrace, one of the important plays Jack Yeats wrote during that period, remained unpublished until 1971, when it was published in a posthumous edition of his collected works edited by Robin Skelton. The play concerns the fantasy world of film, where death is part of everyday production; but Yeats points out that the reverse is likewise true: life is part of the death that is everyday reality. In *The Deathly Terrace* the two ideas intersect. The theme thus created, of which Beckett made prolific use in his own work, recurred often in Yeats's plays. Skelton summarized Yeats's plays with reference to that theme:

In every one there is talk of death and in seven of them a death, or a presumed death, is central to the pattern the play makes. In half of them a central character is a much travelled stranger whose arrival on the scene sets off a chain of events that appears to have its own interior logic. . . . In most of them we are given the strong impression that the characters are caught up in a pattern of destiny which they recognize only dimly, if at all.[82]

In his plays, Yeats also used practical jokes that caught both victim and joker unaware. Moreover, he allowed his principal characters to adopt an ironic perspective, a posture that is not so readily apparent in his paintings. But Yeats described his values—his sense of the importance of emotion and of commitment to a goal, his love of twilight and pictur- esque sunsets—equally well in paint and in language. His descriptions of the characters in his plays recall the miniature theater of the first decades of the twentieth century, when Yeats and John Masefield, "Poet and Painter of the Sea," produced juvenile drama of piracy and high dud- geon, and sailed toy boats on the Gara stream behind Cashlauna Shelmiddy.[83]

The question Yeats was accustomed to ask viewers of his paintings, "Now, what do you think it means?" is implicit in the action of the first scene of *The Deathly Terrace:* Nardock enters, revolver in hand, and advances three paces toward the balustrade, where he stops and places the revolver under his chin. At that moment Andy Carmichael springs from a boat and struggles with Nardock. The gun goes off, Nardock falls to the ground, his hand pressed to his side, and Sheila Delgarvay, a film goddess, moves into view singing from her perch in a rowboat. Is the audience watching a suicide thwarted, a filming sequence of a suicide thwarted, a suicide thwarted by a film crew, or a filming sequence that became a suicide by accident or by design? Is Nardock dead or alive, in fact, in fiction? The only certainty is the melodramatic climax of Sheila's song:

> *Sheila.* Row brothers row, the stream runs fast
> The rapids are near, and the daylight's past!

(95)

Within the dramatic context, Sheila's song appears to have reference both to the time of day and to the passage of life from the man on the balustrade. Nardock has been a great drinker and has suffered business reversals. Andy tells Sheila that Nardock has been paid off in wine and "native paper" to act the part of a stiff for the scene of "the unwanted dead by the sea . . ." (96). The irony is immediately clear; if Nardock is acting the part of a dead man, everything is fine, but if he is dead as the result of an accidental shooting, he is indeed one of the unwanted dead. Meanwhile, Sheila gives instructions to her film crew for the shooting of her next scene in "The Slicer," the main character of which, she tells them, "has the secret of my birth hidden in a place only known to himself" (96).

The shooting of a film scene, juxtaposed with the shooting (with real or fake bullets) of a character who may or may not have been an actor in the film, is simultaneously juxtaposed with the image of a film director who presents life as everyday reality, life as imagined reality, and life as rehearsal:

> *Sheila.* It's like life here. One moment the glad sunshine another moment night, with its velvet pall, palls, falls, over all. *(Shivers.)* Ah death where is thy sting.
>
> (97)

The stage light is just sufficient to make the filming sequence plausible. As the scene on film concludes, reality, in the form of postrehearsal, everyday reality, resumes: Nardock has not moved; the members of the film company realize that they have filmed a real suicide, not a reel suicide. Death has intruded on life, as life intrudes on death in films. Sheila's only question to Andy is whether the shooting was a suicide or an accident:

> *Andy. (to Sheila)* As God's my judge, Del, I found him with his revolver under his chin and when I struggled to get it from him, it got down by his side and blew through him.
>
> (98)

In a scene that beggars Pirandello's *Six Characters in Search of an Author,* spectators watch a film crew shoot a movie, but in fact watch real life, made accidentally into a movie, in which a real dead man takes the role of an actor. However, the irony of the situation quickly changes; as the sun sets, the characters leave the stage and the moon rises:

> *Nardock moves a little . . . stands up. . . .*
>
> (99)

A dead man, playing a live man playing dead, has come back to life. Simple irony, transformed into dramatic irony, becomes even more ironic as Nardock stages his fake suicide, complete with note, dabs of blood, footprints on the balustrade, gun laid carefully to one side, and hat tossed into the water. A dead man, playing a live man playing dead, has come back to life to stage his own death himself on the terrace, though he really exits up a cliff path. The act is a *tour de force* of theatrical reality in conflict with lifelike illusion, and a vivid reenactment of life in death and death in life, onstage or offstage. But even at the height of the pathos Yeats adds his own brand of humor: Nardock writes his last message in his own blood. Because there is not enough, he adds to it from a bottle of red ink, and finishes his job of "Impresario of Despair." In a sunset or a moonrise anything is possible. Beckett learned the lesson; in *Godot*, at precisely that twilight moment, a messenger from Godot arrives.

At the end of act 1 of *The Deathly Terrace*, Yeats develops the dramatic irony; he lets the viewer know exactly what Nardock is doing, in contrast to the opening scene, in which he hides Nardock's intentions from the viewer. In the first act, real life is reel life. In the second act, reel life is real life. Sheila watches some of the day's "takes":

> *Sheila.* I find this bit a bit low brow. If I had my absolute way there would be nothing in this picture but the pure, straight, noble, refining drama of life seen once and seen nobly acted by a natural nobility like you and I and all of us.

> (100)

Sheila's character seems to be that of an imperious cinema actress— shallow, self-centered, willful, and inconsiderate. The real life of Sheila's reel-life fantasies is less real than the fantasy of being real on a reel of film. Suddenly, Nardock appears in the screening room, and real life takes on a new luster. Yeats concludes the act with a chase, Nardock escapes from the area, and Andy pursues him in earnest. Sheila screams and faints, exhibiting the first real emotion of her life.

Act 3 is a self-contained unit with its own internal logic. The play of truth and reality, fantasy and illusion, death in life, and life in death that permeate the first two acts almost disappears in the final scenes of the play, in which Yeats returns to another of his favorite themes, the projection of his own character into the two halves of a pseudocouple.

During an elaborate picnic lunch in act 3, Andy and Nardock disclose their respective pasts. Because of a change in his personal fortunes, Nardock has altered his original suicide plan. No longer the despondent man who foresaw no future, he has become an independently wealthy man. However, his brush with death has given him an idea, and an opportunity that he does not want to forgo. "Everybody isn't my fellow man," Nardock reminds Andy. Now that he is missing, "supposed dead, certainly a case of suicide," no one will bother him or the house of his deadly sin (105).

> *Nardock.* We will take our ease here, read the papers and laugh gently at the world, I will re-name the house—SHARK's BELLY HALL—. . . .

(105)

Nardock has decided to legally *reconstruct* himself, and to spend his days with his close friends on the terrace. For entertainment, they will tell each other their life stories. Nardock begins: "I have been a wandering, gambling orator, speaking when I was not listened to and picking often the subjects of my discourse at haphazard like sweep numbers from a hat" (105). His past failure, ridiculed and ignored, has been transformed by success, a comfortable income, and a *chance encounter* with Andy. Memory and chance, the elements with which life must be reconstructed or constructed, are the subjects Yeats treats in the final act of *The Deathly Terrace*. Nardock finds that he has values, and he expounds them to Andy in graphic terms:

> *Nardock.* I have been among the gales of the mountain tops, and among the lacey rollers of the beaches. I have journeyed over all the worlds, either in body or in spirit and sometimes in both. . . . Time has no meaning to me. I am embedded in time, and floating in eternity. I have seen the Peruvians in pigtails and the Chinese in kilts. I have gone down into the heart of the volcano, and placed my hand where the pulse should be and called on it to shake. And I have stepped from the fragment of one star to the nucleuary [*sic*] fragment of another, and I have looked at myself so doing. . . .
>
> (106)

Nardock expresses the artist's sensibility, his function as a conduit for the emotional experience of sensation. Nardock's words come from Jack Yeats's mouth. "Myself so doing" has more than a double meaning, as the artist demonstrated via pseudocouples in his novels, and in scenes in his paintings—*Glory* (1952), *The Last Voyage* (1946) and *The Showground Revisited* (1950)—in which he included portraits of himself or his counterparts.

Nardock speaks of "continuosity," which George Bernard Shaw and others called "Life Force," as the organizing principle of his career:

> *Nardock.* I had invented continuosity and thrown away stepping stones. . . . For a moment of every day or every age I bit into the crust of the rainbow, and that is only a figure of speech for what I bit into. . . . There is no such thing as redundancy . . . because if there is too much of anything at any moment, we only hold it over in the heel of the fist and later link it up with the coming event, and so linked together we get continuosity, impetuosity and exuberance.
>
> (109)

Through Nardock, Yeats gives his spectators the full flavor of what he had called years earlier the "living ginger of life." Nardock embodies the

principle of organizing experience that is process itself, in all its immediacy and transcendency.

Andy is the other half of Jack Yeats, the pseudocouple, and the artist's
credo. Andy is pure chance; Nardock is pure process; chance (luck) and
process (continuosity) join to form Jack Yeats's philosophy. At Andy's
birth, his father luckily did not bet on a touted horse that failed to win:

> *Andy.* But he decided that I must be dedicated to luck, that chance should rule
> my life not premeditation. So when at the age of five years, my education
> having got beyond my mother's powers, I chanced to spell out the word
> "School" . . . I was taken to board school. . . .
>
> (109)

Andy tells of the time that he lost his shoe, by accident, across from
Dowton College, and he was enrolled there. Five years later, he says, the
school burned down, by accident, and his school days came to an end.
Andy says he delivered newspapers, and by chance, vastly increased
business at his father's newsagent's shop, because customers who failed to
get their paper delivered, came to the store to buy additional sundries.
After a long series of chance encounters, Andy enters the employ of
Sheila Delgarvay, and rescues Nardock from suicide. Now the two creatures of fortune—Andy, who believes in luck, and Nardock, who marvels
in sensation—are prepared to enjoy their lives together.

Andy looks for "sharks" through the binoculars; sharks are the un-
natural influences that "city-folk" use against mankind. Sharks can be
many things—they can even be Turks who mix explosive sherbets to blow
up natives (105). Andy sights a crab boat on the horizon, as well as the
ever-present sharks:

> *Andy.* Yes, they are basking about closing in, chewing
>
> (111)

The scene presages *Fin de Partie,* in which Clov turns his telescope on the
world, in another deathly terrace:

> *Clov.* (. . . *picks up the telescope, turns it on auditorium.*)
>   I see . . . a multitude . . . in transports . . . of joy. . . .
> *Hamm.* Look at the ocean!
> *Clov.* Never seen anything like that!
> *Hamm.* What? A sail? A fin? Smoke?
> *Clov.* The light is sunk.[84]

In *The Deathly Terrace,* the sky, too, has sunk, as the sun sinks lower on
the horizon. The moment allows Nardock, who is never at a loss for
words, to compose a breathtaking image of twilight:

> *Nardock.* Some people are afraid of stylish sky. Nature drawing up its embattled and highly colored wonders to proclaim that when it comes to glory, profundity, high spots, tiger stripes, and whirlygigging refulgences the palette of the painter . . . is but half a half brother to the towering jars of luminosity spilling themselves through the cracks in the firmaments and sweeping to the very feet of the observor, standing bare foot waiting for the flood to lave his ten toes.
>
> (113)

Pozzo's celebrated apostrophe to the firmament in *Waiting for Godot* is a ghost of its literary forebear:

> *Pozzo.* . . . . What is there so extraordinary about it? Qua sky. It is pale and luminous like any sky at this hour of the day. *(Pause.)* In these latitudes. *(Pause.)* When the weather is fine. *(Lyrical.)* An hour ago . . . after having poured forth even since *(he hesitates, prosaic)* say ten o'clock in the morning *(lyrical)* tirelessly torrents of red and white light it begins to lose its effulgence, to grow pale. . . .[85]

Yeats did not incorporate his wonderful description of the sunset into his text as well as Beckett did in *Godot*. Nor did he achieve the tautness of meaning or the dramatic sense of the lines as effectively as did the later playwright. But Yeats discovered and used the raw materials that enticed the mind's eye of his viewers. His "painterly eye" fell everywhere. And he delighted in the display of its continuosity, its impetuosity, and its exuberance, in writing and speaking words; in singing songs in Nardock's croaky voice, "There's a land that is fairer than this" (112); and in painting word pictures for the stage:

> *Nardock.* I talked all day to a fat man on an Arab horse crossing a desert and I was hanging to his stirrup, and, not knowing the language I spoke, he thought I praised his horse, and when we reached his camp he gave me the horse.

The image in Nardock's speech is that of *My Beautiful, My Beautiful!* (1953), which Yeats painted in honor of Caroline Norton's poem "The Arab's Farewell to his Steed."[86] Nardock describes the ride on the back of the Arab's horse, which is ridden "over the ridge pole of the world":

> Ridge pole is the place for philosophy, the essential essence of philosophy drifting upward through the hoofs of the horse, through the horse's body along the horse's ridge pole, into my body and mounting so to my brain.
>
> (112)

The painting shows a man whose head lies along the plane of the horse's "ridge pole," contemplating the loss of his most prized possession. Nardock's croaking song in *The Deathly Terrace* is a match for the Krapp's quavering voice in *Krapp's Last Tape:* both have pretensions to philosophy. Nardock believes that there were important moments in his past: "I felt that one quiver of my eyelashes and I would be master of understanding knowing all things." Krapp is also a believer in the absolutes of factual experience:

> *Krapp.* . . . memorable night in March, at the end of the jetty, in the howling wind, never to be forgotten, when suddenly I saw the whole thing. The vision, at last.[87]

But thirty years later, the vision is so insignificant that an impatient Krapp cuts off the recording, without even waiting for a sentence break:

> *Krapp.* . . . for the miracle that . . . the belief I had been going on all my life, namely—*(Krapp switches off impatiently, winds tape forward, switches on again)*— . . . in reality my most—*(Krapp curses, switches off, winds tape forward, switches on again)*—. . . light of the understanding and the fire—*(Krapp curses louder, switches off. . . .)*
>
> (20–21)

What is significant, and memorialized, in this scene is an emotional memory of lying with a young woman in a punt on a river:

> *Tape.* We lay there without moving. But under us all moved, and moved us, gently, up and down, and from side to side.
>
> (27)

Genuine emotion and commitment is everything for Yeats's Nardock; in the end, it is everything for Beckett's Krapp, who stares before him, wordless, as the foolishness of a tape made three decades earlier plays to its conclusion. Krapp's rejection of happiness and love for "the fire in me now" is no more a solution than are Krapp's tapes. Nardock needs Andy. Krapp's tapes are not enough. An exuberance of feeling needs a great deal of luck to get through life safely. At the critical moment of Nardock's life, Andy Carmichael comes to the rescue; in *Godot*, Didi and Gogo serve each other's purposes, as do Pozzo and Lucky. In *Fin de Partie*, Hamm and Clov are a similar pseudocouple. But no one comes to Krapp. He has only one dimension to explore. The alternative, of course—to marry the woman, to have a large family and a menagerie— was unacceptable, as Beckett has himself commented. A tape recorder is hardly a substitute for a genuine exchange of emotions, unless "memory pictures" are the first and only goal of life. Krapp has spent years recording his life on tape, summarizing its intellectual contents, and jettisoning its emotional values. In the end he realizes that what he had wanted to preserve, the intellectual contents, are nothing, but that what he had wanted to jettison, the emotional values, are everything. Reconstituted memory is as important for Beckett's characters as it is for Yeats's characters, and is a measure of the mind's underside.

The last scene of *The Deathly Terrace* restores Sheila Delgarvay to the action, and ties off the real/reel knots that were strung together in the first two acts. It also allows Yeats to engage in another of his favorite enterprises—leg pulling—which Nardock had explained earlier to Andy:

> *Nardock.* A poet has shown us the sadness of the last man, the hangman with no one in the world left to pull his legs. But I see another picture of the last man looking with desolated eyes searching for the last leg but two, just to pull it, and his mind will be brimming with splendid schemes for leg pulling—too late, and he could not stoop to pull his own leg.
>
> (108)

One final scene of the film remains to be shot. Nardock, ever the exuberant exponent of the goodness of life, is determined not to disappoint the film star. Real life comes to the aid of reel life, as it did, unintentionally, in the first act's staged double suicide—Nardock writes a note on a visiting card, "I cannot live any more, therefore I depart." Andy follows suit, "I go, I step off here" (117). Two shots are fired in the air, the business of the shoes and the footprints of act 1 is repeated, and the men exit up a bank beside the balustrade.

Sheila Delgarvay appears at the top of the balustrade following a very specific stage direction, *"A WAIT,"* and change of lighting, *"Sun sinks more towards the west and the edge of the sea"* (117). She reads the two cards and protests that her two lovers have died "for love of me" (since neither could bear to live in the knowledge that the other would win her hand). She begins to pace back and forth, searching for words to describe the loss of love, the sunset, the tropical twilight, and the ineffable moment in which she finds herself. At last, inspired, she bids her farewell, to the pits, the stalls, the gods, and the dress circle:

> *Sheila.* DELGARVAY THE IRRESISTIBLE
> DELGARVAY THE GRAND
> DELGARVAY—*(here she sees her rope going. . . .)*
>
> (119)

The irony of the moment is topped by the figure of the star, the actress, upstaged by the rope from her row boat, that slowly disappears. A bad melodrama comes to an end. As the sun disappears, the memory of Nardock's celebration of the sunset is echoed in Sheila's coarse dismissal of its natural beauty:

> *Sheila.* Ah so, flop, ends the tropic day. That gets me. *(She sinking on the ground*

with her back against the balustrade, takes the yellow rose out of her hair and twiddles it as the curtain goes down.)

(119)

Yeats had, of course, prepared his audience for this ending. He had chosen Nardock to comment on the function of language, ineffective though it may be:

> *Nardock.* Ah words, I often do talk about them and with them too. It's a superstition, using words for speech, and I suppose the day will come when it'll be found it, like most superstitions. . . . When all speech dies at last the sniff superior will be the last comment, because of course you can sniff flowers silently if you like.

(114)

Sheila Delgarvay, on the contrary, does not even possess the good sense of Nardock's epigram: when speech ends for her, she twiddles, rather than sniffs, her flower. There is no art in real reel, nor in her real life. There is only shallow make-believe. Nardock's practical joke, a mock suicide, neutralizes all the pretensions of the melodrama, which is itself an ironic statement of life's real values.

The practical joke plays a central role in the three plays Jack Yeats published in 1933—*The Old Sea Road, Rattle,* and *Apparitions*—under the general title *Apparitions.* In these short works, leg-pulling, of the brand discussed by Nardock in *The Deathly Terrace,* becomes high art. Death becomes part of the game of life that makes leg-pulling possible. Skelton noted the link that Yeats made between death and the practical joke:

> The essence of the practical joke is the way it makes its victim feel insecure and unable to trust his eyes or his ears. It peoples his world with delusions; it takes his realities and proves them illusion. Thus it might be said that Death is the greatest practical joker of all. In the midst of life we are in death; in the midst of reality we are insubstantial.[88]

The internal analysis is accurate. But what is of critical importance to the spectator is the ironic perspective of the playwright. At any moment in his plays, a practical joke may be played on the sensibilities of the viewer, as well as on the characters in the piece. Until the final curtain comes down, the action depicted can never be certified as real or as illusion, either within the context of the play, or within the mind's eye of the viewer. "Now, what do you think?" is a key question in Jack Yeats's plays, as it is in his paintings. Process, once again, is the essential bond between artist and observer.

Yeats's artistic vision is immediately apparent in the stage directions for

The Old Sea Road, in which he asks that the sky, sea, and land be "brighter than the people" (142). As the play begins, a meadow lark sings overhead, and the faint sound of the surf breaking over rocks echoes in the distance. In the course of the day, the play, Yeats's *petit peuple* of Ireland talk as they pass along the old sea road, and take comfort in themselves, the sea, and the land around them. Laborer and teacher, ballad singer and postman, all find relationships to their environment that are relevant to everyday things:

> *Josephine.* Did you hear the bees buzzing about the heather? That's happy
> sound, Miss Julia. *(Turning to the sea)* There's the old sea, listen how he
> sounds.
> *Julia.* He makes a noise like a child that'd be eating stirabout.
> *Josephine.* Stirabout yourself, pupil and teacher will be late for school.[89]

The one exception is Ambrose Oldbury, known locally as the joker, and a man about whom the local inhabitants are wary:

> *Dolan.* He's standing now looking out over the ocean and plotting some
> mouldy old divilment. . . .
> *Nolan.* And now we'll get first whiff of whatever he's up to, the common
> omadhawn.
>
> (146)

But at nightfall an itinerant poet, who does not know Ambrose as the locals do, establishes an acquaintance with him. Oldbury complains to Michael of the Song that the folks do not appreciate a good practical joke, even when it is shown them: "What a genuis like me wants is a large canvas, as the saying is, to spread myself on, and by God I'll get it or die in the attempt" (155). The statement is ironic. Ambrose learns all there is to learn about practical jokes before the night is out. Once again, Yeats discusses leg-pulling, as he did in *The Deathly Terrace:*

> *Ambrose.* I'm only a second-hand leg-puller. I mean I'm second-hand at leg-
> pulling. I don't mean that the legs I pull are second-hand, if you get my
> meaning.
>
> (156)

On this occasion Ambrose has apparently burned all his money. But appearances are deceiving; only the top and bottom bills in the burned pile were bank notes. Everything else was newspaper.

Ambrose has always wanted to find a joke with four dimensions, but so far he has been unsuccessful. Tonight, however, he has two jokes left: one is to really burn all the money, which he does—"Naked I came and naked I go" (157). The second joke is:

Ambrose. I don't think you've seen even this joke.
  Never mind, we'll have a drink on it.

(157)

The two men drink, and die. In fact, the imbibers almost seem to be welcoming death. Each man takes a second drink to make sure the poison "trick" works:

Michael. (Taking another deep drink from the cup. . . .) So you think you've done
  the trick.
Ambrose. (Sinking on the bank beside Michael. . . .) I think I have.

The trick with four dimensions, a deadly trick, springs its own surprise on the spectators. Michael of the Song, poisoned to death by the Trickster, does not die cursing his murderer, but praising him:

Michael. Would it be any offence if I said a prayer for you?

(158)

At this moment, an attentive audience experiences an emotion quite different than it might have thought possible. Ambrose has played a last joke on a "benighted people." The ecstasy of death—when creatures again become part of the sky, the sea, the land, the song of the meadowlark, and the roar of the lacey rollers of the beaches—is also a part of Jack Yeats's continuosity, impetuosity, and exuberance—terrible though it may seem. The last scene of the play takes place on the following morning, when Michael and Ambrose are discovered. Police are summoned, and each villager expresses shock at the sight of the dead bodies. Then all sit listlessly in their places. A silence descends on the crowd, broken only by muted expressions of the passing of "great creatures" like Michael, "a handsome man . . . a lovely man," and the meadowlark's song. The last practical joke but one has yet to be played, by death, the last leg-puller.

The title of the second of the three plays—*Rattle*—derives from the death rattle of a family business, Gardeyne & Golback. It is also a death rattle of a man, Ted Golback. The play contains another sunset, and another picnic supper in an exotic clime, both reminiscent of those in *The Deathly Terrace.* There are also passages that remind the reader of the resemblance between the Yeats/Pollexfen family shipping business and the fictional Gardeyne & Golback concern. References to the death of Ted Golback's father in the state of Pakawana ten years earlier coincide with the death of John Butler Yeats, in New York in 1921, approximately ten years before the play was written. And there are amusing speeches by William Gardeyne, brother of the deceased husband who married

Ted's sister (sufficiently removed from both the Golbacks and the Yeatses), that recall the excesses of sentiment in which W. B. Yeats was prone to indulge:

> *John.* . . . if we dwell any longer on a settling-up of some kind, we will find ourselves manufacturning cobwebs in our brains.
> *William.* Never while reason holds her sway!
> *Christie.* Good for you, William.[90]

During a subsequent discussion of John Gardeyne's business perspicuity, the widow remonstrates with her brother:

> *Christie.* People with second sight should only see roses.

William's *non sequitur* leaves everyone in stony silence:

> *William.* Scratch no more fair heart, scratch no more!
> *Alec.* You're thinking of a thorn in the side.
> *William.* I don't think I was thinking of anything at all, if you asked me.
> *John.* Well, let us get on to business.

(183)

The family even discusses all the possible symbolic associations a broken packing case with the letters "P. E. A. C." written on it can have for them. But the final act of the play concerns Ted's investiture in the Order of the Wave, Cloak and Collar, and his visit to Pakawana, where he receives his inheritance:

> (*. . . there is a rattle of shots on the right and Ted falls forward on his face. . . .*)

(204)

Ted forgives all, makes out a will leaving half of everything to Pakawana and the rest to his relations—in whatever proportion they themselves shall decide—and dies (205). The rattle at the door that announced the opening scene becomes the death rattle of the family business, which leads in turn to the rattle of gunfire and the death rattle of Ted Golback. The game of words, of meanings, and of leg-pulling goes on.

Apparitions is about the town of Pullickborough, and the economic downturn of its principal business, the Little Bridge Hotel, after the appearance of ghosts has frightened away its paying guests. The main thrust of the play is the elaborate joke Charlie Charles, the village barber, plays on the townsmen. He conducts a séance to discover the reason that the specter is haunting the hotel. Six of the most prominent men of the community are invited to participate. When the lights are turned off, the ghost makes his appearance. When the lights are turned on, all the visiting dignitaries' hair has turned white. The barber explains the situation to his hapless victims:

> *Charles.* Why, you bunch of old fools, don't you know you're Brave men. The Spirit was willing, but the coloring matter supplied by nature was weak and disappeared when you wanted. But I'll show you how Art can put right the mistakes of nature.[91]

Charles shows each man a black shaving brush, and promises to paint each man's hair raven black. Charles has played the trick on the townsmen for revenge because they had slighted his foster-father, who was the town barber before him. But the real trick is obvious when Charles, pretending to paint each head of hair black, instead paints each with red ink. Each man sees the other's red hair and says nothing, so each one is guilty of leg-pulling. Finally, draped in antimacassars, the chagrined men creep out of the hotel and board an open car for their trip home. The last apparition but one, Jimmy the waiter, enters with the ghost costume. He leads a tall, willowy young woman carrying a typewriter. As the last scene ends, Jimmy begins to describe the indignities he had to put up with from "bull-necked, ignorant, inaesthetic clods" (139). As the secretary types his dictation, the last apparition becomes apparent: the events of the first scene come next in Jimmy's monologue. Jack Yeats has been poking fun at the pretensions of the Anglo-Irish of his country; Pullickborough becomes "Pull-leg borough" indeed!

All three plays reveal Yeats's predilections for dramatic irony, and for staging practical jokes that neutralize all pretensions. They also reveal his predilection for the subject of life in death and death in life. They show his particular fondness for moments of transition, sunset, and moonrise when all things are possible. Above all, they demonstrate his belief that the emotional values of life and the commitment to its goals—continuosity, impetuosity, and exuberance—are everything. In eighty-six years he never tired of repeating his message.

6
Stages of an Image: No Symbols Where None Intended

Summer 1945 I had a walk with Jack Yeats. I had not seen him
for five years. Did he feel his work had changed and in what
way? He finally replied: "Less—(long pause)—conscious."

—Samuel Beckett

THE themes Jack Yeats developed in his plays and novels of the late
twenties and early thirties—continuosity, impetuosity, and exuberance—
represented his personal as well as his artistic maturation. But beyond his
ironic perspective, his love of the practical joke, his creation of characters
who expressed life in death in everything they touched, and his predilection for twilight settings that approximated that creative process itself,
Yeats achieved an innovation in his painting in 1936 that changed the
nature of the last and greatest period of his art. He discovered a means
of portraying freedom in his work that had never been attempted
before. He would summarize the process in an ethereal metaphor that
could be considered his epitaph. But he described its genesis in more
earthly terms to T. de Vere White, who recorded his conversation with
Yeats in his book, *A Fretful Midge*. The painter explained, in the semi-
chant of the ballad singers of Sligo:

> I have travelled all my life without a ticket: and, therefore, I was never
> to be seen when Inspectors came round because then I was under the
> seats. It was rather dusty, but I used to get the sun on the floor
> sometimes. When we are asked about it all in the end, we who travel
> without tickets, we can say with that vanity which takes the place of
> self-confidence: even though we went without tickets we never were
> commuters.[1]

The image of the noncommuter, the "clochard sans billet" (tramp without a ticket)—of whom Beckett's Watt is an excellent example—represented for Yeats a denial of the tyranny of the middle class. Such a
disavowal had special meaning for a man from Ireland. The division of

the country had left deep wounds that created ugly scars along class lines. It was not simply a matter of loyalty to, or rebellion against, England. Nor was it merely upper-class Ireland versus lower-class Ireland. The problem was that of the Irish middle class versus the Irish peasant class. Pyle described the feelings of the deeply idealistic artist:

> To him the Free Staters were middle-class, while the Republicans represented all that was noble and free. His patriotism had nothing to do with war or the practicalities of the situation, but was rather a dedication to perfect life, without blemish, where no man was subject to another.[2]

Ordinary politics played no part in Yeats's art; only politics that did not interfere with any other man's freedom entered his work.

In his prescient study of Yeats's work, O'Doherty suggested another aspect of the ticketless traveler who, he argued, was the stereotypical native Irishman who escaped conflict through constant travel. The artist, in turn, dignified the stereotype, making heroes "of those of no fixed abode—those vagrants in motion as much across the country's imaginative as well as physical landscape."[3] The heritage of Beckett's tramps is no less clear than that of Yeats's figures, who escape the tyranny of the Pozzos of their world:

> The patriot on the run is a romantic figure like those other outsiders approved in the romantic cannon—the madman, the criminal, the clown and acrobat . . . all paradigms for a soul the bourgeoisie felt they had lost. Hence Yeats's repertory . . . of tinkers, gypsies, sailors, circus performers, actors, travellers, tramps, jockeys, gamblers.[4]

The clowns and the madmen of Beckett's literature—Murphy, Belacqua, Vladimir, Estragon, Krapp, the painter of *Fin de Partie*, Pim, Watt, and the creatures of the trilogy of novels—share a heritage shaped by another hand. Their common legator was Jack Yeats, who described his artistic journey to freedom in 1936:

> I have painted the other day a new subject for me—a rose. I painted the rose alive, and then followed it into the ante room of the Rose's Shadow Land, and painted another little panel of it departing. . . .[5]

Yeats felt that he had traveled from objectivity to complete subjectivity, where he found he had become a channel through which all the experience and emotion of his life could be poured into his paintings. He realized his sudden arrival with astonishing vigor and freedom.

The personal symbol he used to explore and explain his new habitat was the rose, the emblem of all that was pure and free and noble. The personal symbol Beckett chose was Watt, a visitor to the house of Knott, deep in Ireland. Watt, a unique tardigrade, moved with a singular gait, a kind of headlong lunge in a straight line that required his torso and opposing leg to be flung at right angles to his intended destination, in a crablike motion, until he gained some ground. In part 4 of the novel (which is really part 3), Watt sees another figure, much like himself, on the road:

> The arms did not end at the hands, but continued, in a manner that Watt could not determine, to near the ground. The feet, following each other in rapid and impetuous succession, were flung, the right foot to the right, the left foot to the left, as much outwards as forwards, with the result that, for every stride of say three feet in compass, the ground gained did not exceed one.[6]

The humor of the image, which is that of Watt watching himself retreat from his self, or the antiself of his mind's eye retire from his conscious view, is finally clear when Watt notes that after half an hour's struggle, the "incomprehensible staffage . . . had made no more headway, than if it had been a millstone" (227). Beckett undertook his journey from objectivity to complete subjectivity with the same vigor as did Yeats, although his arrival meant containment, not freedom. Beckett's expression of what he characterized as "Gaelomania" demonstrated his genuine concern over the seemingly insoluble problems of his homeland.[7] Watt's gait is a parody of Yeats's free Irish, who walked the roads of their land. Watt's speech, in part 3 (that is, part 4, itself a parody of purposeful movement), with its recombinant inversion of words in sentences, letters in words, and sentences in paragraphs, is reported to the auditor as "so much Irish to me" (169). Jack Yeats was always a true celebrant of the people of Ireland; Beckett, on the contrary, used a more Joycean liturgy, and occasionally used darker images, harder words, and more acerbic wit.

Jack Yeats painted the rose, his symbol, as early as 1927, in *The Scene Painter's Rose*. James White reported that William Butler Yeats was "drawn to the rose for its esoteric significance in the eighteen-nineties."[8] Jack Yeats was more practical. He painted *A Rose Dying* (1936), *A Rose in a Basin* (1938), and then a series of rose pictures, *A Rose, A Dusty Rose*, and *A Dying Rose* (1938). Yeats's depiction of a subject that departed from the canvas—that, in effect, developed the dynamic evanescence of the stage in pictorial representation—signified a change in his personal life as well. He developed a certain indifference concerning the obscurity of his subject matter:

His friends observed this change of attitude in him. Not even his most regular visitors were shown new paintings until they appeared in exhibitions and he seemed quietly amused at the various interpretations which critics and collectors put on his subject matter.[9]

But he became increasingly concerned with the loneliness of the soul, and with the difficulty of illustrating or even expressing its actual process.

Yeats depicted the artist and the artist's inspiration obliquely in his 1943 painting *This Grand Conversation Was under the Rose*, which White described succinctly, but only partially, as a representation of the creative process:

> The girl with the whip in her hand from which the rose was suspended symbolized the muse and the clown seated in the tent represented the artist. The grand conversation was the lifetime encounter of the artist and his inspiration.[10]

The title of the work was that of a traditional Irish song that Yeats had illustrated for *A Broadsheet* of August 1903. In the artist's illustration, Napoleon, wearing a long green coat and the familiar black hat, rides a horse with a red saddle blanket and gestures to the crowd. The Irish ballad "This Grand Conversation Was under the Rose" describes Bonaparte's attempt to stir the people to war, in an effort to return the world to prosperity:

> Come, stir up a war, and the world will be flourishing—
> This grand conversation was under the rose.
> . . . .
> The Farm and Comedian would wish the great Bonaparte
> Was brought on the stage to act a new play.
> . . . .
> But the All-seeing Eye would not let him o'er the world run—
> This grand conversation was under the rose.[11]

Nineteen forty-three was a dark year in World War II. There is no reason to believe that the weeping, seated clown of Yeats's painting has not been restrained by the "All-seeing Eye" of the woman with the whip in her hand. The partially visible world is waiting, Napoleon is nowhere to be seen, and clowns do not ride horses. Yeats had moved quite beyond symbols, to a purely emotional statement of reality. The white face, painted lips, and stylized eyebrows of *The Clown among the People* (1932), which represented Yeats's memory picture of an Irish clown, Johnny Patterson, who performed in Athlone at the end of the nineteenth century, now reveal an isolated figure filled with remorse.[12] More than one interpretation is, however, possible. In the interplay of possibilities, the process of becoming—or retreating from meaning—had become paramount. Yeats used no symbols in his painting because he had moved beyond its intellectual components into the shadow land of objects that departed from sense, or arrived from the unconscious. His painting had become, in fact, less conscious.

Yeats soon transferred the singular insight into the creative process that he had discovered in his painting to his written work. His novel *The Amaranthers* was published in 1936 and reviewed by Samuel Beckett for *Dublin Magazine,* under the magazine's title, "An Imaginative Work!":

> There is no allegory. . . . There is no symbol . . . but . . . stages of an image. There is no satire. . . . The landscape is superb, radiant and alive, with its own life. . . . The end, the beginning, is among the hills, where imagination is not banned.[13]

In 1938, Yeats wrote another novel, *The Charmed Life,* in which he interpreted the opposite halves of his personality in two distinct characters, Mr. No Matter and Bowsie.[14] The characters derived from the rose paintings, in which images come and go in consciousness. Mr. No Matter going:

> He had at times, without any effort as far as anyone could know, a way of almost floating into the invisible. He was there. He wasn't there. A slow tick of the clock and he was there again. A shoulder coming forward, an arm raised, a bosom heaved, and he was hidden. That was all.[15]

and Bowsie, coming:

> There was one man from whom No Matter never vanished, that was his worn old friend, Bowsie (2).

The Charmed Life represented Yeats's prodigious effort to come to terms with his sixty years as an artist. Publication of the novel caused W. B. Yeats to comment on its importance and its value:

> And now comes my brother's extreme book, *The Charmed Life.* He does not care that few will read it, still fewer recognize its genius; it is his book, his *Faust,* his pursuit of all that through its unpredictable, unarrangeable reality least resembles knowledge. His style fits his purpose, for every sentence has its own taste, tint, and smell.[16]

Bowsie and No Matter became points of reference for Yeats's later paintings, *The Last Voyage* (1946) and *Glory* (1952), in which the figure of No Matter waves to a dawning day in the west of Ireland, and a small, golden-haired child, standing on the shoulder of Bowsie and the arm of his companion, expectantly points his finger. The painterly "lost and found quality" that figural art can create, but that narrative art traditionally has been unable to duplicate, found its first expression in Yeats's written work precisely because Yeats found a voice for his images. *Glory* is a powerful, triumphant, and vivid painting that, as Douglas Archibald described it, "celebrates generational continuity and expansive life."[17] Jack Yeats painted because, as he told anyone who asked, he was the son of a painter: he might have added that he wrote for an even better reason—because he had something to say.

The artist who drew the figure of Mr. No Matter onto the page, and off again—first the shoulders, then the arm, then the bosom, the way a painter would shade an outline, or compose the elements of his picture, to reveal first one aspect, then another—was equally adept at presenting his philosophy of continuosity, impetuosity, and exuberance:

> Seeing funny things is a protection, but when the curtain falls on fun, what then my children? Then we, you and I, must take what comes. And here comes chance leading a horse by a hay rope, but the horse in a sudden lurch of his stride breaks the hay rope and passes by me like a wind. The man stands foolishly with the broken rope in his hand, he says to me, "That horse was the star horse of all the world and what will I do now? I know what I will do." And so he makes a slipping loop in the end of the rope, and the other end he throws over a low branch of a tree, jutting out convenient to his hand, he brings the end down and makes it fast to a fairy's archway of a root that comes above the ground, then he puts his neck through the noose, makes himself into a spider's ball, and launches for eternity (6).

The familiar image of the ironic leg-puller, whom Nardock personified in *The Deathly Terrace,* appears once again in *The Charmed Life:*

> He signed to me to pull up his legs, but I wasn't ready to do that, so I went to hold them up, to take the weight of his body off his neck, but lo, there was no weight in his body, he was just grey air. So I blew at him, and he went up among the leaves, and I cut the hay rope with my pen knife, and my responsibility was ended (6).

The tramps of *Godot* reflect Mr. No Matter's whimsical story of hanging from a tree. Even Pozzo, leading Lucky, "Chance," by a hay rope, derives from *The Charmed Life,* in which two adventurers set out on a journey through the imagination. The countryside is Sligo, from *Memory Harbor* (1900):

Now out along the westerly road towards the port, you know the road well. On the crest of the hill that'll make three quarters of a mile out. We will climb up on the bank beside the gate and look out over the sea hailed down under the moon with the house. Crooked Dell, down below us. . . . Look at the wide melon slice of bay; see how the water lives where the moon spangles it (22–23).

Yeats summons the reader to re-create, in the mind's eye, an ancient vista, and two itinerant rogues: "We gave way for the poor townsmen who knew nothing of the wild bracken and furzy country where we lived" (25). One half of the creative imagination summons the other: Mr. No Matter, the subjective "I," the imagination, introspective and philosophical, summons Bowsie, the objective "being," the memory, extroverted and responsive. Mr. No Matter's summons to Bowsie applies to the reader as well:

You are now away, Bowsie, on your flood of common lies, flowing gently towards the whirlpools and the rapids of your uncommon lies, your adventures in places you never heard of until some geographical memoried spectre of the shadows in the smoke breathed them on to your tongue (27).

Yeats alternately brings Bowsie on, drops him, then brings him back to show him off again, in another light, as it were, just as he might in his painting, in which certain lights—the moon's glow, or the sun's reflection on the water—offer him the opportunity to provide a fleeting glimpse of a torso, or a tree stump, or a nothing. In each case the artist dangles the image in front of the viewer's imagination, then grabs it away. In the village of *The Charmed Life,* Yeats shows the reader figures who appear, then fade away, fog that creeps across the quay, Tim Devany pacing as he plans a Hollywood film career, and Michael Hayden, the Irish ex-Yank hotel keeper of the Pride Hotel ("running water in every room and three baths"), who looks very much like the cigar-smoking man in the foreground of *Memory Harbor.* As the book progresses, the author shows the reader Market Day, when Bowsie and Mr. No Matter meet John Davey (the ballad singer who expresses the freedom of the hills), Willie Dempsey, and John Ogle.

Freedom lives in Davey as it does in perhaps no other creature of Yeats's Ireland. Davey always looks up, since he has never bent his head to read, or to observe the arid land. "A ploughed field of beautifully straight furrows" saddens him, but "the scattered furrowing of the skies . . . the clouds bunching and lengthening themselves above him" thrills his free spirit (63). There is also freedom for Bowsie and his companion, as they stand before the North Atlantic or by a pillar memorializing some ancient warrior killed in battle, before a spring equinoctial gale.

No Matter and Bowsie's freedom is that of Krapp, who was at a moment in his thirty-ninth year, on a jetty in March, when he "suddenly saw the whole thing" (20). Bowsie dreams of freedom in a home he once had in which the sun never shone, "and where every day was too long" (76). He also expresses freedom, walks up and down, then falls asleep to forget everything, "while a comic strip of some ridiculous adventure, of colored figures, bouncing before him in cloudland, will pass before his eyes, comatose eyes" (76). These must be the dreams of Gogo:

> *Estragon.* I dreamt that—
> *Vladimir.* DON'T TELL ME!
> *Estragon. (gesture towards the universe).* This one is enough for You?
>
> (11A)

> *Estragon.* I was dreaming I was happy.
> *Vladimir.* That passed the time.
> *Estragon.* I was dreaming that—
> *Vladimir. (violently).* Don't tell me!
>
> (57B)

Clearly, for Bowsie, as for Estragon, the woven fantasy of a homeland is a necessary prelude to the imbrication of external reality. Murphy's "mote of absolute freedom" in the dark, in the will-lessness of his third zone of being, and Pim's life, in *How It Is,* are extracted by torment, in the consciousness of how it was, before the light interfered:

> he gave it to me I made it mine what I fancied skies especially and the paths he crept along how they changed with the sky and where you were going on the Atlantic in the evening on the ocean going to the isles or coming back. . . . [18]

Murphy's freedom and Pim's life are no less real than the "unique inquisitor" of *Play:* "W1. Is it that I do not tell the truth, is that it, that some day somehow I may tell the truth at last and then no more light at last, for the truth?"[19] Yeats's goal in *Sligo* is to examine the movement of the mind's eye as it is incessantly drained of images by the consciousness. But in *The Charmed Life,* Yeats personifies the old memories he jettisons. Bowsie, like Watt on the high road in his own novel, "appears, at times, to be moving away, and then coming towards the beholder, everlastingly. He goes away, into some ancient air, so choked with dimensions that it's a jamb and no movement. Then, in a flash, he's back again" (101). Plucking the rose from his lapel, Bowsie fastens it to a bush in the hills above Siligo Bay, and departs with the blessing: "Long may you wave over the little young things of the wild—under the rose" (106). This idealization of freedom "under the rose" of Jack Yeats's Republican banner was neither limited nor defined by the political realities of Ireland. But it did serve to inspire those who cared to read his books and to look at his painting. And it inspired Samuel Beckett to protest, on occasion, the loutishness of his countrymen, who never realized that there was once an Irish painter named Jack Yeats.[20]

Yeats concludes the book with some slight adventures: that of a stranger whose tale is as gripping as that of "The Rime of the Ancient Mariner" until it reverts to the imagination of its creator; and that of Bowsie's miraculous sea rescue and return to what might have been his own funeral procession, a prefiguration of his departure to a semi-office job. No Matter and the Judge speak at length of a lifetime of experiences that will soon pass, and that has amounted to *no great matter:*

> I have the experience, constantly now, as I grow old, of viewing the moment of disappearance. . . . "Departure" isn't a good word for it. Have you noticed how difficult it is to get a good word that gives just the right shade for any particular death (240).

In Yeats's twilight, No Matter enjoys the sensation of a community of spirits, where the grass, the soil, the rocks, and the salt still air "have a fondness for each other." The world stands still, or transcends time. Sligo and the memory of Sligo become "a space of earth, a valley, a nest of hills, a lake, a gathering of lakes, where the shadow people met and played their games" (244).

Yeats's *The Charmed Life*, his *Faust*, summons the spirit of the people of a heroic age. The author finds, in the immediacy of a contemporary image, a way to invoke the past in the mind's eye. Life is a *dancing girl:*

> My idea is that there must be an enormous mass of spirits like my own, since the world began, crowding the shores in every place, beyond the dancing floor. Did you ever watch by a roadside dancing floor at night, and if you did, did you notice the way a girl or a young man would pass from the light into the night for a moment, in the dance, and then come into the light again. Well, that is the way the dead die on me. Those I meet passing in the street and then meet no more (245).

"In the midst of life we are in death."[21] Bowsie has passed down the road, but something remains. Just as No Matter holds a flaming match in his hand, then extinguishes the flame, the flame goes on: "That small match has taken the freehold of your memories" (267). Memory Harbor is freedom, beyond all matter, beyond Watt and his trip to the House of Knott, beyond the play of the unique inquisitor, beyond the extracted words of Pim, and Krapp, and all the characters that people the works of Yeats and Beckett. The last conversation of *The Charmed Life* dissolves into a mist, that dissolves in particles, "then goes up into the sky, straight, like a leaping curtain of lace, to melt in the sun" (237). With a last thought of Bowsie getting ready for work in Dublin in the morning, No Matter goes off to a dinner, where he sits between a young woman and an elderly matron, for whom he invents a whole new repertoire of stories—of continuosity, impetuosity, and exuberance. The novel ends in mid-sentence: "I look at the row of human beings opposite, and I begin to name them, from fancy, beginning on the left, Mrs. Wan Lee—" (295). Mr. No Matter is scarcely food for thought when recombinant imagination and reconstituted memory are the bill of fare: that is freedom.

Jack Yeats's first play to be produced, *Harlequin's Positions,* premiered on 5 June 1939 at the Abbey Experimental Theatre in Dublin. It was four months after the death of W. B. Yeats. Jack Yeats took a great interest in the production, as it was his first venture in live theater and he had specific ideas on performance techniques and staging devices. According to Pyle, Yeats believed that the actors should carry the play, not the characters: "if a play was acted it was fatal; dialogue must flow from one actor to another—each becoming nothing but an agent, and putting all of Yeats into his words."[22] Furthermore, Yeats passionately disliked symmetrical settings, and insisted that balance in stage design be achieved by the arrangement of dissimilar elements of mass, shape, and placement. He also felt that a small theater was preferable, because it allowed spectators to better see the feet of the players. Yeats was apparently pleased with the production of his work in Ria Mooney's experimental theater, and wrote a letter complimenting the actors to a friend two weeks after *Harlequin's Positions* opened: "I was in the theatre four times, and each time with more respect for the way the company carried the days along."[23]

Yeats's play was a Chekhovian drama of people caught in mid-stride, at a moment of great and imminent change. In 1939 the world was preparing for World War II. Yeats had completed the draft of his work in 1938, and had submitted it to the Abbey Theatre as "a play about war's alarums."[24] Typically, his work has points of reference in memory, in immediate surroundings, and in the transformation of both in an idealized setting. Yeats worked through his cast of characters the way a painter might complete a painting. He sketched in the principal characters at the beginning of the play—Madam Rose Bosanquet, Claire Gillane, Johnnie Gillane, Annie Jennings, and Alfred Clonboise—very carefully. The major link between those characters and the characters who complete the drama—the ship's pilots, the railway porters, the Guard, the Apple Woman, the Boy, and Kate—is the rumor of war, and Miss Jennings's aborted plan to take the townsfolk of Portnadroleen on a

This Grand Conversation Was under the Rose, 1943, 14 × 21. **Private collection.**

world tour. In *Harlequin's Positions*, Yeats presents his audience with a pastiche of Ireland at a moment when universal calamity had befallen it.

His play was an early statement of his 1943 painting *This Grand Conversation Was under the Rose*. In his conversation with the Apple Woman and the child, the Railway Guard makes Yeats's point clear:

> *Guard.* There was a song once—"This Grand Conversation Was under the Rose." Did you ever hear tell of it? . . . That was a song of great warriors. Greater than the one you see before you now. . . . *(Turning to Boy)* . . . when the sword, shining and bright, falls from my hands, it's you child that will grasp it and wave it, wave it. . . . [25]

Yeats took his image from *A Broadsheet* of August 1903, and enhanced it with the immediacy of war in Ireland and on the European continent in 1939, and the patriotism inspired by the Irishman Robert Emmet, who died in 1803.[26] Yeats's play is anchored securely in the real world, although some of its elements are the artist and his people, deployed in new positions—a circus clown at the edge of the big ring, and a crowd of spectators waiting for the action to begin.

Skelton pointed out the random nature of the play, and suggested a similarity between it and the short works of Beckett:

[Yeats] was not . . . concerned to present a philosophical viewpoint so much as something for philosophical contemplation. In this the play resembles the apparently inconsequential short late plays of Samuel Beckett where little that is dramatic occurs, but where an episode from life is held up to us for our scrutiny, and for us to make of it what we will.[27]

The late plays of Beckett are not, of course, inconsequential and undramatic, as Skelton suggested, but represent Beckett's own artistic development. The notion that a play must contain a rising action in a series of acts, each of which has its own crisis, climax, and resolution that is finally resolved in the last act—the resolution of mistaken identities, long-lost relations, misplaced children, errant letters, and mischievous guardians—is based on a theater of linear perspectives. But Beckett's theater moves inward, like a vortex. Furthermore, by its very nature, a theater of vertical perspectives cannot be grasped all at once, but only segmentally, like a painting by Jack Yeats, with its layers of images and color relationships available for interpretation. Of paramount importance to both artists was the intention of their artwork: they intended not so much that an episode from life would be held up for scrutiny and speculation, but—very specifically—to note the fact that all intention, artistic and otherwise, is arbitrary. Beckett particularized that relationship when he commented on Jack Yeats as an artist who brought light "as only the great dare to bring light, to the issueless predicament of existence":

reducing the dark where there might have been mathematically at least, a door. The being in the street, when it happens in the room, the being in the room when it happens in the street, the turning to gaze from land to sea, from sea to land, the backs to one another and the eyes abandoning, the man alone trudging in sand, the man alone thinking (thinking!) in his box—these are characteristic notations having reference, I imagine, to processes less simple, and less delicious, than those to which the plastic *vis* is commonly reduced. . . . [28]

The fluidity of Jack Yeats's "stages of an image" is the perfect description of the process that Beckett employs in his dramaticules, where the actor, as well as the spectator, is expected to "see the whole inwardly . . . as an image that develops gradually." Skelton was close to the mark in his description, but he missed both the intention and the essential mechanics of the situation.

In *Harlequin's Positions,* Jack Yeats showed the spectator the "order of existence" of his *petit peuple,* as events sweep away their lives and their ambitions:

> *Alfred.* We cannot read our future. At least I cannot read my own, whatever I might do about other people's future. I choose a pattern and stay within it . . . and I discovered that those positions the harlequin takes with the wand in his hand all have names. . . . Admiration, Pas de Basque, Thought, Defiance, Determination. I committed them to memory—Harlequin Positions—and have made them my order of—order of existence, if I may put it that way. I often start a journey in a state of "Admiration" and end it with "Determination."
>
> (258)

Behind the whimsical nonsense of the porter's fantasy of crossing the Atlantic Ocean bed in an old truck on his way to New York, or of the supposed glory of swinging a sword through the skulls of the people, Yeats expressed his genuine concern for events of his day. Alfred's small wisdom is a measure of the resilience and strength Jack Yeats wished to instill in his countrymen. His message was very straightforward. It certainly had nothing to do with the late plays of Samuel Beckett, but it had everything to do with the state of the world, and of Ireland, in 1938 and 1939.

Yeats's message in *The Silencer* (193?) is the same as that he discovered in painting the rose's "shadow land." As important a work as *The Charmed Life,* the drama concerns Hartigan's transformation from corporeal "chatter-box" to incorporeal being. The same ironic framework of *The Deathly Terrace, Rattle,* and *Apparitions*—in which the characters find themselves in situations that admit of several interpretations—sets the stage for Hartigan's transformation.

Hartigan is Yeats's embodiment of the life process. He shares the philosophy of Ted Golbach in *Rattle,* "To know all is to forgive all," and of Michael of the Song in *The Old Sea Road,* "Would it be any offence if I said a prayer for you?" In Yeats's work the most extreme moments of life, when life is lost, reveal a generosity in spirit of forgiveness that amounts to something much more. The spirit Yeats sought to expose, for all who cared to notice, was the transcendent nature of being that extended beyond life itself into all nature. Yeats had done a remarkable painting of the life process in 1937, *Death for Only One,* in which a man, his hands clasped in front of him, mourns the death of another man, his companion, who lies in the foreground. The mourned figure's body has nearly become part of the landscape, but his face, upturned and almost radiant, is still his own. The man standing over him, as bleak as the surrounding terrain, seems drawn to the land embodied in the prone figure. The painting represents Yeats's passionate feelings about a divided Ireland,

and his personal philosophy of life as he described it in his novels and his plays.

Yeats wrote of life processes from another perspective much earlier, in his introduction to *The Old Sea Road* (1933), in which he describes the sky, the sea, and the land as "brighter than the people." In his review of *The Amaranthers* (1936), Samuel Beckett noted Yeats's earlier play in his discussion of the novel, whose landscape he described as "superb, radiant and alive, with it own life.[29] Yeats clearly had something very definite in mind when he wrote of the transformation of being from life to death-in-life, and from death to life-in-death. The transformation of being closed the circle of Jack Yeats's thought begun in the "shadow land" of 1936.

Following the line of the circle took him from his complete disinterest in the occultism of his brother, W. B. Yeats, to his ironic perspective in *The Silencer,* which in some ways resembles the vision of William Blake's "generated soul." One commentator on *The Silencer,* Robin Skelton, even saw it as a modern justification of Blake's vision, as well as a litany of Jack Yeats's thoughts about enduring the follies of mankind:

> We are advised to see the unity of life, to perceive how the good thoughts and the bitter ones, the happiness and the pain, are woven together into unity and are necessary complements to each other. We are warned against self-regard and self-pity; we must see ourselves as part of a total pattern and learn to forget the unimportant details of living and even, finally, our own identities, our own self-consciousness in order that we may become part of the "one thought" which, Blake tells us, "fills immensity."[30]

Yeats's paintings from the end of World War II verify Skelton's speculations. *Rise up Willie Reilly* (1945) shows some elements of dream imagery. In it a young man kneels in the foreground, and a young woman who stands behind him holds in her hands the ends of a veil that drapes around her head, past her shoulder and down below her right side. Pyle described the picture as "not merely . . . a ballad singer entertaining a listener," but as something more.[31] Other suggestions for the true meaning of the work, that the singer is Cathleen ni Houlihan, and that the veil is purely a religious symbol, were not particularly apt interpretations of the painting's meaning, nor of Yeats's intention—which was to wrap the veil of mortality about the kneeling figure, and thereby weave him back into nature. In W. B. Yeats's *The Death of Cuchulain,* Aoife, Cuchulain's great early love, wrapped the veil of nature about her dying warrior-husband. And W. B. Yeats once declared, in *A Vision:* "Those who inhabit the 'unconscious mind' are the complement or opposite of that mind's consciousness and are there . . . because of spiritual affinity or bonds created during past lives."³² Jack Yeats would not have agreed with the "opposition" of spirits, as he makes clear in *The Silencer*. But there is good reason to believe that he made use of an image when it suited his purpose, whether it came from the work of his brother, or Blake, or Swedenborg, or Plotinus. Mediocre artists borrow materials; great artists steal, without apology, when it is appropriate.

The Silencer begins with Hartigan's arrival at a small city bar. He has "just blown in from all round the World in every direction."³³ He is the embodiment of continuosity in life and a great talker, who is described as "Old Chat" on several occasions, and expounds his philosophy on every subject to all and sundry. But Hartigan is particularly good at discussing death:

> *Hartigan.* There is the dignity of the waves that sinks the ship, and there's the dignity of the wreck that sinks. There's a living dignity and there is the dignity of the dead. There is the dignity of the child's rattle and the last rattle of the throat. I have heard them all, and with a new body and a new heart, I'd hear them all again, under different circumstances.
>
> (228)

Through a succession of events that reveals man's ingratitude to his fellow man, Hartigan maintains his composure and his enthusiasm for life. Confronted with personal calamity, he remains silent. But when he senses a man who might benefit from his knowledge, Hartigan becomes eloquent:

> *Buyer.* Floods and storms, and fires and earthquakes. They seem to thrive on these things. The more Chinese are destroyed the more seems to be to take their place. I hope it doesn't mean the survival of the unfittest.
> *Hartigan.* The Chinamen that were swept by the Sceptered elemental forces of their fates . . . died game. All deaths are game deaths; death sees to that.
>
> (231–232)

At this moment Jack Yeats shows his most solemn face.

Through Hartigan, the playwright decries the state of Ireland, in comparison with the state of China (a mythological China, to be sure):

> *Hartigan.* Chinamen in all the parts of the world where I have seen them, appear to me to be neither waiting, nor watching, nor regretting. And you are doing the whole three this moment I know: I know it in my bones.
>
> (232)

The countrymen of whom W. B. Yeats despaired in *The Green Helmet*, because of their incessant, internecine quarrels; the Irish peasants of whom Beckett complained because of their ignorance of the worth of Jack Yeats and their obsession with "Gaelomania"—are now the *petit peuple* whom Jack Yeats assails, because of their incessant waiting, watching, and regretting:

> *Hartigan.* You are afraid and ashamed of what you cannot help. . . . You think I am holding you against your will, and you have no will. You are listening to me because you have nothing to say yourself. You are not going away because you have nowhere to go. You have forgotten you have a home. You have forgotten you have a tongue. . . . You wade in stars and hate the ocean seas that lap over you like a sinking tent.
>
> (232)

As Hartigan expounds on the state of Ireland, which pains him greatly, his executioner, Hill, stalks in the background, carrying a gun with a "silencer: attached." The irony, of course, is that the talker, Hartigan, cannot be silenced, even in death. Hartigan is continuosity. And he will continue, in one form or another, as long as there are artists to convey his message. All Yeats's frustration comes through Hartigan's final words, spoken before the executioner guns him down for a crime that he did not commit. Because Hartigan does not accept his fate passively, Yeats has once more taken the opportunity to say "Rise up, Willie Reilly, and seize your opportunities!":

> *Hartigan.* Look at your boots; they're all smeared with stars. . . . You are speechless because I talk for you. You think you speak yourself. You think I echo your thoughts. You have no thoughts; you never had thoughts. Those things that straggled across your brain were not thoughts, they were wheel tracks in the dust, and you have no idea what wheel made them. When your dust is gathered to its dust, it will make no difference to you. You have never existed in your own right. . . . By my lips you live; by their stillness you pass away or back again into your solidity of a poised dust mote.
>
> (233)

The speech is a devastating criticism of a benighted people who have none of the Nardockian requirements for successs in the world—continuosity, impetuosity, and exuberance of spirit. They do not exist in their own right. Instead they wait, they watch, and they regret; perhaps in another decade they will even wait for Godot!

Six weeks after Hill kills Hartigan, the murderer's guilty conscience takes him to "The Seekers Bridge," a fraudulent séance at which elderly believers contact their departed loved ones. There Snowey, the white-bearded intermediary to the spirit world, with the aid of his assistant, leads the believers in a spirited rendition of "Lead Kindly Light" as the lights are turned out. The séance begins with several miscues, but ends suddenly as Sam, Hill's accomplice, shines a light on Snowey, and exposes the ghostly fraud. Yeats cannot resist adding to the dramatic irony of the situation. Not only is the Snowey ghost in the room, and exposed, but

Hartigan's Ghost, who flits back and forth, has transfixed "Spill" Hill, who "spilled Hartigan" earlier in the play. Snowey and his flock leave quickly. After he has emptied the cashbox, Sam follows, and leaves Hill to face the ghost of his victim. Turning on the dictaphone, "Old Chatagain" begins to chat again, through the mouth of Snowey's intermediary. But the language Hartigan's Ghost speaks is that of the living, and he speaks of a world that is beyond the living, even beyond the living forgetting. Compared to the stars, argues the Ghost, who have forgotten the sky they ploughed, or the seed stars that lie forgotten in forgotten furrows, or the forgotten memories of the breath of the memory of all the birds, what significance can there be in even the forgetting of man's inhumanity to man? Hartigan's Ghost counsels Hill to take heart (or to take *heart-again*), to "think the good thought":

> *Ghost.* As the basket is woven on the uprights, which are the good thoughts . . . so I know that one day by forgetting here and there we will arrive at but one thought—one thought to satisfy all needs.
>
> (244)

This is Yeats's expression of a continuity that reaches beyond the limitations of the physical body. Much as he used the painting *Humanity's Alibi* (1947), Yeats uses *The Silencer* to show that the townsmen of Dublin and many another town are cruel, mercenary killers.

But Hartigan's Ghost forgives all, and does so with a dignity that reaches beyond life itself. He has become a "child of the universe" once more, a tributary of the great stream of process, in which earth, real time, and even "deep time" occupy but an instant of reflection in the consciousness of the stars:

> *Ghost.* In comfort of body I recall dreadful days of old, fighting odds too heavy, far too heavy. But then I was held in a body that could ache and fear. But this body now is the fun of a body which has neither fear nor ache, unless the misty vapor of the lake can ache. Do the clouds ache in their hearts because the lake distorts their reflections? Not they! They say if there were no clouds there'd be no lakes. And what are lakes but little puddles grown up. And what are little puddles but little drops of water, and little grains of sand too; they make the mighty ocean and the pleasant land too. A song of innocence. . . . Oh, dear heart, be glad. . . . So that where we leave down one gangway, we come aboard skipping up the next.
>
> (244–45)

The Ghost's song of innocence is a full statement of Yeats's philosophy of life, quite different from his brother's mystical approach to the ancient heroes of Ireland's glorious past. Jack Yeats engaged the hearts of his countrymen in the immediacy of their situation. He exhorted them:

never again must they abandon their leaders, or sit idly by as events shaped their destiny. They must wait no more, watch no more, regret no more; they must not even forget the troubled spirit that divides neighbor from neighbor. They must try to take heart and be glad; there may be hope "in the wind's eye, in the trough and on the crest, forgetting where the flaming stars come down and the twinkling waters rush up" (245).

Yeats knew that his message could not be accepted, and added one last irony. Hill shoots twice at Hartigan's Ghost, once at the dictaphone, and exists. Policemen, who turn out to be "fancy dress constables," arrest the killer immediately. Hill is then released into the custody of the landlord, whom the constables relieve of four bottles of champagne. As the play ends, Hill is confused, and Hartigan's Ghost dances, seen only by Hartigan's killer. Hill will not soon forget the ghost's forgiveness.

The Silencer represents Jack Yeats's most complete and succinct statement of the continuum of process. To make his message understandable and acceptable, he cajoles, castigates, and encourages his *petit peuple* to break with the traditions of their past. Yeats developed the personal philosophy he expounded in *The Silencer* over a decade of experimental work. He discovered the "shadow land" of the rose at the same time that he discovered his own renewed technical ability, and both discoveries allowed him to direct his creative energy toward his last great period of work—1945 to 1957. His late works—*Freedom* (1947), *Shouting* (1950), *Queen Maeve Walked upon This Strand* (1950), and *Glory* (1952)—capture the exultation of the moment and the images of memory in glowing pigments that leap out at the viewer. Rosenthal described them as "singing with all the joy the artist [could] summon."[34] But even in his late paintings, an ironic framework insulated Yeats the man from Yeats the conduit and conscience of an entire nation. He had a great deal to say to a people who were, at once, the glory and the despair of his life. Both he and Beckett shared an amused tolerance for the limitations of their fellow man, who sat and waited—for help, for Godot, for whatever—in various stages of resignation. Probably no two playwrights have ever painted as many characters who perpetually sleep, who fall asleep, or who prepare for sleep, as did Yeats and Beckett.

In 1957, when Jack Yeats died, a letter from a saddened Samuel Beckett arrived at the home of H. O. White: "The light of Jack Yeats will always come with me."[35] Skelton analyzed and summarized the perspective Jack Yeats brought to the world:

There is, finally, nothing but the current of life itself, and that finds death meaningless, a delusion. The state of the heart, of the soul, is all that matters and that survives to other places, and, maybe, other lives.[36]

The other lives of which Skelton spoke included not only those "embedded in time and floating in eternity," but also the very real, and literary, life of Samuel Beckett.[37]

In his 1922 publication *Modern Art,* Yeats had declared that if a painter were true to himself, the spectator and the truth could be sure to shake hands.[38] He meant, of course, that the subjects represented must be painted as they really are, without ennobled, idealized, or picturesque adornment. But as his attention shifted from objective representation to subjective interpretation, a new tension arose between the artist and the pictorial plane; where, formerly, the relationship between the two-dimensional canvas and representative space of a three-dimensional painting (with elements of perspective and composition) challenged the artist to produce "Truth and Beauty" in his work, Yeats added a new dimension. Imagination became the key to interpreting Jack Yeats's work. The very surface of his canvases and the actual language of his plays both began to play a new and critical role in his work. The nature of two-dimensionality captured his attention. The canvas as a conveyor of meaning, and the paint as a conduit for emotion absorbed his creative energy. He reached into the recesses of his consciousness to create, and in the act of investing meaning in a vehicle, whether it was paint in a painting or language in a play, the process of creation became as important as the art it produced. In the imaginative re-creation of the artist's process, Yeats expected the viewer-spectator of his work to use his own memory patterns and emotional constructs to stand before the work of art in exactly the same manner as the artist had. Pyle noted Jack Yeats's changing techniques; from his decisive brushwork of 1912 to 1917, through the 1920s, during which his outlines vanished completely, into the 1940s, when the freedom and exuberance of his paint was his last and largest artistic statement:

> The brush leaps into action from the start and draws and draws . . . a brush transcended, at times a paint tube transcended. The impatient hand ignores the palette and squeezes pigment directly from the tube onto the canvas, or applies it with thumb and forefingers.[39]

His pictures developed their own palpable textures, both in their heavily painted surfaces, where color exploded off the canvas, and in their almost unpainted spaces, where their lack of texture showed that the artist's powerful hand had hurried across the empty surface, his mind directed toward more compelling emotional images. The spectator was left with the job of completing the images from his own mind-store. The summons Yeats issued to the spectator at his theater pieces was the same as the one he issued to the viewer of his paintings.

La La Noo was performed at the Abbey Theatre on 3 May 1942. It is easy to understand the critics' confusion at the spectacle: Yeats insisted that the actor be the vehicle through which his (the playwright's) own voice be transmitted. The players of his piece were the paint with which he (the artist) expressed his emotions. The honesty and originality of Yeats's stagecraft were startling and revolutionary. Yeats offered the script of *In Sand* to the Abbey Theatre the following year, but the theater company did not undertake production of it until 1949. Yeats fought his disappointment by doing more paintings and writing more plays. Unfortunately, his popularity did not increase noticeably in the last decade of his life, despite the creativity and importance of his work.

Unlike Yeats's earliest plays for the adult theater, *La La Noo*'s meaning is difficult to state baldly. The problem is that Yeats applied the same principles of composition to his theater that he did to his canvas. In *La La Noo*, he juxtaposed the theme of death-in-life with characters who adamantly refused to advance the action of the plot. Skelton partially defined the problem:

> The drama of *La La Noo,* though it seems at first sight to be a presentation of the theme that Death lies in wait for us all and is always both awaited and expected, is something more. It is a portrait of questioning, fearful, speculative mankind. Its dramatic technique is almost that of anti-drama. The talk is unforced, natural, wayward. It is, one might say, a slice of life—and a slice of death.[40]

There can be no question that Yeats intended to develop his drama in the same way as he had developed his painting style. He intended to portray "the rose's shadow land" with three-dimensional players on the stage. Their unforced talk was his invitation to the spectator to share the moment when character was not transcended, but absented from the stage, and to complete the picture from his mind-store.

The play takes place in a small public house, the door of which opens on a vista of the strand, a sandy road, bent grass, nearby low sea islands, and distant high islands. A stranger arrives. He is a world traveler, who can "read the clouds of the sky" and who is convinced that the big cities of the world have spoiled humanity with their "envy, obstruction and throat cutting in the way of business."[41] At sunset, the skies darken with heavy rain, and seven women arrive. The ensuing conversation moves at right angles to the action of the play, embellishing life in the pub and commenting on life in the world. The women leave, thinking the storm has subsided. A few moments, punctuated by laconic utterances of folk wisdom, precede the return of the women, who are drenched and then retire to remove their clothes and dry themselves (hence the title, the French for "nude"). The folk wisdom treats the hardness of life,

> *Publican.* Isn't that a terrible thought that as soon as man finds a well he finds a poison to put in it.
>
> (322)

the progress of the young,

> *Publican.* If it wasn't for youth dashing about and making new inventions we'd be walking backwards into the mists of the past.
>
> (322)

and the legends of ancient Irish heroes:

> If it wasn't that you'd heard them and their deeds told out so well you mightn't think so much of them. They had poets and old shanachies to tell out their great deeds, and it was the poets that had the great thoughts. . . . They could sketch a small little thing, so that it'd look like a gold banner shining above a mountain, and the people would be leaping round with their old swords sweeping holes in the whin bushes, to be fighting the enemy whoever he was. . . . And afterwards whatever they did, be it little or much, make a great song and a giving out about it.
>
> (323)

The play has little sympathy for the golden glow that W. B. Yeats conferred on the legends of Cuchulain. Nor does it have much sympathy for the spectator who attempts to follow its plot. When the final scene erupts, the driver, the playboy of the western world, careening down the road in the smith's lorry makes any action anticlimactic. The Stranger, the driver of the truck, is thrown from its cab and killed. Shortly after the accident it becomes apparent that the seventh woman can drive a truck. All the women leave together in the truck and drive into the sunset, toward the bus stop. The Stranger's accidental death could have been avoided, just as Hartigan's death in *The Silencer* should have been avoided; except that life is not like that. No one asked the seventh woman to drive, and she did not volunteer. According to local superstition it is unlucky for a man to meet a large group of women on the road, but it is even more unlucky for the seventh woman to have remained silent at a critical moment. Nonetheless, the pastiche of ordinary life ends; the continuity of life and death that is process concludes satisfactorily, if the viewer has *eyes to see*.

The irony in Jack Yeats's plays works because he pits unaccommodated man against the ultimate leg-puller—death. The plays' predictable results give them their universal quality. As always, the final irony in any Yeats play is the invitation he extends to his spectators—they are always welcome to join in the leg-pulling games themselves, and "to think the good thought"! *In Sand* was the last of Yeats's plays to be produced during his lifetime. It is an extended invitation to all to "think the good thought." Yeats's prologue, *The Green Wave,* remained unproduced until a version of the entire work was performed in 1964, seven years after the playwright's death.

Bowsie and the Baron made their reappearance in 1944, with the publication of the novel *And to You Also.* A number of other characters from Sligo, also jettisoned in the book, are the Man-Without-a-Shirt, a poet in his autumn, and a young woman who worships twilight ("the dissolving hour between the sunset and the night"). The group strolls gently in the half-light; each figure takes a turn at speaking, in or out of turn. As they stroll through St. Stephen's Green in Dublin, the characters paint word-images of scenes they have known. The novel does not end when they bid each other good-bye, but continues, in twenty-three pages of line drawings of the images drawn from earlier portions of the novel. Yeats moved easily from one medium of expression to another; when words were not meaningful enough, he drew images.

The twilight, the metaphor for process that is part of Yeats's best work, is the basis of Beckett's sixth chapter of *Murphy,* in which the mind of the young hero pictures itself as a closed system. "Light, half light, and dark" are his triad of forms. Dark is a will-less state of absolute freedom; half-light admits of contemplation (during which Murphy is free to move as he pleases "from one beatitude to another"); and light is the simple experience of the physical state recollected in memory.[43]

But Yeats had something much more comprehensive in mind than Beckett's scenario for the inside of Murphy's head. Yeats won his role as Ireland's great realist painter of the *petit peuple* by effectively dissolving his subject matter to avoid distorting the images he portrayed. He gives the voice of his inspiration to the woman of *And to You Also:*

> I love this hour of the sun's retiring. . . . It's the dissolving hour between the sunset and the night. It has always been that hour. Always where Venus holds the position on the rails, but not when the bivouac of Mars is pitched on the edge of the battlefield of blood. It is the woman pecking with her foot upon the threshold of the night (57).

For Yeats the half-light was a civilizing influence, one that could tame reality's harsh glare and night's promise of transforming dark. Because it served as a conduit of pure process, the half-light brought forms to consciousness.

As Yeats developed an aesthetic, however, he found that the subjective mode finally demanded the elimination of all but a trace of the subject itself, a trace of both the coming and going of forms of consciousness. He learned that inspiration was, at best, a vessel that carried the liquors of creation, undistorted by artistic interpretation. The objective criteria of his youth became the basis of his "half-memory," in which images of the past could be evoked and transformed by moments distilled in the present. Rosenthal noted that Yeats almost deceived one into thinking he was an abstract expressionist, like Pollock or Tobey, so freely did he apply his paint, and so creatively did he paint nonfigurative shapes:

> Yet beneath the riotous paint and the exuberant colors lurk strictly figurative paintings; like many a great work of art, a late Yeats requires more than cursory study. Yeats's figures are often skeletal, like the sculpted ones of Giacometti, and again like Giacometti's, they turn out to be substantial and the apparent homunculus is revealed for a Yeatsian giant, as in his masterpiece "Glory".[44]

In the half-light at the edge of consciousness, Yeats issued his summons to the viewer to participate in life, glory, and the joy of creation. As Beckett observed, Yeats's stature as an artist was indisputable because he brought light "as only the great dare to bring light, to the issueless predicament of existence, reduc[ing] the dark where there might have been mathematically at least, a door."[45] He expanded the limits of consciousness. Beckett's own work, both his plays and his novels, has also expanded the limits of consciousness. Beckett wrote *Waiting for Godot* to put limits on the darkness in which he found himself as he wrote his trilogy of novels. [46] At least in Pozzo's eyes, it is a celebration of twilight. In many others' eyes it is an expansion of consciousness.

Jack Yeats did not originate the metaphor of twilight as a moment of artistic creation. William Butler Yeats, who founded the Irish National Theatre Company in the Hall of the Mechanic's Institute in Abbey Street, Dublin, in April 1904, saw twilight as the basis of tragic art:

> Tragic art, passionate art, the drowner of dykes, the confounder to understanding, moves us by setting us to reverie, by alluring us almost to the intensity of trance. . . . It was only by watching my own plays that I came to understand that this reverie, this twilight between sleep and waking, this bout of fencing, alike on the stage and in the mind, between men and phantom, this perilous path as on the edge of a sword, is the condition of tragic pleasure.[47]

The elder brother was clearly aware of all the implications that process represented by twilight held for the theater. But his highly schematic philosophy and his wrenchingly symbolic drama severely limited his insight. And his focus on the distant, heroic past, rather than on the present, led to a charge by Beckett and Joyce—among others—that he concentrated on all the wrong things in Irish life.

Something more than subject matter—the right things in Irish life—and technique—their figurally dramatic presentation—made his younger brother's work effective. That something in Jack Yeats's work changed the nature of Samuel Beckett's work.

Jack Yeats's indissoluble attachment to the country of his forebears was more than just national loyalty. He identified with it because he saw himself as an artist. He felt that an artist had certain responsibilities:

> The true painter must be part of the land and of the life he paints. The artist may travel all the roads of the world and may paint pictures of what he sees, but he can never be part of these roads as he can of the roads of his own land.[48]

During his eighty-six years of visits to the continent and to the United States, and stays in London and in Devon, Yeats never worked with any subject other than Ireland and its people. The *petit peuple* of Ireland responded to the devotion of the Anglo-Irishman who had spent the days of his youth at country fairs in Sligo, watching the traveling circuses, the melodrama troupes, the minstrel shows, and the horse races on the strand. Yeats drew pictures of all he saw, and stored the images in his memory.

In his later years, in a moment of new inspiration, he retrieved the images, "and through imagination . . . converted [them] into a painting which bound all elements together in a poetic complex, with words and with paint."[49] Yeats was interested, not only in the Irish people, but in the landscapes and seascapes where they lived and worked. MacGreevy described his talent for composition:

> I do not think I am claiming too much for Jack Yeats when I say that nobody before him had juxtaposed landscape and figure without subduing the character of either to that of the other.[50]

An early indication of the direction Yeats's art would take can be gleaned from *A Broadsheet* of February 1903, which he illustrated:

> VI
> It's my grief that I am of the race of the poets;
> It would be better for me to be a high rock,
> Or a stone, or a tree, or an herb, or a flower,
> Or anything at all but the thing that I am.[51]

Yeats turned his grief to joy in his work. But his sense of identity with the land itself—a rock, a stone, or a tree—developed poignantly in his work.

Pyle, White, MacGreevy, and others have discussed Yeats's development as an artist.[52] What is of interest is their assessment in his switch from line drawings to paintings that moved beyond the confines of line. At one point in his artistic development he confided to Sir John Rothstein:

> I believe the painter always begins by expressing himself with line— that is, by the most obvious means; then he becomes aware that line, once so necessary, is in fact hemming him in, and as soon as he feels strong enough, he breaks out of its confines.[53]

Yeats's artistic research revealed a consciousness searching for something more than an outline. Pyle reported that he collected newspaper photographs of everything quaint, as well as pictures of groups at parties or race days. He was interested in the curving lines "of the shoulders, behind and in front, in heads starting up from the main mass, in the angles of each head and of individual arms as they combine in number."[54] The sense of rhythms in a group interested him as much as its individuals; the lines of stress, movement, and mass excited him as much as a pleasing figure.

The strongest indication of a change in Yeats's artistic temperament came with his development as a colorist. In a 1936 article he described, in vivid terms, one of the dominant colors of his palette:

> I know that indigo is not a primary color. But it's an axle, the top of a Giant Stride, from which the ropes dangle in quietude, but swing out wide in movement, when from the end of each a strong young boy floats.[55]

His interest in color allowed Yeats to become a great, if not conventional, artist. His drawing appealed to the mind, and to the educated elite, but his color appealed to the emotions, and to everyone. The French painter Watteau, with whom Beckett flatteringly compared Jack Yeats, won entry to the French Royal Academy of Painting and Sculpture because the Academy adopted the revolutionary attitude that a painting could be judged on its colors as well as on its lines. Color predominated Watteau's late works, as it did Yeats's.[56]

Jack Yeats's investigation of color, and particularly his description of its effects in terms of images and motions, accords with clinical investigations a half-century later. The study of neurologically impaired individuals has led to singular breakthroughs in understanding the mechanisms of perception and image processing in the brain. Oliver Sacks and

Robert Wasserman, a practicing neurologist and ophthalmologist, respectively, noted in their research into color that a completely impersonal "processing" of motion, depth, and form occurs at a subconscious level of the brain, along the visual association cortex.[57] At this stage, images are formed and colored by the mind as part of a "primal sketch" of the world, all completely automatically and without reference to memories, expectations, or associations with external reality. When these primal images are taken to the higher levels of the cortex, to be "admixed inseparably with all our visual memories, images, desires, expectations," they become an integral part of ourselves; when Jack Yeats transforms those processes to canvas, one sees the wonder of the mind, metaphorically expressed by Yeats as "an axle, the top of a Giant Stride."[58]

Yeats's late paintings press the limits of this cortex processing, as Beckett so astutely sensed in describing the painter's works as "stages of an image." Color is not a given phenomenon, but the result of a multistage processing by the brain, and as an end-result of complex and specific cerebral functions. Jack Yeats found his way of discriminating between those associations—those formed from the primal sketch of the world, and those which responded to memory, desire, and emotion in that other, more familiar world of external reality. He painted those associations at the instant of their integration with breathless immediacy, as a "great inner real" of the mind that Everyman possessed, but few could comprehend.[59]

No one was better equipped to express emotion than either Jack or W. B. Yeats:

> Those masterful images because complete
> Grew in pure mind, but out of what began?
> A mound of refuse or the sweepings of the street,
> Old kettles, old bottles, and a broken can,
> Old iron, old bones, old rags, that raving slut
> Who keeps the till. Now that my ladder's gone,
> I must lie down where all the ladders start,
> In the foul rag-and-bone shop of the heart.[60]

Intellectual images are sterile bones compared to the inexhaustible energy of the heart. In *The Deathly Terrace*, Nardock finds that energy in the pulse of the volcano.[61] That was only the beginning of Jack Yeats's rainbow, and of two more decades of color and of light, begun on the ladders of W. B. Yeats's "Circus Animals' Desertion."

Jack Yeats's fascination with death and the transitory nature of life culminated in his paintings of the rose's shadow land in 1936. His affirmation of the unity of nature's rhythms, which lay beyond any conceivable extension of objective reality, afforded him new artistic freedom. But his new freedom from objectivity established his ability to function, to be the artist-as-consciousness he wished to be. In the subjective mode that Yeats adopted as a credo, his work, had its own life. In it, the painter (no less than the writer) was irrelevant. To friends who inquired about Yeats's work, White reported a marked change in the artist:

> He became deeply conscious of the importance of the work of art and disliked any reference to himself as an individual, to his age, to his habits or point of view. Only the picture mattered, he felt, and it would have to stand on its own eventually.[62]

The natural rhythms that Yeats discovered as he worked through the difficulties of portraying the rose's shadow were those of death in life and life in death. Those rhythms were the inner strength of the people he had chosen to paint, and of a country whose topography was more colorful than its inhabitants. There is no way to know if the artist's change from objectivity to complete subjectivity came before or after his recognition that his representation of the *petit peuple* of Ireland would necessitate his complete subjection to his subject. Whichever came first, a year after he had painted the rose's shadow, Yeats began to paint masterpieces like *Helen* (1937) and *Tinker's Encampment: The Blood of Abel* (1940). By then Yeats had discovered what MacGreevy called the great truth of the artist's "essential significance to society":

> The artist, poet or painter perceives and in terms of the imagination projects, the idea that the people to whom he belongs have of themselves, and thus creates the attitude that the world will have of them afterwards.[63]

When he realized that he could function as a conduit for the myth of the people, Yeats portrayed his subject matter with renewed freedom and energy. Both his canvases and his rose works exploded with vitality. The latter were filled with images that could scarcely be contained within the pages' margins. When he was not content to portray unalloyed subjectivity, he stepped into his pictures. Pyle recognized the figure of the thin, ascetic Jack Yeats in his paintings of the forties—*Where Fresh Water Meets Sea Water* (1947), *Silence* (1944), *People Walking beside a River* (1947) and *The Great Tent Has Collapsed* (1947). The joy of Yeats's painting captured Rosenthal's imagination. He reviewed *Glory* (1952) as a measure of the artist's stature:

> If one has to sum up Yeats's achievements in a few words, they lie in his

transportation of particularity into universality and in his almost heroic affirmation of life and its forces. . . . A painting like "Glory" is not
simply of three human beings standing looking at the day. It is at the
same time that archetypal trio of son, father, and grandfather which
meant so much to Yeats and it is also youth, maturity and old age all
talking and rejoicing in the glory of life.[64]

Yeats began to use his *medium* to express emotion. Color leaped from his
canvases. Medium, paint, light, and canvas became his principal means
of communication: he joined the great realist tradition of the nineteenth
century. What Yeats did was to adapt that tradition to a people he loved;
to find a way to project the myths of his country—continuosity, impetuosity, and exuberance—into an art form; and to settle on color as a
medium that would be freely understood by even the most untutored of
his country's inhabitants.

Yeats's ironic perspective on life permitted him to tell stories about his
paintings and then turn to a person viewing them and ask him for
another interpretation. Critics are inclined to see both paintings and
plays as vehicles for telling stories. But neither the nature of theater nor
the nature of figural art is limited to the *communicable*. Stories come from
the mind, but communication comes from the "rag-and-bone shop of the
heart." When subjects are neutralized beyond distortion by the artist's
vision, any number of interpretations are possible. If successful, the
conduit of subjectivity becomes a conduit of many subjectivities, if the
viewer has eyes to see, and dares. So Yeats's work followed the realist
tradition. When his subject disappeared, his objectivity of representation
stayed intact. His painting became a celebration of paint and freedom of
color. His theater became a celebration of the playwright's imagination
through its actors, who connected it to the inner eye of the spectator.
Actors became players, not simply characters in a play. He seized a single
moment (not a story) and used his medium to transform it into an
expression of the means of expression. That was all. His rambling,
directionless dialogue that ran at right angles to his plots (slight though
they were), was Yeats's demonstration of actors as players in an emotional
reality, not characters in an intellectual drama.

Both Jack Yeats and Samuel Beckett (in his later plays) issued a summons to the viewer that had a long and obscure pictorial tradition.
Jansen noted that Velásquez's *Las Meninas* (1656), which the art historian
tentatively subtitled "the artist in his studio," depicts little Princess Mar-
garita, "who has just posed for him [the artist], among her playmates and
maids of honor." In a work of this magnitude many interpretations are
possible, but few are as misleading as Jansen's:

The faces of her parents, the king and queen, appear in the mirror on the back wall. Have they just stepped into the room, to see the scene exactly as we do, or does the mirror reflect part of the canvas—presumably a full-length portrait of the royal family—on which the artist has been working?[65]

Svetlana Alpers has pointed out the difficulties of this interpretation by making the simple observation that the artist included the spectator in the picture: the spectator is looked at by those who are looking. A neutral posture with regard to this painting is impossible. Jansen's interpretation, that Velásquez's purpose in painting *Las Meninas* was to show the movement of light itself and the infinite range of its effects on form and color, has nothing to do with the emotional substance of the painting. A painter paints on a canvas while others watch. Velásquez painted an invisible subject because the subject was the viewers, who were probably originally the king and the queen (reflected in the mirror on the far wall). Those who posed for the painting were not its subject. In other words, there is no narrative. As it is depicted, the moment is complete and replete with its own emotion. Velásquez painted a picture of "me," the "me" in everyone else's eyes. In its portrayal of "me" the painting is the same picture that Beckett exhibited in *Not I*. In both works the world outside the picture has become as important as the world inside the picture. The challenge to Velásquez—to paint a picture of the viewer that was not the viewer—inspired his solution—to paint the viewer as his image in the eyes of others, and as the image in the mirror on the wall (if the viewer has the eyes to see).

Jack Yeats took the world outside his picture as a starting point for a more imaginative rendering of a situation or scene. The inventive process consisted of a confrontation between a remembered past experience and an event seen or imagined in the present. The technique provided Yeats's paintings with built-in double exposures, as James White explained:

> The one illuminates the other so that there are at least two trains of thought flowing from separate sources, one contemporary and one historic.[66]

Beckett's explanation of Yeats's works as "stages of an image" derived from this phenomenon. The viewer must play an active part in interpreting the images from the viewer's perspective. There is no narrative in the painting until the viewer supplied it.

There is no traditional grammar or vocabulary with which the iconography of such a painting can be interpreted. Nonetheless, that interpretation must be attempted because of its importance and because of its relevance to the works of Samuel Beckett. Jack Yeats required the viewer of his work to stand in his stead and to re-create the moment of his inspiration. Beckett required the same of his spectators. The playwright placed objects on his stage to be transformed into guides to the boundaries of the mind's eye. The figure of the Auditor in *Not I* derived from Caravaggio's *The Beheading of John the Baptist* (1608), in which the figure of the executioner stands over the hapless victim while the women watch in horror. What seems to be a water vase can be seen in the background behind the grill work. On closer inspection, however, it is clear that the artist painted not a vase, but the figure of a man (the artist perhaps), who watches the viewer observe the scene of horror. The viewer's emotional response to the scene of horror is the subject and the meaning of the painting, not the scene of horror itself. Velásquez, Caravaggio, Yeats, and Beckett all included the viewer in their art.

Not I is the disembodied figure of Mouth, red lips and a tongue that emit the torrential stream of words that suddenly flowed from an old, illegitimate, partially mute, and generally uncomprehending woman, who one day found herself in a field of cowslips: "when suddenly . . . gradually . . . all went out."[67] The other figure in the play is the Auditor, whose sole contribution to the play's action is to raise both his arms four times with greater or lesser intensity, in a *"gesture of helpless compassion."* (Beckett commented that the Auditor's degree of exertion can be determined by the plays' director.) At the beginning of the play the voice of Mouth is unintelligible. Her first audible words signify much: "*Mouth.* out . . . into this world . . . this world . . . tiny little thing" (14). Beckett's perspective and Yeats's continuosity are part of this declaration. More than one world of transformations punctuates the rhythms of the universe. Mouth comes "out" into this world from another consciousness that asks questions, demands clarifications, and requires a certain order. Mouth must get it right, or repeat it until it is right: "tiny little thing . . . before its time . . . in a godfor- . . . what? . . . girl? . . . yes . . . tiny little girl" (14). The questioner is an intelligence that might be the growing consciousness of the spectator. The split image of a Jack Yeats painting, where present event or imagined event confronts a past experience, is found in Beckett's *Not I* as the spectator is required to invent the situation depicted onstage. Mouth fills the pauses by inventing her responses exactly as she might in a stage telephone conversation. The spectator participates by supplying the imagined other half of the dialogue. The narrative in *Not I* is as much a collaborative venture as it is in a Jack Yeats painting. The end result is to illuminate the issueless predicament of existence: Mouth's speech is a broken threnody of life on earth, as was Lucky's speech in *Godot,* in which he stated that the sum of man is a being that "wastes and pines."

In his effort to create a theater of the real modeled on Yeats's plays and paintings, Beckett discovered an ironic inspiration. He eliminated the subject, which allowed him to display any object in such a way that it could be perceived from two equally valid perspectives. Dramatic irony resulted—when the coming consciousness of the spectator reflected the departing consciousness of the onstage object at a moment of transition (twilight again) when process became merely the play of words on the mind's eye.

In this context the narrative of Mouth is unimportant. Context, like subject, is reduced to zero, to permit both the playwright's faithful communication of the image to the stage and the spectator's creation of a personal myth in the mind's eye. The communication is not intellectual but emotional. Beckett staged the play as a torrent of words cascading upon the listener, who had no opportunity to decipher every phrase. In the play certain words are noted and repeated. The old woman suddenly realizes she is no longer suffering. What is more, she cannot remember when she suffered less, "unless of course she was . . . *meant* to be suffering" (16). She is also aware of her tormentor:

> *Mouth.* . . . . all the time this ray or beam . . . like moonbeam . . . but probably not . . . certainly not . . . . always the same spot . . . now bright . . . now shrouded . . . but always the same spot . . . as no moon could . . . no . . . no moon . . . just all part of the same wish to . . . torment . . .
>
> (16–17)

The same image of light as torment appears in *Play,* with its unique inquisitor who appears to extract words from W1, W2, and M, until M learns that it is all play; the light is "mere eye, no mind. Opening and shutting on me." M1 says, "all is falling, all fallen, from the beginning, on empty air. Nothing being asked at all. No one asking me for anything at all."[68] In *Not I,* the inquisitor both solicits and repels the voice. The old woman, nearly insentient in the cow field, finds a voice not her own whose stream of words floods her being. Her lips and tongue move almost reflexively. She becomes a conduit for verbal images—fragments of scenes she once lived, whose sense she once understood as consciousness.

In an attempt to comprehend this turn of events, in which a voice speaks with words that are not her own, Mouth and the spectator find themselves, ironically, in the same situation. At this moment in the play, a transformation of comprehension takes place; the consciousness of Mouth and spectator is interchangeable. Because he abolishes subject, Beckett effects a binding relationship between himself and spectator. Both demand that Mouth "get it right." *Not I* reflects *Play's* "play of light." Flashes of Pim, in *How It Is,* light the final section, in which Mouth protests repeated questioning:

Mouth. something she had to tell . . . (. . . .) could that be it? . . . something that would tell . . . how it was . . . (. . . .) something that would tell how it had been . . . how she had lived.

(21)

At the same moment that the tormentor begs Mouth to say it all, it begs her to stop the babble. The incongruity of that moment is another ironic statement on the meaning of meaning. Consciousness may not be "intelligence" in the ordinary sense, but it may be an extraordinary kind of intelligence in which "meaning" is really only glorified process. Unquestionably, the old woman learns something in her present state. It is a revelation. For the first time in her life she is free from the torment and suffering of seeking consciousness. She declares it—loudly and clearly— four times in the play: "*Mouth.* what? . . . who? . . . no! . . . SHE! . . . *(pause and movement 1)*" (15). The old woman will not say "I" because she is "not I" any longer, but a less-conscious rhythm that consciousness can scarcely torment. (The less-conscious rhythm, derived from Yeatsian "continuosity," generated the elliptical dialogue of *Not I,* the truncated narrative of *How It Is* and *The Unnamable,* the staccato rhythms of *Play,* Lucky's diatribe in *Godot,* and other similar features in Beckett's plays.)

The very movements of the Auditor dramatize the old woman's predicament. His gesture of helpless compassion has its own irony; her loss of consciousness makes her corresponding gain in freedom possible. For the reasons for the Auditor's movements is, Beckett remarked, that "The poor woman won't say 'I.' "[69] The Auditor functions as a chorus, interpreting the meanings and emotions of the play for the spectator. His four successive decreasingly emphatic genuflections reflect his decreasingly sympathetic attitude toward the woman's refusal to say "I." The Auditor also serves as an intermediary for the play in the mind's eye, where Mouth and the spectator's imagination collaborate to create not "I," but something less substantial and more real. In the collaboration Mouth cannot say "I" because she is, finally, less conscious than "I." The spectator's mind's eye perceives and the Auditor reflects her acquiescence to a more powerful reality. The Auditor's genuflections, his bow to reality, becomes his bow to the real, the more powerful reality. The Auditor's bow to reality is a symbol of his tacit approval of Mouth's refusal to say "I"; his bow to the real is a sign of the mind observing itself.

At the end of the play, the unintelligible Voice continues in ten seconds of darkness. The old woman has learned something. Mouth has served as a conduit for verbal garbage, and the Voice continues—Voice and consciousness have been separated from being. The "SHE!" of *Not I* has become a part of the Nardockian universe of continuosity, impetuosity, and exuberance that even Michael of the Song praises at the end of *The*

Old Sea Road. A reminder of that play recurs in the last lines of *Not I:* "*Mouth.* back in the field . . . April morning . . . face in the grass . . . nothing but the larks . . . pick it up—" (23). The last line of *The Old Sea Road* describes the scene in which the bodies of Ambrose Oldbury and Michael lie: "(*The lark sings loud in the air. Nolan and Josephine only, look up*)."[70]

On an interpretive level, Mouth represents the artistic "other" that the playwright listens to and tries to heed, while the Auditor represents the present visible self that accedes to unconscious demands. In this description of artistic process the real Beckett, the soft Dublin accent, the deep furrows of the forehead, the ram-rod stiff deportment, hides silently between the writer of his plays and the ex-patriot Irishman who lived in Paris, and smiled with bemused tolerance at his two puppets.[71]

Beckett and Yeats preserved the ironic frame of reference in their works to the very end. Their irony required the viewers of their work to decipher its inner meaning. In addition to irony, however, the artists offered joy, exuberance, and a promise of freedom to the viewers if they had eyes to see. Both Yeats and Beckett demanded that the viewers of their work re-create in their mind's eye the subject the artists had chosen from memory and from the immediacy of the moment that they, the artists, had removed (for aesthetic reasons) from the field of vision. "Now, what does it mean to you?" was the question Yeats asked of his visitors; Beckett's quizzical stare was no less direct. The viewer's task is difficult. But its immediate reward is a play of forms and language that delights the sensibility, if not the conventional sense.

Jack Yeats died on 28 March 1957. Two days later he was buried in Mount Jerome Cemetery in Dublin. Beckett tried desperately to get to the funeral, but no flights were available. He sent flowers and asked MacGreevy to apologize to mutual friends for his unseemly absence.[72] He had paid an earlier tribute to Jack Yeats on the opening of the April 1954 Paris exhibition of the painter's work that may be exactly what he would have wanted to say:

> In images of such breathless immediacy as these there is no occasion, no time given, no room left, for the lenitive of comment. None in this impetus of need that scatters them loose to the beyonds of vision. None in this great inner real where phantoms quick and dead, nature and void, all that ever and that never will be, join in a single evidence for a single testimony. None in this final mastery which submits in trembling to the unmasterable.
>
> No.
>
> Merely bow in wonder.
>
> Samuel Beckett[73]

Notes

Chapter 1. The Modernist Temper

1. Michael Robinson, *The Long Sonata of the Dead: A Study of Samuel Beckett* (New York: Grove Press, 1969), p. 141.

2. Colin Duckworth, ed., *En Attendant Godot,* by Samuel Beckett (London: George G. Harrap, 1966), p. xiv.

3. Samuel Beckett as quoted in Raymond Federman and John Fletcher, *Samuel Beckett: His Works and His Critics* (Berkeley: University of California Press, 1970), p. 63: "*Godot* is without any doubt between *Malone* and *L'Innomable.*"

4. Alain Robbe-Grillet, "Samuel Beckett, or 'Presence' in the Theatre," in *Samuel Beckett,* ed. Martin Esslin (Englewood Cliffs, N.J.: Prentice-Hall, 1965), p. 113.

5. Arnold Hauser, *The Social History of Art* (New York: Alfred A. Knopf, 1939), p. 169.

6. Franz Kafka, *Notebooks,* as quoted in Robert Corrigan, Preface, *Six Plays of Chekhov* (London: Holt, Rinehart and Winston, 1962), p. xiv.

7. Pierre Chabert, "Samuel Beckett as Director," in *Theatre Workbook 1. Samuel Beckett: Krapp's Last Tape,* ed. and trans. James Knowlson (London: Brutus Books, 1980), p. 103.

8. Samuel Beckett, *Waiting for Godot* (New York: Grove Press, 1954), pp. 40B–41A. Subsequent page citations will appear in the text.

9. Alec Reid, *All I Can Manage, More Than I Could: An Approach to the Plays of Samuel Beckett* (New York: Grove Press, 1968), p. 28.

10. Samuel Beckett, *Murphy* (New York: Grove Press, 1957), p. 2.

11. Samuel Beckett, *Watt* (New York: Grove Press, 1959), p. 73.

12. John Pilling, *Samuel Beckett* (London: Routledge & Kegan Paul, 1976), p. 35.

13. Samuel Beckett, *How It Is* (New York: Grove Press, 1964), p. 133.

14. Samuel Beckett, *Imagination Dead Imagine* (London: Calder and Boyars, 1965), p. 7.

15. John McPhee, *Basin and Range* (Farrar, Straus & Giraux, 1981), p. 124.

16. Maria Jolas, "A Bloomlein for Sam," in *Beckett at Sixty: A Festschrift,* ed. John Calder (London: Calder & Boyars, 1967), p. 16. Maria Jolas is the widow of Eugène Jolas, former editor of *Transition,* a popular English-language literary review published in Paris in the 1930s.

17. Ruby Cohn, *Back to Beckett* (Princeton: Princeton University Press, 1973), p. 14.

18. Personal interview with Samuel Beckett, 4 November 1980.

19. Ihab Hassan, *The Literature of Silence: Henry Miller and Samuel Beckett* (New York: Alfred A. Knopf, 1967), p. 115.

20. Richard Coe, *Samuel Beckett* (New York: Grove Press, 1968), p. 11.

21. Samuel Beckett, *Proust* (New York: Grove Press, 1957), pp. 46–47.

22. Samuel Beckett, Letter to Sighle Kennedy, "Paris 14. 6. 67," printed in Barbara Gluck, *Beckett and Joyce* (Lewisburg, Pa.,: Bucknell University Press, 1979), p. 9.

23. Richard Ellmann, *James Joyce* (New York: Oxford University Press, 1959), p. 579.

24. Hilary Pyle, *Jack B. Yeats: A Biography* (London: Routledge & Kegan Paul, 1970), p. 146: "Thomas MacGreevy wrote to [Jack] Yeats: 'He was completely staggered by the pictures and though he has met many people through me he

dismissed them all with the remark "and to think I owe meeting Jack Yeats and Joyce to you!"'"

25. "Poetry is Vertical," *Transition* (1931), pp. 148–49.

26. Geoffrey Hartman, *Deconstruction and Criticism* (New York: The Seabury Press, 1979), p. viii.

27. Gabor Mihalyi, "Beckett's *Godot* and the Myth of Alienation," *Modern Drama* 9 (December 1966): 280.

28. Ellmann, *Joyce*, p. 661.

29. Deirdre Bair, *Samuel Beckett: A Biography* (New York: Harcourt Brace Jovanovich, 1978), p. 121.

30. Ibid., pp. 526–27. John Montague recorded the conversation.

31. See Samuel Beckett, "Homage to Jack B. Yeats," *Les Lettres Nouvelles* (April 1954); rpt. in James White, *Jack B. Yeats 1871–1957: A Centenary Exhibition* (London: Martin Secker & Warburg, Ltd., 1971), p. 10, for a particularly laudatory forward by Beckett.

32. Richard Ellmann, *The Identity of Yeats* (New York: Oxford University Press, 1964), pp. 86–88.

33. Ibid., p. 89.

34. Richard Ellmann, *Yeats, The Man and the Masks* (New York: W. W. Norton & Company, 1979), p. 166.

35. Letter received from Samuel Beckett, dated "Paris. 4.23.81."

36. Ellmann, *Man and Masks*, p. 289.

37. Kathleen Raine, "Death-in-Life and Life-in-Death: 'Cuchulain Comforted' and 'News for the Delphic Oracle,'" *New Yeats Papers* 8 (Dublin: The Dolmen Press, 1974), p. 11.

38. W. B. Yeats, *Fighting the Waves*, from *Wheels and Butterflies* (1934), in *Explorations* (New York: Macmillan, 1962), p. 371.

39. Ellmann, *Man and Masks*, p. 290.

40. W. B. Yeats, letter to Fiona MacLeod, 1897, as quoted in George Mills Harper, *The Mingling of Heaven and Earth: Yeats's Theory of Theater* (Dublin: The Dolmen Press, 1975), p. 34.

41. Beckett, *Proust*, p. 57.

42. W. B. Yeats, *The Body of Father Christian Rosencrux*, in *Essays and Introductions* (New York: Macmillan, 1961), p. 197; W. B. Yeats, "Samhain: 1904. First Principles," in *Explorations*, p. 152.

43. W. B. Yeats, "Samhain: 1905," in *Explorations*, p. 197.

44. W. B. Yeats, "Samhain: 1904," in *Explorations*, p. 86.

45. W. B. Yeats, *Per Amica Silentia Lunae*, in *Mythologies* (New York: Macmillan, 1980), p. 337.

46. W. B. Yeats, "Swedenborg, Mediums, and the Desolate Places" (1914), in *Explorations*, p. 32.

47. Ibid., p. 35.

48. W. B. Yeats, *Per Amica Silentia Lunae*, in *Mythologies*, p. 343.

49. W. B. Yeats, Introduction to *The Cat and the Moon*, from *Wheels and Butterflies* (1934), in *Explorations*, p. 403.

50. W. B. Yeats, *The Variorum Edition of the Plays of W. B. Yeats*, ed. Russell K. Alspach (New York: Macmillan, 1966), p. 566.

51. John Rees Moore, *Masks of Love and Death* (Ithaca, N.Y.: Cornell University Press, 1971), p. 18.

52. W. B. Yeats, *Per Amica Silentia Lunae*, in *Mythologies*, p. 344.

53. Peter Ure, *Yeats the Playwright* (New York: Barnes and Noble, 1963), p. 46.

54. Beckett, *Murphy*, pp. 112–13.

55. Barton R. Friedman, *Adventures in the Deeps of the Mind* (Princeton: Princeton University Press, 1977), p. 6.

56. W. B. Yeats, *The Letters of W. B. Yeats*, ed. Allan Wade (New York: Macmillan, 1955), p. 309.

57. W. B. Yeats, "The Poet and the Actress," in Ellmann, *Identity*, p. 105.

58. W. B. Yeats, "J. M. Synge and the Ireland of his Time," in *Essays and Introductions*, p. 339.

59. W. B. Yeats, *Per Amica Silentia Lunae*, in *Mythologies*, p. 341.

60. W. B. Yeats, "Samhain: 1904. The Play, the Player, and the Scene," in *Explorations*, pp. 166–67.

61. W. B. Yeats, *Essays and Introductions*, pp. 169–70.

62. Friedman, *Adventures*, p. xiii.

63. Ellmann, *Man and Masks*, pp. 165–66.

64. W. B. Yeats, "If I were Four-and-Twenty" (1919), in *Explorations*, p. 267.

65. G. C. Barnard, *Samuel Beckett: A New Approach* (London: J. M. Dent & Sons, Ltd., 1970), p. 4.

66. Raine, "Death-in-Life," p. 13.

67. Lewis Carroll, "Preface to Sylvie and Bruno Concluded," in *The Complete Works of Lewis Carroll*, ed. A. Woolcott, (New York: Modern Library, 1936), pp. 512–13.

68. W. B. Yeats as quoted in Montrose J. Moses, "With William Butler Yeats," in *W. B. Yeats, Interviews and Recollections*, ed. E. H. Mikhail (New York: Harper and Row, 1977), p. 129.

69. Beckett, *Murphy*, p. 113.

70. W. B. Yeats, *The Poetical Works of William Blake* (London: Barnard Quaritch, 1893), p. 276.

Chapter 2. Presence, Myth, and Discourse in Beckett's Dramaticules after *Not I*

1. Samuel Beckett, *Cahiers d'art*, nos. 20 and 21 (Paris, 1945–46), trans. John Pilling, in Pilling, *Samuel Beckett*, p. 34.

2. Katherine Worth, *The Irish Drama of Europe from Yeats to Beckett* (Atlantic Highlands, N.J.: Humanities Press, 1978), p. 2.

3. Virginia Woolf, "The Last Act," *The Diary of Virginia Woolf*, vol. 5, 1936–1941, *New York Review of Books*, vol. XXXI, no. 17, Nov. 1984, p. 3.

4. Woolf, p. 4.

5. Beckett, "From an Abandoned Work," *No's Knife* (London: Calden & Boyars, 1967), p. 149.

6. Linda Ben Zvi, "The Schismatic Self in *A Piece of Monologue*," *Journal of Beckett Studies* 7 (Spring 1982): 8.

7. Martin Esslin, *Plays and Players*, Vol. 20, no. 6 March, 1973, p. 39.

8. Samuel Beckett, "Eleutheria," n.p., n.d., manuscript completed in March 1947. There are no plans for publication.

9. Paul Lowry, "Symbolic Stillness and Creative Obligation in *Endgame*," *Journal of Beckett Studies* 5 (1979): 53.

10. Samuel Beckett, *Endgame* (New York: Grove Press, 1957), p. 39. Subsequent page citations will appear in the text.

11. Lowry, "Stillness," p. 58.

12. Beckett, *Murphy*, pp. 107–13. See in particular: "The third, the dark, was

a flux of forms, a perpetual coming together and falling asunder of forms. . . . Here there was nothing but commotion and the pure forms of commotion. Here he was not free, but a mote in the dark of absolute freedom. He did not move, he was a point in the ceaseless unconditioned generation and passing away of line."

13. Samuel Beckett, *The Unnamable,* in *Three Novels by Samuel Beckett* (New York: Grove Press, 1958), p. 414.

14. Eric P. Levy, *Beckett and the Voice of Species* (Totowa, N.J.: Barnes and Noble, 1980), p. 58.

15. Barbara Gluck, *Beckett and Joyce: Friendship and Fiction* (Lewisburg, Pa.: Bucknell University Press, 1979); David Hayman, "Joyce/Beckett/Joyce," *Journal of Beckett Studies* 7 (1982): 101–7.

16. Hayman, "Joyce," p. 101.

17. Billy Whitelaw, "Practical Aspects of Theatre, Radio and Television," *Journal of Beckett Studies* 3 (1978): 89.

18. Stan Gontarski, *Beckett's Happy Days: A Manuscript Study* (Columbus: Ohio State University Libraries, 1977), p. 44.

19. Beckett, "Homage to Jack B. Yeats," April 1954.

20. See Colin Duckworth, "The Making of Godot," *Casebook on Waiting for Gobot,* ed. Ruby Cohn (New York: Grove Press, 1967), p. 94.

21. Douglas Hofstadter, "Mind, Body and Machine," *New York Review of Books,* 13 November 1983, p. 6–7. See also Hofstadter, *Godel, Escher, Bach* (New York: Basic Books, 1979).

22. Erwin Schrödinger, *What is Life? The Physical Aspects of the Living Cell* (Cambridge: Cambridge University Press, 1945), p. 72.

23. Hassan, *Literature of Silence,* p. 72.

24. Gontarski, *Happy Days,* p. 18.

25. Coe, *Samuel Beckett,* p. 11.

26. James D. Knowlson, *Light and Darkness in the Theatre of Samuel Beckett* (London: Turret Books, 1972), p. 27.

27. Gontarski, *Happy Days,* p. 25.

28. See Ruby Cohn for further discussion of this topic, particularly in her *Samuel Beckett* (Princeton: Princeton University Press, 1978), pp. 255–56.

29. Richard Coe, "God and Samuel Beckett," *Meanjin Quarterly* 24, no. 100 (1965): p. 67.

30. Beckett, "Homage to Jack B. Yeats."

31. John Pilling, "The Living Ginger: Jack B. Yeats's 'The Charmed Life,'" *Journal of Beckett Studies* 4 (Spring 1979): 55–65.

32. Ronald Rollins, "Old Men and Memories: Yeats and Beckett," *Eire-Ireland: A Journal of Irish Studies* 13, no. 3, pp. 106–19; and Thomas Kilroy, "Two Playwrights: Yeats and Beckett," in *Myth and Reality in Irish Fiction,* ed. Joseph Ronsey (Waterloo, Ont.: Wilfred Laurier University Press, 1977), pp. 329 ff.

33. Friedman, *Adventures,* p. 77.

34. Worth, *Irish Drama,* p. 2.

35. Ibid., p. 2–3.

36. Ibid., p. 12.

37. "Beckett by the Madelaine," *Columbia University Forum* 4, no. 3 (Summer 1961): 23.

38. Samuel Beckett, *Le Monde* (1945), p. 352, trans. John Pilling, in his *Samuel Beckett,* p. 19.

39. Ben Zvi, "Schismatic Self," p. 13.

40. See in particular Lawrence Harvey, "A Poet's Initiation," in *Samuel Beckett Now,* ed. M. Friedman (Chicago: University of Chicago Press, 1970), p. 443.

41. Worth, *Irish Drama,* p. 194.

42. Donald Davis, "American Premiere: Provincetown Playhouse, New York," in *Theatre Workbook 1,* ed. James Knowlson (London: Brutus Books, 1980), p. 63.

43. Pierre Chabert, "Samuel Beckett as Director," trans. M. A. Bonney and J. Knowlson, in *Theatre Workbook 1,* pp. 102–3.

44. Walter D. Asmus, "Practical Aspects of Theatre, Radio and Television," trans. Helen Watanabe, *Journal of Beckett Studies,* 2 (Summer 1977): 83.

45. Ibid., p. 84.

46. Ibid., pp. 89–90.

47. Ibid., p. 91.

48. Samuel Beckett, "An Imaginative Work," *Dublin Magazine* 11 (July–September 1936): 80–81.

49. William B. Yeats, "Anima Mundi," in *Mythologies,* p. 366.

50. Beckett, *Proust.*

51. Ibid., pp. 4–5.

52. Ibid., p. 8.

53. Ibid., pp. 10–11.

54. Ibid., p. 11.

55. Ibid., p. 54.

56. Ibid., p. 42.

57. Ibid., p. 47.

58. Ibid., p. 55.

59. Samuel Beckett, *Film* (New York: Grove Press, 1969), p. 11.

60. Sylvie Debevec Henning, "Film: A Dialogue between Beckett and Berkeley," *Journal of Beckett Studies* 7 (Spring 1982): 92.

61. Beckett, *Murphy,* pp. 107–8.

62. Ibid., p. 110.

63. Samuel Beckett, "Three Dialogues," in *Samuel Beckett: A Collection of Critical Essays,* ed. Martin Esslin (Englewood Cliffs, N.J.: Prentice-Hall, Inc., 1965).

64. Hersh Zeifman, "Being and Non-Being: Samuel Beckett's *Not I,*" *Modern Drama* 19 (March 1976): 35–46.

65. Ben Zvi, "Schismatic Self," p. 10.

66. Ibid., pp. 9–10.

67. Paul Lowry, "Beckett's *Not I,*" *Modern Drama* 26 (December 1983): 409.

68. Katherine Kelly, "The Orphic Mouth in *Not I,*" *Journal of Beckett Studies* 6 (Autumn 1980): 76.

69. Samuel Beckett, *Not I,* in *Ends and Odds* (New York: Grove Press, 1976), p. 15.

70. Samuel Beckett, "Dante. . .Bruno. Vico . . Joyce," *Our Exagmination round His Factification for Incamination of Work in Progress* (London: Faber and Faber, 1962), p. 22.

71. Beryl Fletcher, *A Student's Guide to the Plays of Samuel Beckett,* ed. Beryl Fletcher, John Fletcher, B. Smith, and W. Bachem (London: Faber and Faber, 1978), pp. 197, 198.

72. Samuel Beckett, as told to Gordon Armstrong, Café Francaise, Paris, 16 September 1985.

73. Knowlson, *Light,* p. 32.

74. Martin Esslin, *The Theatre of the Absurd* (New York: Grove Press, 1957), p. 26.

75. Bert O. States, "The Actor's Presence: Three Phenomenal Modes," *Theatre Journal* 35, no. 3 (October 1983): 359–75.

76. Ibid., p. 359.

77. Ibid., p. 375.

78. Ibid., p. 362.

79. Ibid., p. 374.

80. Jacques Derrida, *Of Grammatology*, trans. Gayatri Spivak (Baltimore: The Johns Hopkins Press, 1976), deals extensively with this aspect of communications, and the transition from an aural to a literate civilization in the past two thousand years, which has profoundly changed the borders of conscious experience.

81. Fletcher, *Student's Guide*, p. 33.

82. The stage script for *Not I*, premiered at Lincoln Center, New York City, in December 1972, reveals the evolution of a script from production to published version. The passive repetitions of Mouth are shortened, from "what. .what?. .no. .no!" to "what?. . .no!"; descriptions are filled out in describing the Auditor: "figure" becomes "figure, sex undeterminable"; and verbal images are given new dimensions in the printed version: "love such as normally visited" becomes "love such as normally vented." While the majority of changes are editorial rather than contextual, there are significant differences in the two versions that bear further study. The Grove edition contains at least forty-four additions to the Lincoln Center script, whereas the production version contains eighteen phrases that were not included in the final published version. The evidence suggests that for Beckett at least, the image is established first; then language is adjusted to sharpen or to vaguen the context, and to polish the rhythm of the piece.

83. Jean-Jacques Rousseau, *Essaies,* cited in Derrida, *Grammatology,* p. 270.

84. Derrida, *Grammatology,* pp. 271 ff.

85. Jean-Jacques Rousseau, *Essaies,* cited in ibid., pp. 272–73.

86. Samuel Beckett, *Play,* in *Play and Two Short Pieces for Radio* (London: Faber and Faber, 1964), pp. 21–22. Subsequent page citations will appear in the text.

87. Derrida, *Grammatology,* pp. 273–76.

88. Marilyn Gaddes Rose, "The Sterne Ways of Beckett and Jack B. Yeats," *Irish University Review* 2, ii (1972): 164.

89. Knowlson, *Light,* p. 15.

90. Rose, "Sterne," p. 164.

91. Ibid., p. 165.

92. Beckett, *No's Knife,* p. 148.

93. Esslin, ed., *Beckett: A Collection of Critical Essays,* p. 4.

94. Samuel Beckett, *Play,* in *Collected Shorter Plays of Samuel Beckett* (London: Faber and Faber, 1984), p. 157.

95. Samuel Beckett, *Happy Days* (New York: Grove Press, 1964), p. 49. Subsequent citations will appear in the text. See also p. 40 of playscript for additional references to "another."

96. Stan Gontarski, "The Anatomy of Beckett's *Eh Joe,*" *Modern Drama* 26, no. 4 (December 1983): 425.

97. Beckett, *Murphy,* p. 250.

98. Ibid., pp. 9, 253.

99. Samuel Beckett, *Rockaby* (New York: Grove Press, 1981), p. 16. Subsequent page citations will appear in the text.

100. Beckett, "An Imaginative Work," pp. 80–81.

101. Enoch Brater, "Fragment and Beckett's Form in *That Time* and *Footfalls*," *Journal of Beckett Studies* 2 (Summer 1977): 73–74.

102. Samuel Beckett, to author, Paris, November 1980.

103. Samuel Beckett, notes to original production of *Krapp's Last Tape*, permanent Beckett exhibition, University of Reading, England; cited in Knowlson, *Light*, pp. 21–22.

104. Samuel Beckett, *Ohio Impromptu*, in *Rockaby and Other Short Pieces* (New York: Grove Press, 1981), p. 34.

105. Samuel Beckett, "Catastrophe," *New Yorker*, 19 February 1983, pp. 26–27.

106. Beckett, production notes for *Krapp's Last Tape*.

107. Beckett, "Homage to Jack B. Yeats," pp. 619–20.

Chapter 3. The Geography of the Mind's Eye

1. Francis A. C. Wilson, *Yeats's Iconography* (New York: Macmillan, 1960), pp. 20, 33.

2. See Samuel Beckett, letter to Alan Schneider, in Alan Schneider, "Working with Beckett," *Chelsea Review* (Autumn 1958): p. 16.

3. A. E. F. Horniman, letter to W. B. Yeats, April 1904, as quoted in *Samhain (An Occasional Review)*, ed. W. B. Yeats (Dublin: Sealy Bryers and Walker and T. Fisher Unwin, 1904), p. 53.

4. Ellmann, *Man and Masks*, pp. 164–81 ff.

5. Ibid., pp. 130–31.

6. Peter Ure, *Yeats the Playwright* (New York: Barnes and Noble, 1963), p. 26.

7. Ibid., pp. 26–27.

8. W. B. Yeats, *The Countless Cathleen*, in *Collected Plays of W. B. Yeats* (London: Macmillan and Company, 1953), p. 31. Subsequent page citations will appear in the text.

9. W. B. Yeats, *Literary Ideals in Ireland* (London and Dublin: 1899), p. 19.

10. C. Bridge, ed., *W. B. Yeats and T. Sturgis Moore, Their Correspondence* (London: Routledge & Kegan Paul, 1953), p. 2.

11. Wilson, *Iconography*, p. 20.

12. Ibid., p. 42.

13. Ure, *Yeats*, p. 62.

14. Friedman, *Adventures*, p. xii.

15. Friedman, p. 8.

16. W. B. Yeats, "*Magic*," in *Essays and Introductions*, p. 41.

17. W. B. Yeats, *On Baile's Strand*, in *Collected Plays of W. B. Yeats* (London: Macmillan, 1953), p. 272. Subsequent page citations will appear in the text.

18. W. B. Yeats, *Deirdre*, in *Collected Plays*, p. 192.

19. W. B. Yeats, *The Green Helmet*, in *Collected Plays*, p. 225. Subsequent page citations will appear in the text.

20. Beckett, *How It Is*, p. 121.

21. Wilson, *Iconography*, pp. 59–61.

22. W. B. Yeats, *Certain Noble Plays of Japan*, in *Essays and Introductions*, p. 221.

23. W. B. Yeats, *At the Hawk's Well*, in *Collected Plays*, p. 207.

24. Ibid., p. 208.

25. Friedman, *Adventures*, p. 58.

26. W. B. Yeats, *Per Amica Silentia Lunae*, in *Mythologies*, p. 337.

27. W. B. Yeats, *The Only Jealousy of Emer*, in *Collected Plays*, p. 281.

28. Friedman, *Adventures*, p. 95.

29. W. B. Yeats, *"The Theatre,"* in *Essays and Introductions*, p. 170.

30. Ellmann, *Identity*, p. 183.

31. W. B. Yeats, "Swendenborg, Mediums, Desolate Places" (1914), in *Explorations*, p. 64.

32. W. B. Yeats, "At Stratford-on-Avon," in *Essays and Introductions*, pp. 96–110.

33. Ellmann, *Man and Masks*, p. 296.

34. W. B. Yeats, *Per Amica Silentia Lunae*, in *Mythologies*, p. 340.

35. Ibid., p. 339.

36. Ellmann, *Man and Masks*, p. 293.

37. Ibid., p. 295ff.

38. W. B. Yeats, *The Variorum Edition of the Plays of W. B. Yeats*, ed. Russell K. Alspach (New York: Macmillan, 1966), pp. 415–16.

39. M. C. Stopes, *Plays of Old Japan: The No* (London, 1912), p.22.

40. Tatsuro Ishii, "Zeami's Mature Thoughts on Acting," *Theatre Research International* 12, no. 2 (Summer 1987): 111.

41. Ibid., p. 117.

42. Ibid., p. 117–18.

43. Ibid., p. 123.

44. Ure, *Yeats*, p. 93.

45. Wilson, *Iconography*, pp. 59–63.

46. Ezra Pound, as quoted in Ellmann, *Man and Masks*, p. 216.

47. Ibid., p. 278.

48. Ellmann, *Identity*, p. xvii.

49. W. B. Yeats, *At the Hawk's Well*, in *Collected Plays*, p. 208. Subsequent page citations appear in the text.

50. Ure, *Yeats*, p. 71.

51. Beckett, *Proust*, p. 16.

52. Ellmann, *Man and Masks*, p. 219.

53. W. B. Yeats, "Samhain: 1904. First Principles," in *Explorations*, p. 152.

54. Friedman, *Adventures*, p. 8.

55. W. B. Yeats, "Certain Noble Plays of Japan," in *Essays and Introductions*, p. 224.

56. Ellmann, *Man and Masks*, p. xviii.

57. W. B. Yeats, *Per Amica Silentia Lunae*, in *Mythologies*, p. 324.

58. Friedman, *Adventures*, p. 133.

59. Thomas Parkinson as quoted in Ure, *Yeats*, p. 65.

60. Samuel Beckett, letter to Rick Cluchey, as quoted in "Beckett's San Quentin Theater Workshop Production," in *Krapp's Last Tape: Theater Workbook 1*, p. 127.

61. Samuel Beckett as quoted in *Krapp's Last Tape: Theater Workbook 1*, p. 128.

62. Samuel Beckett, *Krapp's Last Tape* (New York: Grove Press, 1960), p. 25.

63. Samuel Beckett as quoted in *Krapp's Last Tape: Theater Workbook 1*, p. 128.

64. Friedman, *Adventures*, p. 107.

65. Ibid., 77.

66. Ellmann, *Identity*, p. 107.

67. Kathleen Raine, "Death-in-Life," p. 13.

68. Beckett, *Watt*, p. 145.

69. Ibid., p. 196.

70. Samuel Beckett as quoted by Alan Schneider in "Working with Beckett," pp. 3–20.

71. W. B. Yeats, letter to Olivia Shakespear, 1 October 1937, as quoted in Raine, p. 13.

72. Raine, "Death-in-Life," p. 12.

73. Ibid., 12–13.

74. W. B. Yeats, *Calvary*, in *Collected Plays*, p. 449. Subsequent page citations will appear in the text.

75. Ure, *Yeats*, p. 119.

76. W. B. Yeats, *The Only Jealousy of Emer*, in *Collected Plays*, p. 289. Subsequent page citations will appear in the text.

77. Samuel Beckett, *Imagination Dead Imagine* (London: Calder & Boyars, 1965), p. 13. Subsequent page citations will appear in the text.

78. Samuel Beckett, *Play*, in *Play and Two Short Pieces for Radio* (London: Faber and Faber, 1964), p. 22. Subsequent page citations will appear in the text.

79. W. B. Yeats, *A Vision* (New York: Macmillan, 1965), p. 223. Subsequent page citations will appear in the text.

80. W. B. Yeats as quoted in Ure, *Yeats*, p. 88.

81. W. B. Yeats, *Per Amica Silentia Lunae*, in *Mythologies*, pp. 355–56.

82. Ure, *Yeats*, pp. 84–5.

83. W. B. Yeats, *The Dreaming of the Bones*, in *Collected Plays*, pp. 433–34.

84. Ure, *Yeats*, p. 97.

85. Wilson, *Iconography*, p. 213.

86. Ibid., p. 225.

Chapter 4. "The Painter's Brush Consumes His Dreams"

1. I. A. Richards, cited by T. S. Eliot, "After Strange Gods," *Science and Poetry* (New York, 1926), pp. 86–87.

2. W. B. Yeats, letter to Allen Wade, as quoted in *The Letters of W. B. Yeats*, ed. Allen Wade (New York: Macmillan, 1955), p. 97.

3. Ellmann, *Identity*, pp. xxii, xxiv.

4. A further discussion of this type of semiotic structure can be found in Jacques Ehrman, ed., "Game, Play and Literature" issue of *Yale French Studies* 41 (1968); see particularly A. J. Greimas and F. Rastier, "The Interaction of Semiotic Constraints," pp. 81–105.

5. W. B. Yeats, "The Great Day," in *Collected Poems of W. B. Yeats* (London: Macmillan, 1961), p. 358.

6. Moore, *Masks*, p. 310.

7. W. B. Yeats, *Purgatory*, in *Collected Plays*, p. 686. Subsequent page citations will appear in the text.

8. Personal notes taken at the "Permanent Beckett Exhibition," University of Reading, England, August 1971. Information partially reprinted in *New Theatre Magazine* 11, no. 3 (1971).

9. Personal notes taken at the "Permanent Beckett Exhibition."

10. Moore, *Masks*, pp. 313–14.

11. Donald Torchiana, *Yeats and Georgian Ireland* (Evanston, Ill.: Northwestern University Press, 1966), pp. 357–8.

12. See Kathleen Raine, "Death-in-Life," pp. 11–53, in particular, for a discussion of this problem.

13. W. B. Yeats, letters to Ethel Mannin and Ernst Töller, as quoted in Ellmann, *Man and Masks*, pp. 281–82.

14. W. B. Yeats, *The Theatre*, in *Essays and Introductions*, p. 166.

15. W. B. Yeats, *The Death of Cuchulain*, in *Collected Plays*, p. 693. Subsequent page citations will appear in the text.

16. Samuel Beckett, *Endgame* (New York: Grove Press, 1957), p. 84. Subsequent page citations will appear in the text.

17. A. J. Leventhal, "The Thirties," in *Beckett at Sixty*, p. 11.

18. Beckett, *Murphy*, p. 42.

19. Friedman, *Adventures*, p. 130.

20. Michael Benedikt and George Wellwarth, *Modern French Theatre* (New York: E. P. Dutton, 1966), p. ix.

21. Benedikt and Wellwarth, *Theatre*, p. xv.

22. William B. Yeats, *The Autobiography of W. B. Yeats* (Garden City, N.Y.: Doubleday, 1958), pp. 233–34.

23. Ibid., p. 234.

24. Samuel Beckett, *Company* (New York: Grove Press, 1980), p. 7. Subsequent page citations will appear in the text.

25. Samuel Beckett as quoted in Raymond Federman and John Fletcher, eds., *Samuel Beckett: His Works and His Critics* (Berkeley: University of California Press, 1970), pp. 62–63: "*Godot* is without any doubt between *Malone* and *L'Innomable*."

26. Samuel Beckett, *The Unnamable*, in *Three Novels*, p. 414. Subsequent page citations will appear in the text.

27. Leventhal, "The Thirties," in *Beckett at Sixty*, p. 11.

28. John McPhee, *Basin and Range*, p. 124. McPhee is much indebted to the pioneering efforts of the geologist-theologian Pierre Teilhard de Chardin.

29. Samuel Beckett, letter to Alan Schneider, as quoted in *Village Voice Reader* (New York: Grove Press, 1967), p. 182.

30. W. B. Yeats, "Samhain: 1904, The Play, the Player, and the Scene," in *Explorations*, p. 172.

31. William B. Yeats, "The Tower," *Collected Poems of W. B. Yeats* (New York: Macmillan, 1961), p. 223. Subsequent page citations will be found in the text.

32. Samuel Beckett, *. . .but the clouds. . .* , *Collected Shorter Plays of Samuel Beckett* (London: Faber and Faber, 1984), pp. 255–262. Subsequent page citations will appear in the text.

33. Friedman, *Adventures*, p. 136.

34. Moore, *Masks*, p. 43.

35. Ellmann, *Man and Masks*, p. 289.

36. W. B. Yeats, "Samhain: 1904, The Play, the Player, and the Scene," in *Explorations*, pp. 176–77.

37. W. B. Yeats, "A General Introduction for My Work," in *Essays and Introductions*, p. 520.

38. Personal interview with Samuel Beckett, 4 November 1980: "American actors are quite difficult."

39. Bair, *Samuel Beckett*, pp. 489–91.

40. S. E. Gontarski, "Krapp's Last Tape," in *Theatre Work-book 1. Samuel Beckett: Krapp's Last Tape*, p. 16.

41. W. B. Yeats, *Per Amica Silentia Lunae*, in *Mythologies*, p. 331.

42. Ibid., p. 341.

43. Samuel Beckett, "Three Dialogues," in *Beckett: A Collection of Critical Essays*, p. 21.

44. Ibid., pp. 21–2.

45. W. B. Yeats, "The Return of Ulysses," in *Essays and Introductions*, p. 198.

46. Ibid., p. 199.

47. Ellmann, *Man and Masks*, p. 298.

48. W. B. Yeats, "Samhain: 1905," in *Explorations*, p. 201.

49. Wang Wei, "The Bamboo Studio," in *A Chinese Garden Court*, ed. Alfreda Murck and Wen Fong (New York: The Metropolitan Museum of Art, 1981), p. 22.

50. Samuel Beckett, *Rockaby* (New York: Grove Press, 1981), pp. 17–18.

Chapter 5. "Continuosity, Impetuosity and Exuberance"

1. Terence de Vere White, "The Personality of Jack B. Yeats," in *Jack B. Yeats: A Centenary Gathering*, ed. Roger McHugh (Dublin: The Dolmen Press, 1971), p. 28.

2. Thomas MacGreevy, *Jack B. Yeats: An Appreciation and An Introduction* (Dublin: Victor Waddington Publications Ltd., 1945), p. 14.

3. Hilary Pyle, *Jack B. Yeats: A Biography* (London: Routledge & Kegan Paul, 1970), p. 133.

4. Ibid., 38.

5. Jack Yeats, letter to John Quinn, 17 November 1920, Berg Collection, New York Public Library.

6. Thomas MacGreevy, letter to Jack Yeats, 22 December 1930, in Pyle, *Jack B. Yeats*, p. 146.

7. Andrew Belis (Samuel Beckett), "Recent Irish Poetry," *Bookman* 86 (1934): 235.

8. John Gruen, "Samuel Beckett Talks about Beckett," *Vogue Magazine*, London edition, February 1970, p. 108.

9. Jack Yeats, *Modern Art* (Dublin: Cuala Press, 1922), pp. 3–4.

10. Ibid., p. 9.

11. Pyle, *Jack B. Yeats*, p. 128.

12. James White, *Yeats 1871–1957: A Centenary Exhibition* (London: Martin Secker & Warburg, 1971), p. 146.

13. Pyle, *Jack B. Yeats*, p. 17.

14. Anne Yeats, Introduction, *Broadside Characters: Drawings by Jack Yeats* (Dublin: Cuala Press, 1971), p. 24.

15. Brian O'Doherty, "Jack B. Yeats; Promise and Regret," in *Jack B. Yeats: A Centenary Gathering*, p. 89.

16. Pyle, *Jack B. Yeats*, pp. 128–29.

17. Beckett, *Imagination Dead Imagine*, pp. 13–14.

18. Beckett, *Company*, p.11.

19. Beckett, *Proust*, p. 20.

20. James White, "Memory Harbor: Jack Yeats's Painting Process," in *Yeats Studies: An International Journal*, ed. Robert O'Driscoll and Lorna Reynolds, no. 2 (Shannon: Irish University Press, 1972), p. 15.

21. Anne Yeats, *"Jack Yeats: Comments on Painting Exhibition,"* in *Yeats Studies* ed. O'Driscoll and Reynolds, p. 1.

22. Beckett, *Proust*, p. 72.

23. Beckett, *Rockaby*, p. 20.

24. Asmus, "Practical Aspects of Theater, Radio, and Television," pp. 89–90.

25. O'Doherty, "Jack B. Yeats," p. 78.

26. Ibid., p. 83.

27. William M. Murphy, *The Yeats Family and the Pollexfens of Sligo* (Dublin: The Dolmen Press, 1971), p. 54.

28. Pyle, *Jack B. Yeats*, p. 20.

29. John Butler Yeats's unpublished memoirs as quoted in Murphy, *Yeats Family*, p. 16.

30. Lily Yeats's unpublished scrapbook as quoted in ibid., p. 38.

31. John Butler Yeats's unpublished letter to Edward Dowden, 8 January 1884, as quoted in ibid., p. 17.

32. In his later years, Yeats was in the habit of adding a seagull to completed paintings, thereby signifying that they were "ready to fly."

33. Murphy, *Yeats Family*, p. 19.

34. MacGreevy, *Jack B. Yeats: An Appreciation*, p. 21.

35. Lilly Yeats, "Grandfather William Pollexfen," as quoted in Murphy, *Yeats Family*, p. 21; Pyle, *Jack B. Yeats*, p. 13; Jack Yeats, *Modern Art*, p. 6.

36. Jack Yeats, *Modern Art*, p. 7.

37. James White, *John Butler Yeats* (Dublin: The Dolmen Press, n.d.), p. 15.

38. Pyle, *Jack B. Yeats*, p. 15.

39. MacGreevy, *Jack B. Yeats: An Appreciation*, p. 19.

40. W. B. Yeats, Preface to *Gods and Fighting Men*, by Lady Gregory (Toronto: Macmillan, 1976), p. 19.

41. Earnan O'Malley, *On Another Man's Wound*, as quoted in MacGreevy, p. 17.

42. Samuel Beckett, letter to Alan Schneider, as quoted in *Village Voice Reader*, pp. 182–83.

43. Jack B. Yeats, letter to John Quinn, 16 September 1907, Berg Collection, New York Public Library.

44. Murphy, *Yeats Family*, p. 55.

45. I am indebted to Professor Robin Skelton of the University of Victoria for pointing out the importance of the influence of Synge on the development of Jack Yeats's artistic credo.

46. Pyle, *Jack B. Yeats*, p. 56.

47. Robin Skelton, "J. M. Synge," reprinted from *Essays by Divers Hands* (Oxford: Oxford University Press, 1970), pp. xxxviii, 97.

48. Jack Yeats, "A Letter about J. M. Synge," *New York Evening Sun*, 20 July 1909.

49. Skelton, "Synge," p. 107.

50. Ibid., p. 96.

51. Ibid., p. 100.

52. W. B. Yeats, "J. M. Synge and the Ireland of His Time," in *Essays and Introductions*, p. 341.

53. Pyle, Jack B. Yeats, p. 97.

54. Jack Yeats, "The Scourge of the Gulph," in *The Collected Plays of Jack B. Yeats*, ed. Robin Skelton (New York: Bobbs-Merrill, 1971), p. 80.

55. Skelton, ed., *Collected Plays*, p. 4.

56. White, *Yeats 1871–1957*, p. 14.

57. Pyle, *Jack B. Yeats*, p. 117.

58. Ibid., p. 119.

59. O'Doherty, "Jack B. Yeats," p. 85.

60. MacGreevy, *Jack B. Yeats: An Appreciation*, p. 27.

61. Skelton, ed., *Collected Plays*, p. 4.

62. Jack Yeats, as spoken to Sir John Rothenstein, as quoted in Pyle, *Jack B. Yeats*, 127.

63. Jack Yeats, Letter to W. B. Yeats, 31 October 1925, as quoted in Pyle, p. 124.

64. Jack Yeats, *Sligo* (London: Wishart and Co., 1930), p. 28. Subsequent page citations will appear in the text.

65. Robin Skelton, "Themes and Attitudes in the Later Drama of Jack B. Yeats," in unidentified journal, n.p., n.p., n.d.

66. Jack Yeats, *Modern Art,* pp. 8, 9.

67. Alan Denson, letter to Anthony Piper, following his interview with Jack Yeats, 30 September 1954, as quoted in Pyle, *Jack B. Yeats,* p. 146.

68. Bair, *Samuel Beckett,* p. 281.

69. Samuel Beckett, letter to Thomas MacGreevy, as quoted in ibid., p. 282.

70. Samuel Beckett, letter to John Kobler, 24 September 1971, as quoted in ibid., p. 283.

71. Beckett, letter to Alan Schneider, in *Village Voice Reader,* p. 182.

72. Jack Yeats, *Modern Art,* p. 10.

73. Vivian Mercer, *Beckett/Beckett* (New York: Oxford University Press, 1977); David H. Hesla, *The Shape of Chaos: An Interpretation of the Art of Samuel Beckett* (Minneapolis: University of Minnesota Press, 1977).

74. Beckett, *The Unnamable,* in *Three Novels,* pp. 327, 414, 353. Subsequent page citations will appear in the text.

75. Maurice Blanchot, Review of *The Unnamable,* trans. Richard Howard, in *Nouvelle Revue Francaise,* October 1953, pp. 678–86, as quoted in *Samuel Beckett: The Critical Heritage,* ed. Lawrence Graver and Raymond Federman (London: Routledge & Kegan Paul, 1979) p. 120.

76. Beckett, *Watt,* p. 247. Subsequent page citations will appear in the text.

77. White, *Yeats 1871–1957,* p. 155.

78. Jack Yeats, *The Deathly Terrace,* in *Collected Plays,* ed. Skelton, p. 108. Subsequent page citations will appear in the text.

79. Erwin Schrödinger, *What is Life? The Physical Aspects of the Living Cell* (Cambridge: Cambridge University Press, 1945), p. 72.

80. Beckett, *How It Is,* pp. 145–46.

81. E. M. Cioran, "Encounter With Beckett," *Partisan Review* 43, no. 2 (1976): 280, trans. Raymond Federman and Jean Sommermeyer, as quoted in *Beckett: Critical Heritage,* p. 338.

82. Skelton, "Themes and Attitudes in the Later Drama of Jack B. Yeats," *Yeats Studies* 2 (1972): 101.

83. Pyle, *Jack B. Yeats,* p. 75.

84. Beckett, *Endgame,* pp. 30–31.

85. Beckett, *Waiting for Godot,* p. 25A.

86. White, *Yeats 1871–1957,* p. 158.

87. Beckett, *Krapp's Last Tape,* p. 20. Subsequent page citations will appear in the text.

88. Skelton, "Themes and Attitudes," p. 105.

89. Jack Yeats, *The Old Sea Road,* in *Collected Plays,* ed. Skelton, p. 146. Subsequent page citations will appear in the text.

90. Jack Yeats, *Rattle,* in *Collected Plays,* ed. Skelton, p. 181.

91. Jack Yeats, *Apparitions,* in *Collected Plays,* ed. Skelton, p. 133.

Chapter 6. Stages of an Image: No Symbols Where None Intended

1. Jack Yeats as quoted in T. de Vere White, *A Fretful Midge,* as quoted in Pyle, *Jack B. Yeats,* p. 172.

2. Pyle, *Jack B. Yeats*, p. 119.

3. O'Doherty, "Jack B. Yeats," p. 84.

4. Ibid., p. 81.

5. Jack Yeats, letter to Thomas Bodkin, 31 August 1936, partially reprinted in White, *Yeats 1871–1957*, p. 151.

6. Beckett, *Watt*, p. 226. Subsequent page citations will appear in the text.

7. Letter received from Samuel Beckett, 4 February 1982.

8. White, *Yeats 1871–1957*, p. 151.

9. Ibid., p. 15.

10. Ibid., p. 14.

11. "The Grand Conversation under the Rose," Irish ballad quoted on *A Broadsheet* (1903), illustrated by Jack Yeats.

12. White, *Yeats 1871–1957*, p. 152. See also Yeats's painting *This Grand Conversation Was under the Rose* (1943) for another treatment of the clown image.

13. Beckett, "An Imaginative Work," pp. 80–81. This review also contains an interesting note on Jack Yeats's *The Old Sea Road*.

14. White, *Yeats 1871–1957*, p. 158.

15. Jack Yeats, *The Charmed Life* (London: Routledge & Kegan Paul, 1938), p. 1. Subsequent page citations will appear in the text.

16. W. B. Yeats, "From 'On the Boiler,'" in *Explorations*, p. 450.

17. Douglas N. Archibald, *John Butler Yeats* (Lewisburg, Pa.: Bucknell University Press, 1974), p. 99.

18. Beckett, *Murphy*, p. 112; Beckett, *How It Is*, p. 72.

19. Samuel Beckett, *Play*, pp. 16, 23.

20. Samuel Beckett, letter to Thomas MacGreevy, 31 January 1938, as quoted in Bair, *Samuel Beckett*, p. 282.

21. "Burial of the Dead," *Book of Common Prayer* (American revision, 1928).

22. Pyle, *Jack B. Yeats*, p. 154.

23. Jack Yeats, letter to Hertha Phyllis Eason, partially quoted in ibid., p. 154.

24. Pyle, *Jack B. Yeats*, p. 154.

25. Jack Yeats, *Harlequin's Positions*, in *Collected Plays*, ed. Skelton, p. 295. Subsequent page citations will appear in the text.

26. Robert Emmet (1778–1803) was a celebrated Irish patriot who studied at Trinity College, Dublin, but was forced to leave there in 1798 because of his nationalist sympathies. During 1801–2, with other exiles, he planned the United Irishmen's uprisings. In July 1803, Emmet and 100 disorderly men staged a march on Dublin Castle. Their rebellion disintegrated into a brawl, and Emmet was forced to flee for his life. He returned to Dublin to be near Sarah Curren and was finally captured there. Tried and condemned to death, Emmet made a stirring speech from the gallows platform that assured his place as a great Irish patriot. Following his death it was discovered that Emmet's attorney and many of his associates had been in the pay of the English Crown.

27. Skelton, ed., *Collected Plays*, p. 8.

28. Samuel Beckett, "MacGreevy on Yeats," in *Jack B. Yeats: A Centenary Gathering*, ed. McHugh, p. 73.

29. Beckett, "An Imaginative Work," p. 81.

30. Skelton, "Themes and Attitudes," p. 112.

31. Pyle, *Jack B. Yeats*, p. 132.

32. W. B. Yeats, *A Vision*, p. 237.

33. Jack Yeats, *The Silencer*, in *Collected Plays*, ed. Skelton, p. 212. Subsequent page citations will appear in the text.

34. T. G. Rosenthal, *Jack Yeats 1871–1957* (London: Knowledge Publications, 1966), pp. 5–6.

35. Samuel Beckett, letter to H. O. White, 15 April 1957, Trinity College Library, Dublin, as partially quoted in Bair, *Samuel Beckett,* pp. 482–83.

36. Skelton, ed., *Collected Plays,* p. 7.

37. Jack Yeats, *The Deathly Terrace,* in *Collected Plays,* ed. Skelton, p. 106.

38. Jack Yeats, *Modern Art,* p. 11.

39. Pyle, *Jack B. Yeats,* p. 128.

40. Skelton, "Themes and Attitudes," p. 115.

41. Jack Yeats, *La La Noo,* in *Collected Plays,* ed. Skelton, p. 301. Subsequent page citations will be found in the text.

42. Jack Yeats, *And to You Also* (London: Routledge & Sons, Ltd., 1944), pp. 47, 56.

43. Beckett, *Murphy,* pp. 107–13.

44. Rosenthal, *Jack Yeats 1871–1957,* p. 5.

45. Samuel Beckett, "MacGreevy on Yeats," in *Jack B. Yeats: A Centenary Gathering,* ed. McHugh, p. 73.

46. Personal interview with Samuel Beckett, 4 November 1980.

47. W. B. Yeats, "The Tragic Theatre," in *Essays and Introductions,* p. 245 ff.

48. Jack Yeats, *Modern Art,* p. 4.

49. Pyle, *Jack B. Yeats,* p. 129.

50. MacGreevy, *Jack B. Yeats: An Appreciation,* p. 14.

51. *A Broadsheet* (1903), illustrated by Jack Yeats, Special Collections University of Victoria Library, Victoria, British Columbia.

52. See also Anne Yeats in *Yeats Studies: An International Journal,* ed. O'Driscoll and Reynolds, pp. 1–2; Rosenthal, *Jack Yeats 1871–1957,* p. 6: "John Berger once observed of Yeats that 'he teaches us to hope' and this remark is particularly apt in the case of these two paintings [*Helen* and *The Blood of Abel*] because Yeats the painter, in the end, triumphs over Yeats the historical pessimist"; Earnan O'Malley, Introduction, *Jack B. Yeats National Loan Exhibition,* June–July 1945 (Dublin: National College of Art, 1945), pp. 6–16.

53. Pyle, *Jack B. Yeats,* p. 127.

54. Ibid., 131.

55. Jack Yeats, "Indigo Heights," *The New Statesman and Nation,* 5 December 1936, pp. 899–900.

56. See H. W. Jansen, *History of Art* (Englewood Cliffs, N.J.: Prentice-Hall, 1967), pp. 447–49 in particular.

57. Oliver Sacks and Robert Wasserman, "The Case of the Colorblind Painter," *New York Review of Books* 34, no. 18 (19 November 1987): 32.

58. Sacks and Wasserman, "Painter," pp. 32–33; Jack Yeats, "Indigo," p. 899.

59. Beckett, "Homage to Jack B. Yeats," rpt. in White, *Yeats 1871–1957,* p. 10.

60. W. B. Yeats, "The Circus Animals' Desertion," in *Collected Poems,* p. 392.

61. Jack Yeats, *The Deathly Terrace,* in *Collected Plays,* ed. Skelton, p. 106.

62. White, *Yeats 1871–1957,* p. 15.

63. MacGreevy, *Jack B. Yeats: An Appreciation,* p. 34.

64. Rosenthal, *Jack Yeats 1871–1957,* p. 6.

65. Jansen, *History of Art,* p. 433.

66. James White, "Introduction," *Jack B. Yeats, Drawing and Paintings* (London: Secker and Warburg, 1971), p. 13.

67. Beckett, *Not I,* in *Ends and Odds,* p. 15.

68. Beckett, *Play,* pp. 18, 21.

69. Personal interview with Samuel Beckett, 4 November 1980.

70. Jack Yeats, *The Old Sea Road,* in *Collected Plays,* ed. Skelton, p. 162.

71. Question: Are you ever going to write your autobiography? Beckett: There are two answers to your question, one from Francis Bacon: *"De nobis ipsis silemus"* ["Let us be silent about ourselves"] and one from Rene Descartes: *"Bene qui latuit bene vixit"* ["He lived well who hid well"], Paris, 14 September 1985.

72. Bair, *Samuel Beckett,* p. 482.

73. Beckett, "Homage to Jack B. Yeats," rpt. in White, *Yeats 1871–1957,* p. 10.

Select Bibliography

Samuel Beckett

Primary Sources

"An Imaginative Work." *Dublin Magazine* 11 (July–September 1936): 80–81.

All Strange Away. New York: Grove Press, 1974.

Cascando and Other Short Dramatic Pieces. New York: Grove Press, 1977.

Collected Poems in English and French. New York: Grove Press, 1977.

Company. New York: Grove Press, 1980.

"Dante. . .Bruno. Vico. .Joyce." *Transition* 16–17 (1929): 242–53.

En Attendant Godot. Paris: Editions de Minuit, 1952.

Endgame. New York: Grove Press, 1957.

Ends and Odds: Eight New Dramatic Pieces. New York: Grove Press, 1976.

"The Expelled." *I Can't Go On, I'll Go On.* Edited by Richard W. Seaver. New York: Grove Press, 1976.

Film. New York: Grove Press, 1972.

Fin de partie. Paris: Editions de Minuit, 1957.

First Love and Other Shorts. New York: Grove Press, 1974.

Fizzles. New York: Grove Press, 1976.

From an Abandoned Work. Stüttgart: Manus Press, 1967.

Happy Days. New York: Grove Press, 1961.

How It Is. New York: Grove Press, 1964.

Ill Seen Ill Said. New York: Grove Press, 1981.

Imagination Dead Imagine. London: Calder and Boyars, 1965.

Krapp's Last Tape. New York: Grove Press, 1960.

"Lessness." *New Statesman* 79 (May 1970): 635.

The Lost Ones. New York: Grove Press, 1972.

Mercier and Camier. New York: Grove Press, 1974.

More Pricks Than Kicks. New York: Grove Press, 1970.

Murphy. New York: Grove Press, 1957.

Not I. In *Ends and Odds.* New York: Grove Press, 1977.

Ohio Impromptu, Catastrophe, What Where. New York: Grove Press, 1984.

Play In *Play and Two Short Pieces for Radio.* London: Faber and Faber, 1964.

Proust. New York: Grove Press, 1957.

Quad, Collected Shorter Plays by Samuel Beckett. New York: Grove Press, 1984.

Radio II. Ends and Odds. New York: Grove Press, 1976.

Rockaby. New York: Grove Press, 1981.

Stories and Texts for Nothing. New York: Grove Press, 1967.

"Three Dialogues." In *Samuel Beckett: A Collection of Critical Essays.* Edited by Martin Esslin. Englewood Cliffs, N.J.: Prentice-Hall, 1965.

Three Novels: Molloy, Malone Dies, The Unnamable. New York: Grove Press, 1965.

Waiting for Godot. New York: Grove Press, 1954.

Watt. New York: Grove Press, 1959.

Worstward Ho. London: John Calder, 1983.

SECONDARY SOURCES

Abbott, H. Porter. *The Fiction of Samuel Beckett: Form and Effect*. Berkeley: University of California Press, 1973.

———. "A Poetics of Radical Displacement." *Texas Studies in Literature and Language* 17 (Spring 1975).

Acheson, James, and Kateryna Arthur, eds. *Beckett's Later Fiction and Drama: Texts for Company*. London: Macmillan, 1986.

Admussen, Richard. "The Manuscripts of Beckett's Play." *Modern Drama* 16 (June 1973).

———. *The Samuel Beckett Manuscripts*. Boston: G. K. Hall, 1970.

Albright, Daniel. *Representation and the Imagination: Beckett, Kafka, Nabokov, and Schoenberg*. Chicago: University of Chicago Press, 1981.

Alvarez, A. *Samuel Beckett*. New York: Viking Press, 1973.

Asmus, Walter. "Beckett Directs Godot," *Theatre Quarterly* 5 (1975): 19–26.

Bair, Deirdre. *Samuel Beckett: A Bibliography*. New York: Harcourt Brace Jovanovich, 1978.

Barnard, G. C. *Samuel Beckett: A New Approach*. London: J. M. Dent & Sons, Ltd., 1970.

Beja, Morris, S. E. Gontarski, and Pierre Astier, eds. *Samuel Beckett: Humanistic Perspectives*. Columbus: Ohio State University Press, 1983.

Belis, Andrew [Samuel Beckett]. "Recent Irish Poetry." *Bookman* 86 (1934): 235.

Ben-Zvi, Linda. *Samuel Beckett*. Boston: Twayne, 1986.

———. "Samuel Beckett, Fritz Mauthner, and the Limits of Language." *PMLA* 95 (March 1980): 183–200.

———. "The Schismatic Self in a Piece of Monologue." *Journal of Beckett Studies* 9 (1984): 65–86.

Blanchot, Maurice. Revision of *The Unnamable*. *Nouvelle Revue Francaise*, October 1953, pp. 678–86. Rpt. in *Samuel Beckett: The Critical Heritage*. Edited by Lawrence Graver and Raymond Federman. Translated by Richard Howard. London: Routledge & Kegan Paul, 1979.

Brater, Enoch., ed. *Beckett at 80/ Beckett in Context*. New York: Oxford University Press, 1986.

———. *Beyond Minimalism*. New York: Oxford University Press, 1987.

Busi, Frederick. *The Transformations of Godot*. Lexington: University of Kentucky, 1980.

Calder, John, ed., *Beckett at Sixty: A Festschrift*. London: Calder and Boyars, 1967.

Carey, Elaine. "Donald Davis Brings Beckett Back Home." *Toronto Star*, March 10, 1984.

Chabert, Pierre. "Samuel Beckett as Director." In *Theatre Workbook 1. Samuel Beckett: Krapp's Last Tape*. Edited and translated by James Knowlson. London: Brutus Books, Ltd., 1980.

Chevigny, Bell Gale, ed. *Twentieth Century Interpretations of "Endgame."* Englewood Cliffs, N.J.: Prentice-Hall, 1969.

Cioran, E. M. "Encounter with Beckett." *Partisan Review* 43, no. 2 (1976): 280. Rpt. in *Samuel Beckett: The Critical Heritage.* Edited by Lawrence Graver and Raymond Federman. Translated by Raymond Federman and Jean Sommermeyer. London: Routledge & Kegan Paul, 1979.

Coe, Richard. *Samuel Beckett.* New York: Grove Press, 1968.

Cohn, Ruby. *Back to Beckett.* Princeton: Princeton University Press, 1973.

———. "Beckett's Recent Residua." *Southern Review* 5 (1969): 1045–54.

———. *Just Play: Beckett's Theater.* Princeton: Princeton University Press, 1980.

———. "Philosophical Fragment in the Works of Samuel Beckett." *Criticism* 6 (1964): 33–43.

———. *Samuel Beckett: The Comic Gamut.* New Brunswick: Rutgers University Press, 1962.

———. "Samuel Beckett, Self Translator." *PMLA* 76 (December 1961): 613–21.

———, ed. *Disjecta: Miscellaneous Writings and a Dramatic Fragment.* New York: Grove Press, 1984.

Copeland, Hannah C. *Art and the Artist in the Works of Samuel Beckett.* The Hague: Mouton, 1975.

Cooke, Virginia, ed. *Beckett on File.* London: Methuen, 1985.

Dearlove, Judith E. *Accommodating the Chaos: Samuel Beckett's Nonrelational Art.* Durham, N.C.: Duke University Press, 1982.

Driver, Tom. "Beckett by the Madeleine." *Columbia University Forum* 4 (Summer 1961).

Duckworth, Colin, ed. *En Attendant Godot.* By Samuel Beckett, London: George G. Harrap and Co., 1966.

Esslin, Martin, ed. *Samuel Beckett: A Collection of Critical Essays.* Englewood Cliffs, N.J.: Prentice-Hall, 1965.

———. *The Theatre of the Absurd.* New York: Doubleday, Anchor Books, 1961.

Federman, Raymond. *Journey to Chaos: Samuel Beckett's Early Fiction.* Berkeley: University of California Press, 1970.

Federman, Raymond, and John Fletcher. *Samuel Beckett, His Work and His Critics: An Essay in Bibliography.* Berkeley: University of California Press, 1974.

Fehsenfeld, Martha. "Beckett's Late Works: An Appraisal." *Modern Drama* 25 (September 1982).

Fletcher, Beryl, et al. *A Student's Guide to the Plays of Samuel Beckett.* London: Faber and Faber, 1978, 1985.

Fletcher, John. *The Novels of Samuel Beckett.* London: Chatto and Windus, 1967.

Gluck, Barbara. *Beckett and Joyce.* Lewisburg, Pa.: Bucknell University Press, 1979.

Gontarski, S. E. *Beckett's "Happy Days": A Manuscript Study.* Columbus: Ohio State University Libraries, 1977.

———. "Krapp's Last Tape." In *Theatre Workbook 1. Samuel Beckett: Krapp's Last Tape.* Edited and translated by James Knowlson. London: Brutus Books, Ltd., 1980.

———. *The Intent of Undoing in Samuel Beckett's Dramatic Texts.* Bloominton: Indiana University Press, 1985.

———, ed. *On Beckett: Essays and Criticism.* New York: Grove Press, 1986.

Gontarski, S. E., and John Pilling. *Frescoes of the Skull: The Later Prose and Drama of Samuel Beckett.* London: John Calder 1979.

Graver, Lawrence, and Raymond Federman, eds. *Samuel Beckett: The Critical Heritage.* London: Routledge & Kegan Paul, 1979.

Gruen, John, "Samuel Beckett Talks about Beckett." *Vogue Magazine,* London edition, February 1970, p. 108.

Harvey, Lawrence E. *Samuel Beckett, Poet and Critic.* Princeton: Princeton University Press, 1970.

Hassan, Ihab. *The Literature of Silence: Henry Miller and Samuel Beckett.* New York: Knopf, 1967.

Hayman, Ronald. *Samuel Beckett.* New York: Frederick Ungar, 1973.

Hesla, David H. *The Shape of Chaos: An Interpretation of the Art of Samuel Beckett.* Minneapolis: University of Minnesota Press, 1977.

Hoffman, Samuel, *Samuel Beckett: The Language of Self.* Carbondale: Southern Illinois University Press, 1962.

Homan, Sidney. *Beckett's Theater: Interpretations for Performance.* Lewisburg, Pa.: Bucknell University Press, 1984.

Jacobsen, Josephine, and William Mueller. *The Testament of Samuel Beckett.* New York: Hill and Wang, 1964.

Jolas, Maria. "A Bloomlein for Sam." In *Beckett at Sixty: A Festschrift.* London: Calder & Boyars, 1967.

Journal of Beckett Studies, nos. 1–9.

Kennedy, Sighle. *Murphy's Bed: A Study of Real Sources and Sur-Real Associations in Beckett's First Novel.* Lewisburg, Pa.: Bucknell University Press, 1971.

Kenner, Hugh. *Flaubert, Joyce, and Beckett: The Stoic Comedians.* Boston: Beacon Press, 1962.

———. *Samuel Beckett: A Critical Study.* Berkeley: University of California Press, 1968.

———. *A Reader's Guide to Samuel Beckett.* New York: Farrar, Strauss and Giroux, 1973.

Kern, Edith. "Beckett and the Spirit of the Commedia dell'arte." *Modern Drama* 9 (1966): 260–67.

Knowlson, James, ed. *Happy Days: The Production Notebook of Samuel Beckett.* New York: Grove Press, 1985.

———. *Light and Darkness in the Theatre of Samuel Beckett.* London: Turret Books, 1972.

Knowlson, James, ed. *Theatre Workbook 1. Samuel Beckett: Krapp's Last Tape.* London: Brutus Books, Ltd., 1980.

Knowlson, James, and John Pilling. *Frescoes of the Skull: The Later Prose and Drama of Samuel Beckett.* New York: Grove Press, 1980.

Leventhal, A. J. "The Thirties." In *Beckett at Sixty: A Festschrift.* London: Calder & Boyars, 1967.

Levy, Eric. *Beckett and the Voice of Species: A Study of the Prose Fiction.* Totowa, N.J.: Barnes and Noble, 1980.

Lyons, Charles. *Samuel Beckett.* New York: Grove Press, 1983.

Mercier, Vivian. *Beckett/Beckett.* New York: Oxford University Press, 1977.

Mihalyi, Gabor. "Beckett's Godot and the Myth of Alienation." *Modern Drama* 9 (December 1966): 280–87.

Moorjani, Angela B. *Abysmal Games in the Novels of Samuel Beckett.* Chapel Hill: University of North Carolina Studies in the Romance Language and Literatures. 1982.

Morrison, Kristin. *Canters and Chronicles: The Use of Narrative in the Plays of Samuel Beckett and Harold Pinter.* Chicago: University of Chicago Press, 1983.

O'Brien, Eoin. *The Beckett Country: Samuel Beckett's Ireland.* London: Faber and Faber, 1986.

Pilling, John. *Samuel Beckett.* London: Routledge & Kegan Paul, 1976.

"Poetry is Vertical." *Transition* (1931): 148–49.

Reid, Alec. *All I Can Manage, More Than I Could: An Approach to the Plays of Samuel Beckett.* New York: Grove Press, 1968.

Robbe-Grillet, Alain. *For a New Novel: Essays on Fiction.* Translated by Richard Howard. New York: Grove Press, 1966.

———. "Samuel Beckett, or 'Presence' in the Theatre." In *Samuel Beckett: A Collection of Critical Essays.* Edited by Martin Esslin. Englewood Cliffs, N.J.: Prentice-Hall, 1965, pp. 108–16.

Robinson, Michael. *The Long Sonata of the Dead: A Study of Samuel Beckett.* New York: Grove Press, 1969.

Rollins, Ronald. "Old Men and Memories: Yeats and Beckett. *Eire* 13 (Fall 1978).

Rose, Marilyn Gaddis. "The Lyrical Structure of Beckett's Texts for Nothing." *Novel* 4 (Spring 1971).

Rosen, Stephen J. *Samuel Beckett and the Pessimistic Tradition.* New Brunswick: Rutgers University Press, 1976.

Schneider, Alan. *Entrances: An American Director's Journey.* New York: Viking Press, 1986.

———. "On Directing Film." In Samuel Beckett, *Film.* New York: Grove Press, 1969.

———. "Working with Beckett." *Chelsea Review* (Autumn 1958): 3–20.

Worth, Katharine, ed. *Beckett the Shape Changer.* London: Routledge and Kegan Paul, 1973.

———. *The Irish Drama of Europe from Yeats to Beckett.* London: Athlone Press, 1978.

Zeifman, Hersh. "Being and Non-Being: Samuel Beckett's *Not I.*" *Modern Drama* 19 (March 1976).

Ziliacus, Clas. *Beckett and Broadcasting.* Abo, Finland: Acta Academia Aboensis, Ser. *A Humaniora* 51, no. 2 (1976).

Jack B. Yeats

PRIMARY SOURCES

Ah Well. London: Routledge, 1942.

The Amaranthers. London: Heinemann, 1936.

And to You Also. London: Routledge & Sons, Ltd., 1944.

Apparitions, The Old Sea Road, Rattle. Illustrated by Jack B. Yeats. London: Jonathan Cape, 1933.

The Bosun and the Bob-tailed Comet. London: Elkin Mathews, 1904.

The Careless Flower. London: The Pilot Press, 1942.

The Charmed Life. London: Routledge & Kegan Paul, 1938.

"Indigo Heights." *The New Statesman and Nation* 5 (December 1936): 899–900.

In Sand. Edited by Jack MacGowran. Dublin: The Dolman Press, 1964.

James Flaunty or The Terror of the Western Seas. London: Elkin Mathews, 1901.

La La Noo. Dublin: The Cuala Press, 1943.

Letter to Joseph Hone. 7 March 1922. Special Collections, University of Kansas Library, Lawrence, Kansas.

Letter to John Quinn. 16 September 1907. Berg Collection. New York Public Library, New York, New York.

Letter to John Quinn. 17 November 1920. Berg Collection. New York Public Library, New York, New York.

Life in the West of Ireland. Dublin: Maunsel and Company, Ltd., 1912.

A Little Fleet. London: Elkin Mathews, 1909.

Modern Aspects of Irish Art. Dublin: Cumann Leigheacht an Phobail, 1922.

Sailing, Sailing, Swiftly. London: Putnam, 1933.

The Scourge of the Gulph. London: Elkin Mathews, 1903.

Sligo. London: Wishart and Co., 1930.

The Treasure of the Garden. London: Elkin Mathews, 1903.

SECONDARY SOURCES

Archibald, D. N. *John Butler Yeats.* Lewisburg, Pa.: Bucknell University Press, 1974.

Arnold, B. *A Concise History of Irish Art.* London: Thames and Hudson, 1969.

Beckett, Samuel. "Homage to Jack B. Yeats." *Les Lettres Nouvelles,* April 1954. Rpt. in James White, *Jack B. Yeats 1871–1957: A Centenary Exhibition.* London: Martin Secker & Warburg Ltd., 1971.

———. "MacGreevy on Yeats." In *Jack B. Yeats: A Centenary Gathering.* Edited by Roger McHugh. Dublin: The Dolman Press, 1971.

MacGreevy, Thomas. *Jack B. Yeats: An Appreciation and an Introduction.* Dublin: Victor Waddington Publications Ltd., 1945.

McHugh, Roger. "Jack B. Yeats 1871–1957." In *Ireland and Its Welcomes* 20, no. 2 (July–August 1971).

Murphy, W. M. *Prodigal Father: The Life of John Butler Yeats 1838–1922.* Ithaca: Cornell University Press, 1978.

Pyle, Hilary. *Jack B. Yeats in the National Gallery of Ireland.* Dublin: National Gallery of Ireland, 1986.

———. *Jack B. Yeats: A Bibliography.* London: Routledge & Kegan Paul, 1970.

Rosenstein, J. "A Least-Known Master: Jack B. Yeats." *London Magazine* 17, no. 2 (June–July 1977).

Rosenthal, T. G. *The Masters, No. 40.* England: Knowledge Publications, 1966.

Skelton, Robin, ed. *The Collected Plays of Jack B. Yeats.* New York: Bobbs-Merrill, 1971.

———. "J. M. Synge." Rpt. from *Essays by Divers Hands.* Oxford: Oxford University Press, 1970.

———. "Themes and Attitudes in the Later Drama of Jack B. Yeats." *Yeats Studies* 2 (1972): 100–120.

White, James. *Jack B. Yeats 1871–1957: A Centenary Exhibition.* London: Martin Secker & Warburg Ltd., 1971.

Jack B. Yeats 1871–1957: A Centenary Exhibition. Catalogue. Dublin: National Gallery of Ireland, 1971.

Jack B. Yeats and His Family. Exhibition Catalogue. Sligo County Museum and Library, 1971.

John Butler Yeats and the Irish Renaissance. Exhibition Catalogue. Dublin: National Gallery of Ireland, 1972.

W. B. Yeats

PRIMARY SOURCES

At the Hawk's Well. In *Collected Plays of W. B. Yeats.* London: Macmillan, 1953.

The Body of Father Christian Rosencrux. In *Essays and Introductions.* New York: Macmillan, 1961.

Introduction to *The Cat and the Moon.* In *Wheels and Butterflies,* 1934. Rpt. in *Explorations.* New York: Macmillan, 1962.

Certain Noble Plays of Japan. In *Essays and Introductions.* New York: Macmillan, 1961.

"The Circus Animals' Desertion." In *Collected Poems of W. B. Yeats.* London: Macmillan, 1961.

The Countess Cathleen. In *Collected Plays of W. B. Yeats.* London: Macmillan, 1953.

The Death of Cuchulain. In *Collected Plays of W. B. Yeats.* London: Macmillan, 1953.

Deirdre. In *Collected Plays of W. B. Yeats.* London: Macmillan, 1953.

Fighting the Waves. In *Wheels and Butterflies,* 1934. Rpt. in *Explorations.* New York: Macmillan, 1962.

"The Great Day." In *Collected Poems of W. B. Yeats.* London: Macmillan, 1961.

The Green Helmet. In *Collected Plays of W. B. Yeats.* London: Macmillan, 1953.

"If I Were Four-and-Twenty." In *Explorations.* New York: Macmillan, 1962.

Letters to Ethel Mannin and Ernst Töller. In Richard Ellmann, *Yeats: The Man and the Masks.* New York: W. W. Norton & Company, 1979.

Letter to Fiona Macleod. 1897. In George Mills Harper, *The Mingling of Heaven and Earth: Yeats's Theory of Theater.* Dublin: The Dolman Press, 1975.

Letter to Olivia Shakespear. 1 October 1937. In *New Yeats Papers.* No. 8. Dublin: The Dolman Press, 1974.

Letter to Allan Wade. In *The Letters of W. B. Yeats.* Edited by Allan Wade. New York: Macmillan, 1955.

The Letters of W. B. Yeats. Edited by Allen Wade. New York: Macmillan, 1955.

Literary Ideals in Ireland. London and Dublin, 1899.

Magic. In *Essays and Introductions.* New York: Macmillan, 1961.

On Baile's Strand. In *Collected Plays of W. B. Yeats.* London: Macmillan, 1953.

"From 'On the Boiler.'" In *Explorations.* New York: Macmillan, 1962.

The Only Jealousy of Emer. In *Collected Plays of W. B. Yeats.* London: Macmillan, 1953.

The Poetical Works of William Blake. London: Barnard Quaritch, 1893.

Purgatory. In *Collected Plays of W. B. Yeats.* London: Macmillan, 1953.

Per Amica Silentia Lunae. In *Mythologies.* New York: Macmillan, 1980.

Preface to *Gods and Fighting Men,* by Lady Gregory. Toronto: Macmillan, 1976.

"Samhain: 1904, The Play, the Player, and the Scene." In *Explorations.* New York: Macmillan, 1962.

"Swedenborg, Mediums, Desolate Places." 1914. Rpt. in *Explorations.* New York: Macmillan, 1962.

The Theatre. In *Essays and Introductions.* New York: Macmillan, 1961.

"The Tragic Theatre." In *Essays and Introductions.* New York: Macmillan, 1961.

A Vision. New York: Macmillan, 1965.

SECONDARY SOURCES

Alspach, Russell K., ed. *The Variorum Edition of the Plays of W. B. Yeats.* New York: Macmillan, 1966.

Allt, Peter, and Russell K. Alspach, eds. *The Variorum Edition of the Poems of W. B. Yeats.* New York: Macmillan, 1957.

Bloom, Harold. *Yeats.* New York: Oxford University Press, 1970.

Bridge, C., ed. *W. B. Yeats and T. Sturge Moore: Their Correspondence.* London: Routledge & Kegan Paul, 1953.

Cowell, Raymond. *Critics on Yeats.* London: George Allen and Unwin, Ltd., 1971.

Donoghue, Dennis. *William Butler Yeats.* New York: Viking Press, 1971.

Ellmann, Richard. *James Joyce.* New York: Oxford University Press, 1959.

———. *The Identity of Yeats.* New York: Oxford University Press, 1964.

———. *Yeats: The Man and the Masks.* New York: W. W. Norton & Co., 1979.

Friedman, Barton R. *Adventures in the Deeps of the Mind.* Princeton: Princeton University Press, 1977.

Henn, Thomas. *The Lonely Tower.* New York: Pellegrine and Cudahy, 1952.

Horniman, A. E. F. Letter to W. B. Yeats. April 1904. In *Samhain (An Occasional Review).* Edited by W. B. Yeats. Dublin: Sealy Bryers and Walker and T. Fisher Unwin, 1904.

Jeffares, A. Norman. *The Circus Animals.* Stanford: Stanford University Press, 1970.

———. *W. B. Yeats.* New York: Humanities Press, 1949.

———, ed. *W. B. Yeats: Selected Criticism.* London: Macmillan, 1964.

Koch, Vivienne. *W. B. Yeats: The Tragic Phase.* London: Routledge and Kegan Paul, 1951.

Moore, John Rees. *Masks of Love and Death.* Ithaca, N.Y.: Cornell University Press, 1971.

Moses, Montrose J. "With William Butler Yeats." In *W. B. Yeats: Interviews and Recollections.* Edited by E. H. Mikhail. Vol. 1. New York: Harper and Row, 1977.

Nathan, Leonard. *The Tragic Drama of William Butler Yeats: Figures in a Dance.* New York: Columbia University Press, 1965.

O'Brien, Conor Cruise. *The Suspecting Glance.* London: Faber and Faber, 10972.

Parkinson. Thomas. *W. B. Yeats: The Later Poetry.* Berkeley: University of California Press, 1964.

Raine, Kathleen. "Death-in-Life and Life-in-Death: 'Cuchulain Comforted' and 'News for the Delphic Oracle.'" *New Yeats Papers.* No. 8. Dublin: The Dolman Press, 1974.

Skelton, Robin, and Anne Saddlemyer. *The World of W. B. Yeats.* Dublin: Dolmen Press, 1965.

Stopes, M. C. *Plays of Old Japan: The No.* London, 1912.

Tindall, William York. *W. B. Yeats.* New York: Columbia University Press, 1966.

Ure, Peter. *Yeats the Playwright.* New York: Barnes and Noble, 1963.

Wade, Allen. *A Bibliography of the Writings of W. B. Yeats.* London: Rupert Hart-Davis, 1968.

———, ed. *The Letters of W. B. Yeats.* New York: Macmillan, 1955.

Wilson, F. A. C. *Yeats Iconography.* New York: Macmillan, 1960.

Zwerdling, Alex. *Yeats and the Heroic Ideal.* New York: New York University Press, 1965.

Realism and Ireland

Archibald, Douglas N. *John Butler Yeats.* Lewisburg, Pa.: Bucknell University Press, 1974.

Birmingham, G. A. *Irishmen All.* London: Foulis, 1913.

Book of Common Prayer. American edition, 1928.

Borthwick, N. *Ceachta Beaga Gaelige* [Irish Reading Lesson]. Illustrated by Jack B. Yeats. 3 parts. Dublin: Irish Book Company, 1902–6.

A Broad Sheet. Illustrated by Jack B. Yeats. London: Elkin Mathews, 1902–3.

A Broadside. Illustrated by Jack B. Yeats. 84 nos. Dublin: Dun Emer Press and Cuala Press: 1908–15.

Carroll, Lewis. *The Complete Works of Lewis Carroll.* Edited by A. Woolcott. New York: Modern Library, 1936.

Colum, Padraic. *The Big Tree of Bunlahy.* Illustrated by Jack B. Yeats. New York: Macmillan, 1933.

Cowie, Donald. *Ireland: The Land and the People.* San Diego: A. S. Barnes, 1976.

Greimas, A. J., and F. Rastier. "The Interaction of Semiotic Constraints." *Yale French Studies* 41 (1968).

Hartman, Geoffrey. *Deconstruction and Criticism.* New York: Seabury Press, 1979.

Hauser, Arnold. *The Social History of Art.* New York: Alfred A. Knopf, 1939.

Jansen, H. W. *History of Art.* Englewood Cliffs, N.J.: Prentice-Hall, 1967.

Kafka, Franz. *Diaries of Franz Kafka.* Edited by Joseph Kresh. New York: Schocken Books, 1965.

Lynch, Patricia. *The Turf-Cutter's Donkey.* Illustrated by Jack B. Yeats. London: Dent, 1943.

McPhee, John. *Basin and Range.* New York: Farrar, Straus and Giraux, 1981.

Marriott, E. *Jack B. Yeats: His Pictorial and Dramatic Art.* London: Elkin Mathews, 1911.

Murphy, John. *Ireland in the Twentieth Century.* New York: Irish Book Center, 1975.

Murphy, William M. *The Yeats Family and the Pollexfens of Sligo.* Dublin: The Dolmen Press, 1971.

O'Connor, Frank, trans. *A Lament for Art O'Leary.* Dublin: The Cuala Press, 1940.

O'Doherty, Brian. "Jack B. Yeats: Promise and Regret." In *Jack B. Yeats: A Centenary Gathering,* edited by Roger McHugh. Dublin: The Dolman Press, 1971.

O'Kelly, Seamus. *Ranns and Ballads.* Illustrated by Jack B. Yeats. Dublin: Candle Press, 1918.

———. *The Weaver's Grave.* Illustrated by Jack B. Yeats. Dublin: Talbot Press, 1922.

O'Malley, Earnan. *On Another Man's Wound.* Dublin, 1943.

Reynolds, J. H. *The Fancy.* Illustrated by Jack B. Yeats. London: Elkin Mathews, 1905.

Russell, G. W. [AE], ed. *New Songs.* Illustrated by Jack B. Yeats. Dublin: O'Donoghue, 1904.

Sanford, William B. *Ireland and the Classical Tradition.* Totowa, N.J.: Rowman and Littlefield, 1976.

Schrödinger, Erwin. *What is Life? The Physical Aspects of the Living Cell.* Cambridge: At the University Press, 1945.

Synge, J. M. *The Aran Islands.* Illustrated by Jack B. Yeats. Dublin: Maunsel and Company, 1907.

———. *In Wicklow, West Kerry and Connemara.* Illustrated by Jack B. Yeats. Dublin: Maunsel and Company, 1910.

Torchiana, Donald. *Yeats and Georgian Ireland.* Evanston, Ill.: Northwestern University Press, 1966.

Uris, Leon, and Jill Uris. *Ireland: A Terrible Beauty.* New York: Doubleday, 1975.

Wei, Wang. "The Bamboo Studio." In *A Chinese Garden Court,* edited by Alfreda Murck and Wen Fong. New York: Metropolitan Museum of Art, 1981.

White, James. *John Butler Yeats.* Dublin: The Dolmen Press, n.d.

———. "Memory Harbor: Jack Yeats's Painting Process." In *Yeats Studies: An International Journal.* edited by Robert O'Driscoll and Lorna Reynolds. No. 2. Shannon: Irish University Press, 1972.

Yeats, Ann. Introduction to *Broadside Characters: Drawings by Jack B. Yeats.* Dublin: The Cuala Press, 1971.

———. "Theatre and the Visual Arts." In *Yeats Studies: An International Journal,* edited by Robert O'Driscoll and Lorna Reynolds. No. 2. Shannon: Irish University Press, 1972.

Yeats, Jack. "A Letter About J. M. Synge." *New York Evening Sun,* 20 July 1909.

———. *Modern Art.* Dublin: The Cuala Press, 1937.

———, illus. "The Grand Conversation under the Rose." In *A Broadsheet,* 1903.

Yeats, W. B. "J. M. Synge and the Ireland of His Time." In *Essays and Introductions.* New York: Macmillan, 1961.

———. *On the Boiler.* Dublin: The Cuala Press, 1939.

Yeats, W. B., and F. R. Higgins, eds. *A Broadsheet.* Illustrated by Jack B. Yeats. Dublin: The Cuala Press, 1935.

Yeats, W. B., and Dorothy Wellesley. *A Broadsheet.* Illustrated by Jack B. Yeats.

Index

RITTER LIBRARY
BALDWIN-WALLACE COLLEGE